Postcard History Series

# *Finger Lakes*

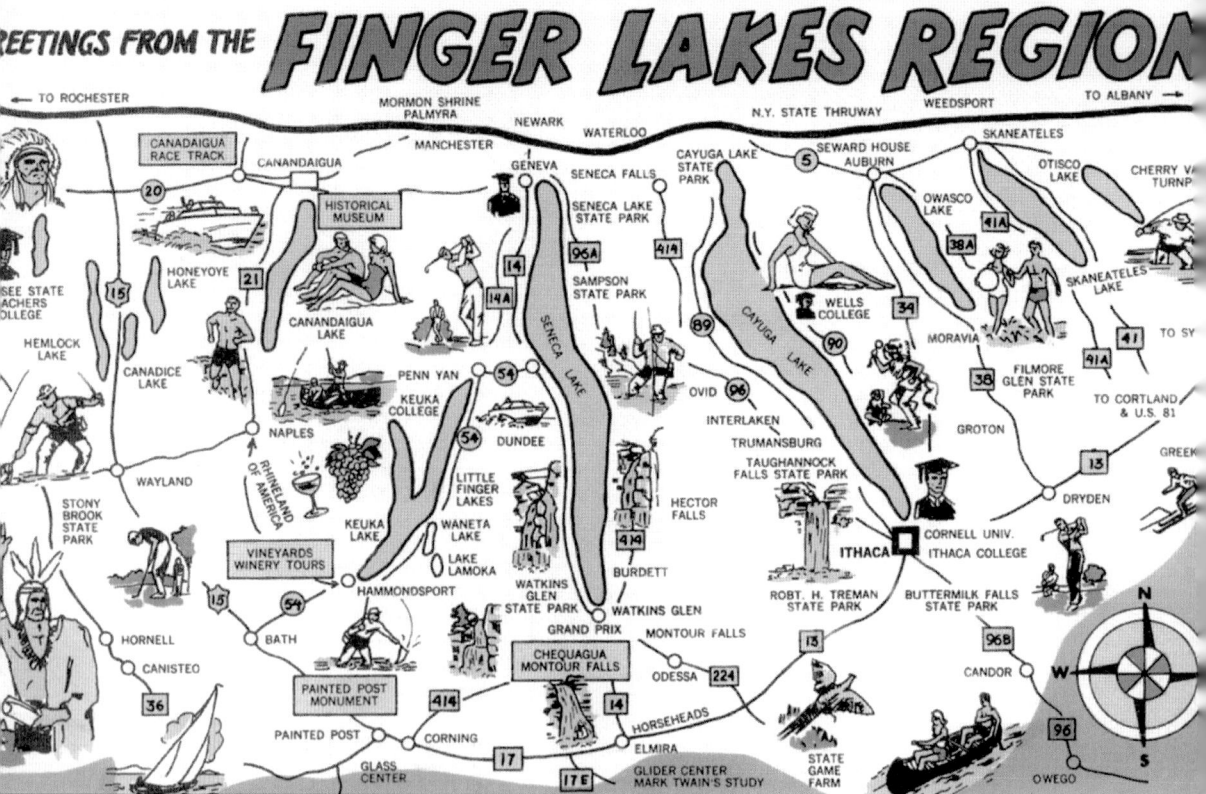

Greetings, and welcome to the Finger Lakes.

*On the front cover:* A steamboat leaves Hammondsport on Keuka Lake, where the vineyards still bloom every spring. (Collection of Yates County Genealogical and Historical Society.)

*On the back cover:* Gorges and falls helped form Ithaca on Cayuga Lake, just as much as Cornell University has. (Collection of L. Caroline Underwood Museum.)

Postcard History Series

# Finger Lakes

*Kirk W. House and Charles R. Mitchell*

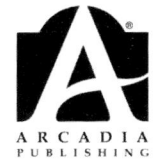

Copyright © 2008 by Kirk W. House and Charles R. Mitchell
ISBN 978-0-7385-5730-4

Published by Arcadia Publishing
Charleston, South Carolina

Printed in the United States of America

Library of Congress Catalog Card Number: 2007937269

For all general information contact Arcadia Publishing at:
Telephone 843-853-2070
Fax 843-853-0044
E-mail sales@arcadiapublishing.com
For customer service and orders:
Toll-Free 1-888-313-2665

Visit us on the Internet at www.arcadiapublishing.com

# CONTENTS

| | | |
|---|---|---:|
| Acknowledgments | | 6 |
| Introduction | | 7 |
| 1. | On the Lakes | 9 |
| 2. | Above the Lakes | 51 |
| 3. | Between the Lakes | 61 |

# Acknowledgments

We are very grateful to the following collectors and repositories for their help in assembling the postcards for this volume: Glenn H. Curtiss Museum, Hammondsport; Joshua B. House; Kirk W. House; Charles R. Mitchell; Ontario County Historical Society, Canandaigua; Steuben County historian's office, Bath; Yates County Genealogical and Historical Society, Penn Yan; and L. Caroline Underwood Museum, Penn Yan.

# Introduction

The Finger Lakes were Iroquois country before the brand-new white settlers arrived, and other cultures made their home here before the Iroquois. The Erie Canal skirted the northern fringe of the lakes, turning that stretch into America's first boom region. The New York Central Railroad and the New York State Thruway rode through that same corridor, tracking the route that Native Americans had paced out centuries before.

The people who lived here were vivid thinkers, if a bit cranky at times. They developed women's rights campaigns, Underground Railroad routes, Mormonism, revivalism, Spiritualism, fiber optics, aeronautic innovations, Pyrex, photographic film, and the Northern Spy.

Nathaniel Hawthorne toured the region, along with Lafayette, Daniel Webster, and the future King Louis Philippe of France. Millard Fillmore lived here, and Stephen A. Douglas, and Glenn Curtiss—not to mention Frederick Douglass, Harriet Tubman, Elizabeth Cady Stanton, and Susan B. Anthony. Mark Twain wrote here, along with Rod Serling and Kurt Vonnegut Jr.

Tens of thousands of seamen did their boot camp at Sampson Naval Training Station in World War II. Hundreds of thousands of people fondly remember college days in the region. Millions have hiked the glens, boated the lakes, shopped the marketplaces, and fished the streams.

# *One*

# ON THE LAKES

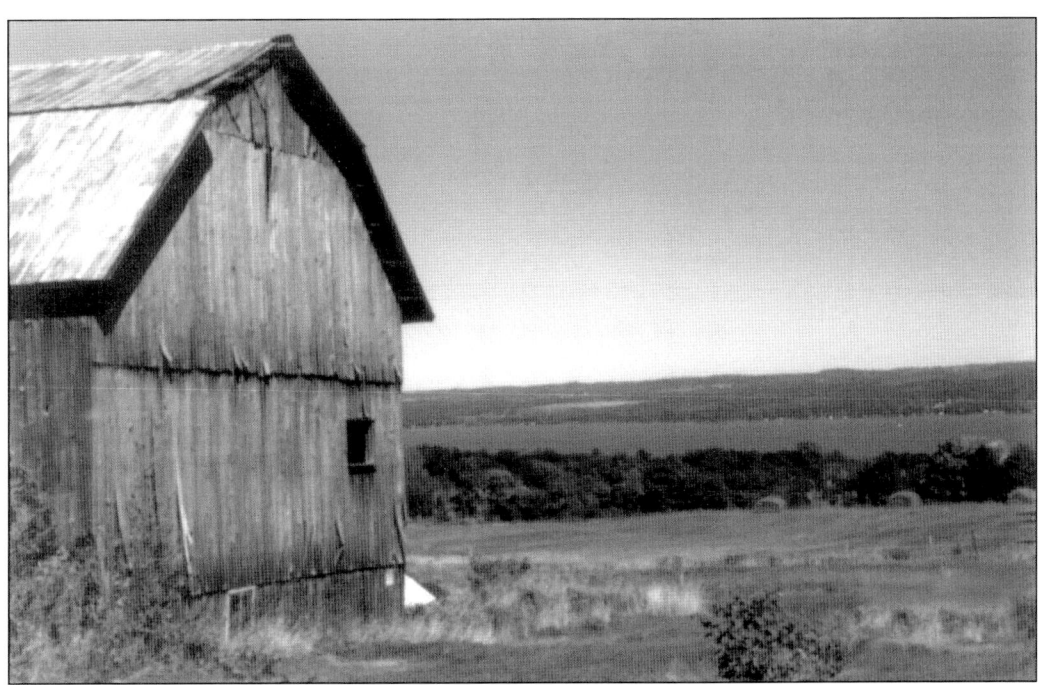

A line of 11 lakes runs across western New York, covering an area the size of Connecticut. Ever-running inflow from tiny streams now keeps them full. In 1816, an excursion boat launched onto the waves of Skaneateles, originating a flood of tourism that still continues. On the shores of Crooked Lake, Rev. William Bostwick cultivated the region's first vineyard; by the time production went commercial, the lake was called Keuka.

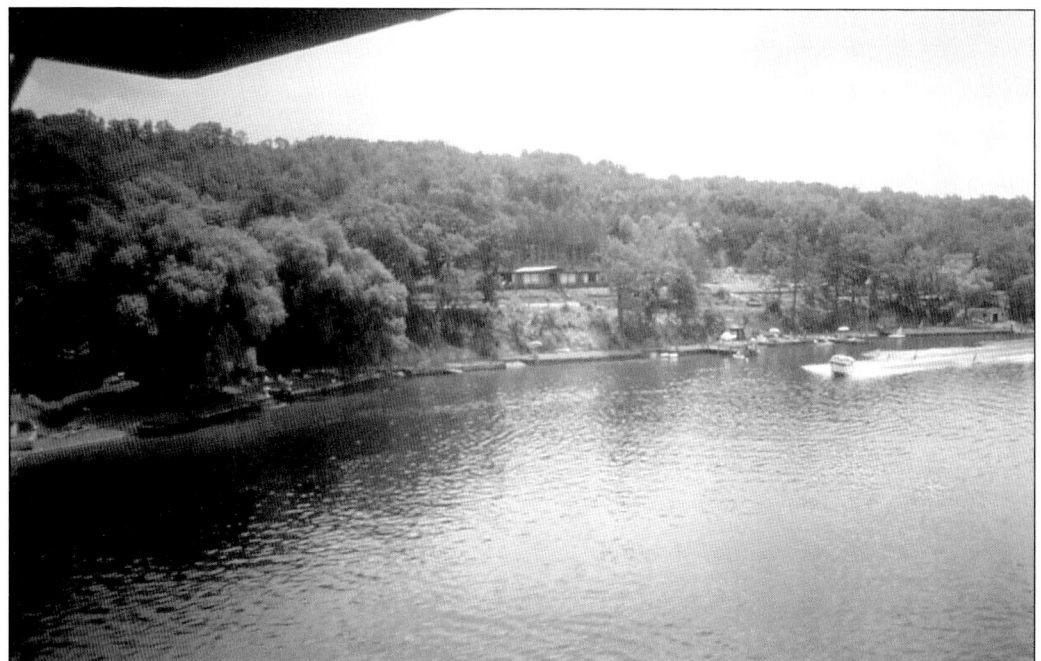

Summer cottages, camps, and year-round homes ring most of the Finger Lakes. The cottages are becoming scarce as they are being replaced by larger homes with people coming back to the lakes where they grew up to retire and live.

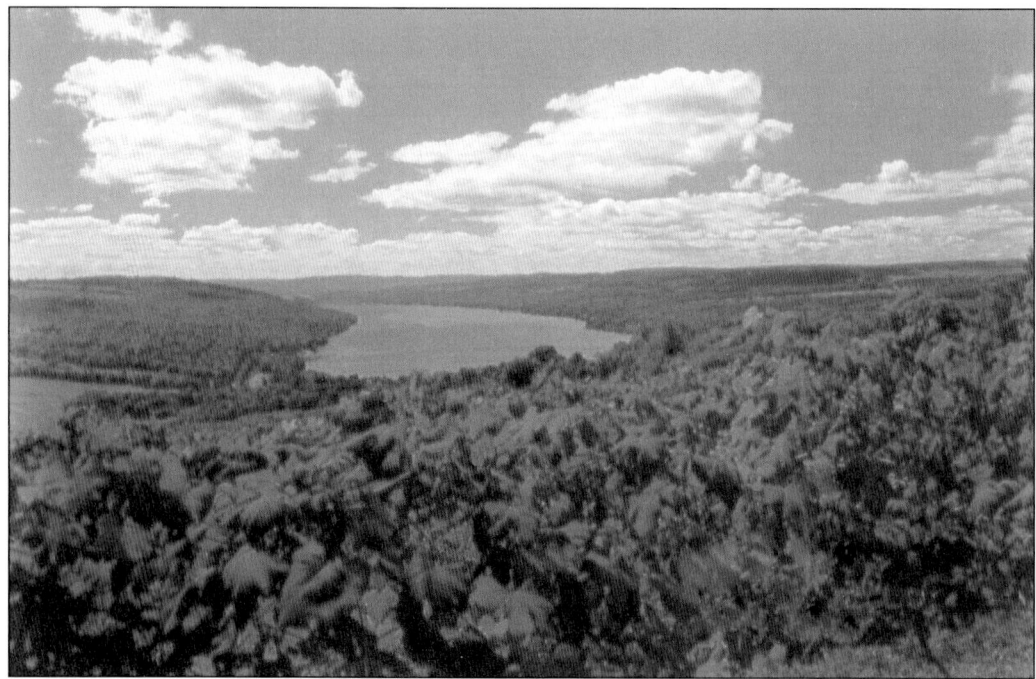

Conesus may be one of the smaller lakes, but there are those who love it—and rightly so. Like the larger Finger Lakes, it has a year-round population and plenty of seasonal visitation. To the Native Americans, Conesus means "always beautiful."

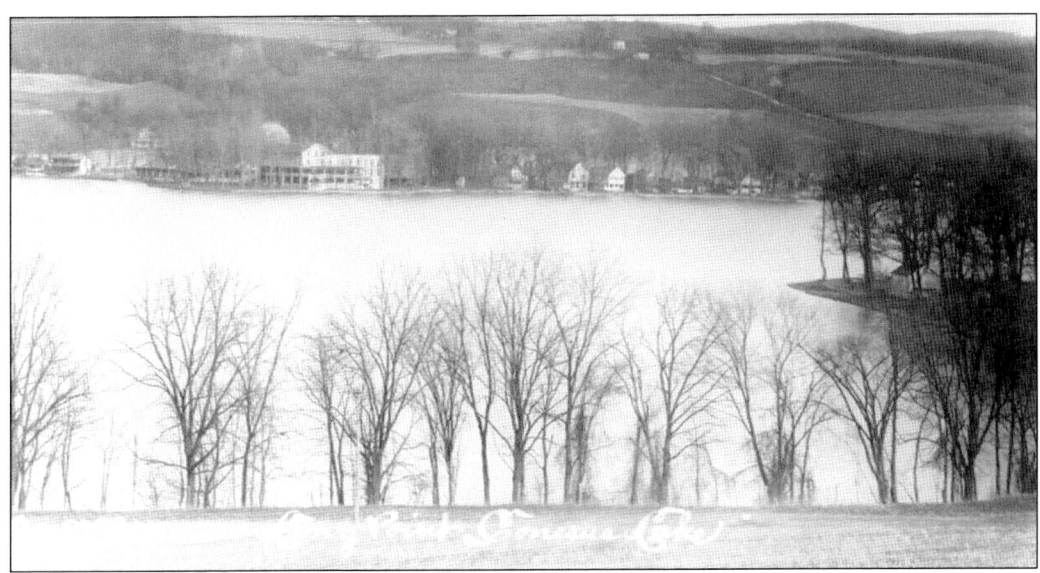

In the postcard showing all the Finger Lakes on page 2, the name for the westernmost lake, Conesus, was omitted. Many of the old cottages remain, but as on the other lakes, they are being replaced by larger year-round homes.

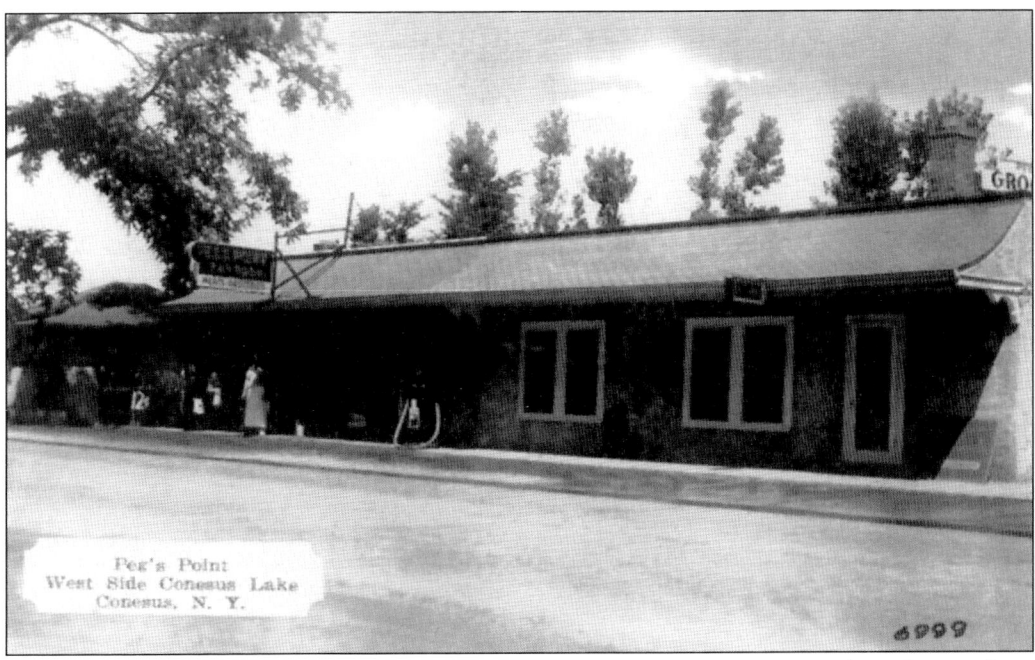

Many businesses throughout the lakes country sell to road traffic out one side and waterfront traffic out the other.

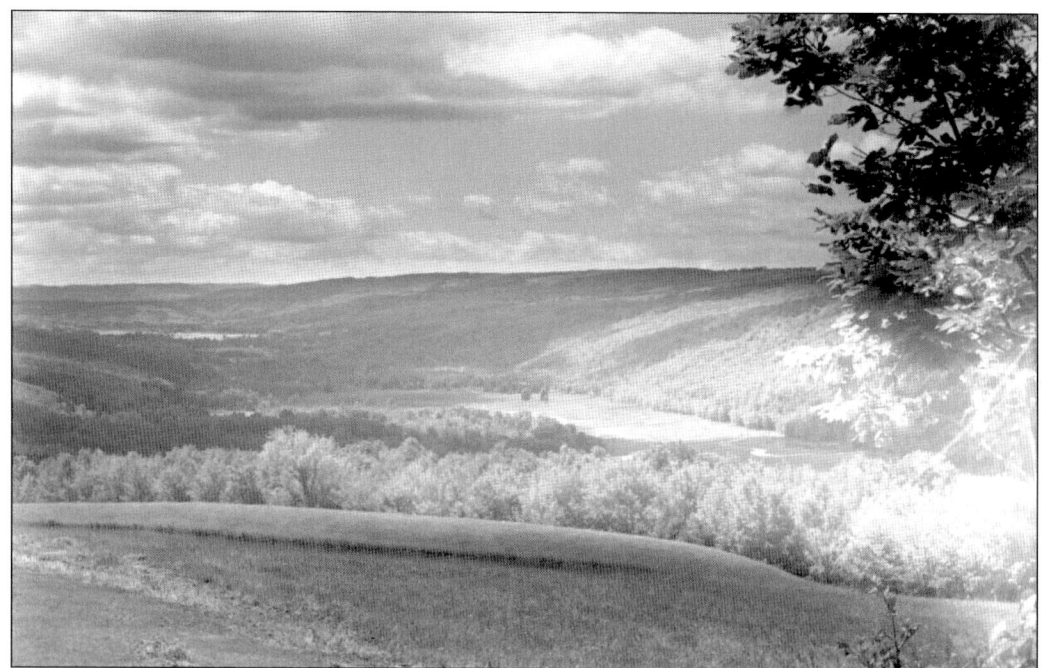

One small lake bears a special honor. When New York Department of Environmental Conservation scientists wanted to reintroduce bald eagles to the area, they decided that Hemlock was the perfect choice and the eagles agreed. Hemlock is the only Finger Lake that does not carry a Native American name, although its Iroquois name means hemlock.

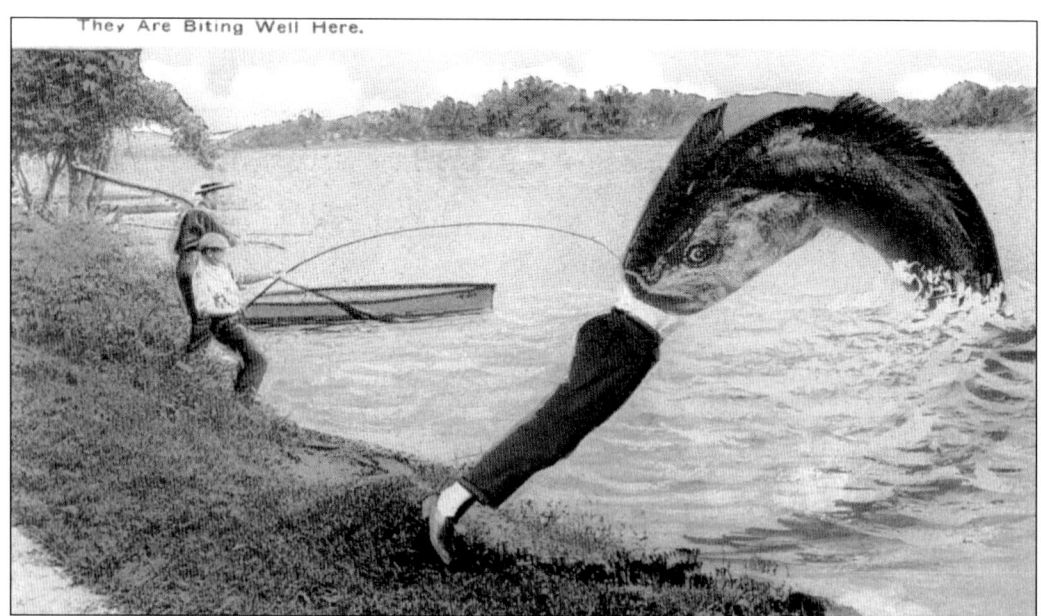

Fish stories from the Finger Lakes are legend, but this one may be a bit tall. See page 20 for a true fishing tale. This generic postcard was used on all of the Finger Lakes and who knows where else.

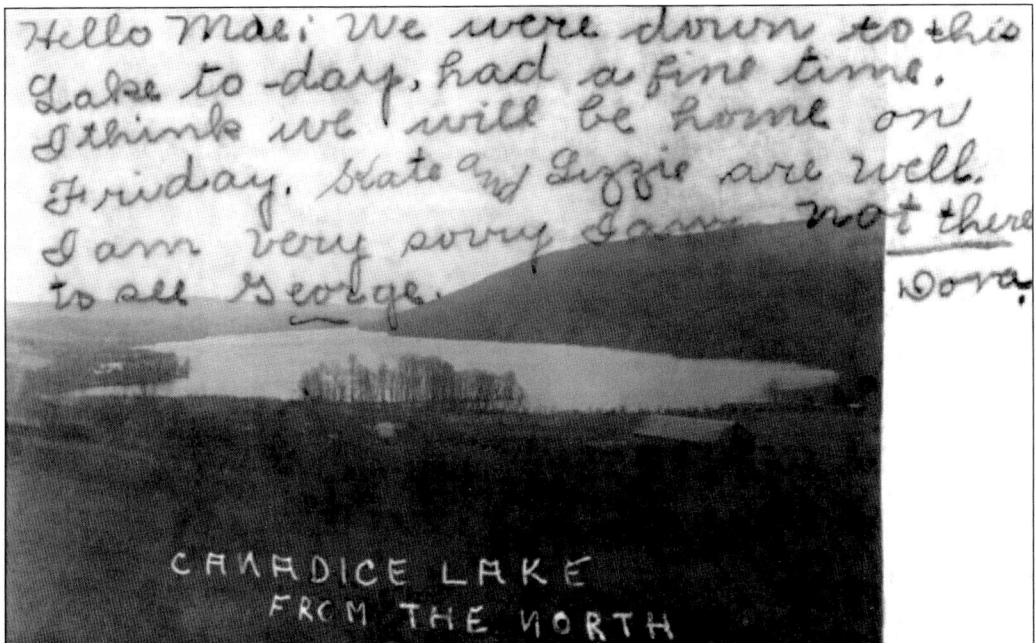

Tiny Canadice Lake, in addition to Hemlock, supplies drinking water for the city of Rochester. A New Jersey family settling in 1795 had the town to themselves for nine years; in the second half of the 1800s, Canadice was a popular tourist destination.

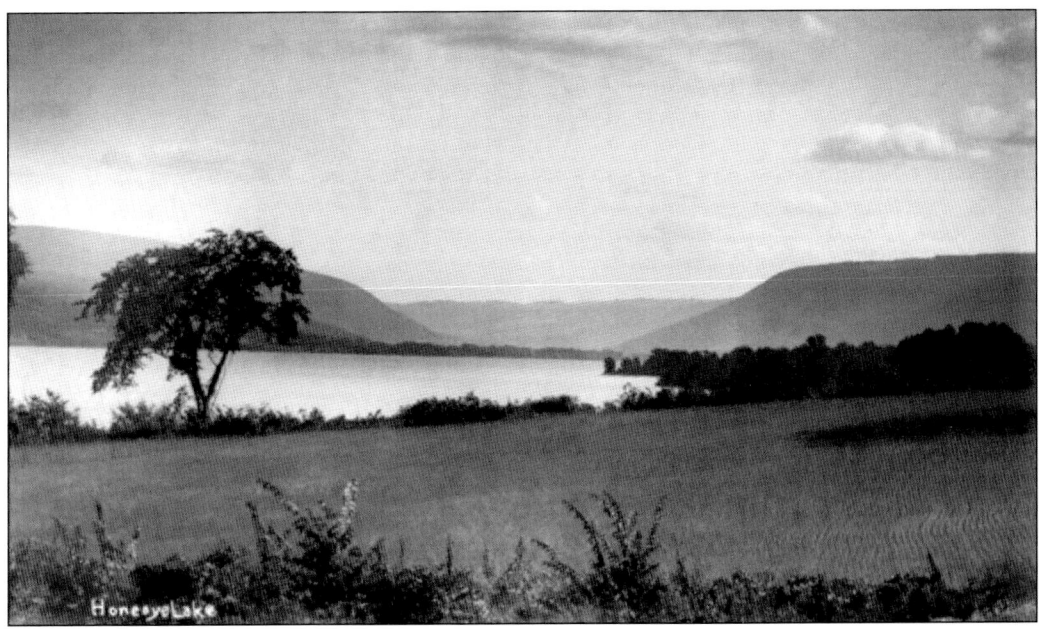

Honeoye Lake is now ringed with private homes and laced by private boaters. To Native Americans Honeoye means "finger lying." The landscape, especially to the southeast of the lake, is heavily wooded.

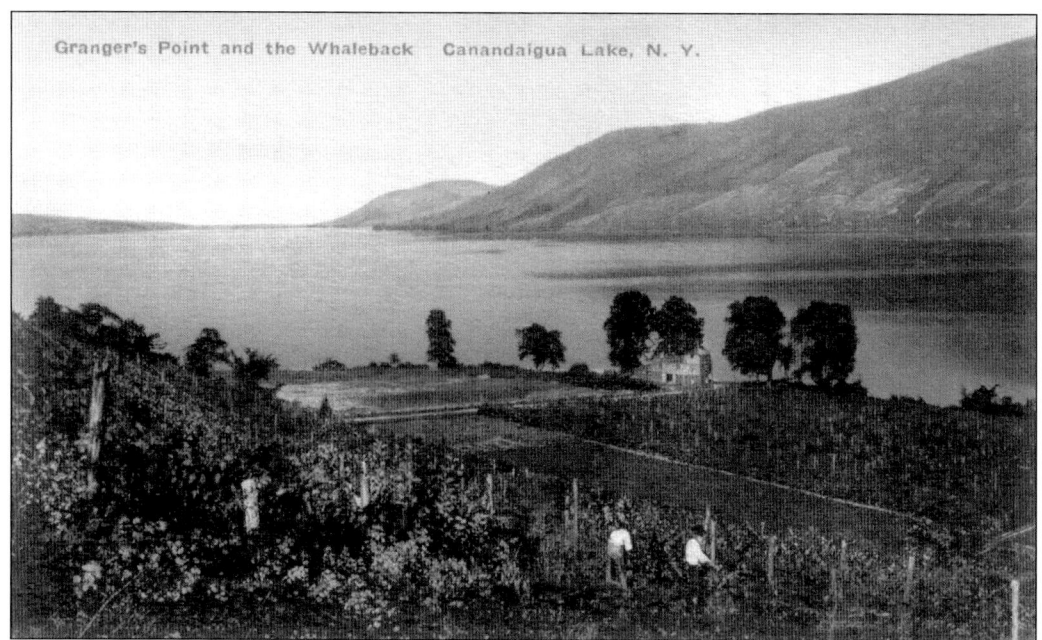

Vineyards still line most of the Finger Lakes, especially on the west shores, where climates favor production. Canandaigua Lake is no exception. The New York Wine and Culinary Center, located in the city of Canandaigua, is helping to build the reputation of Finger Lakes wines.

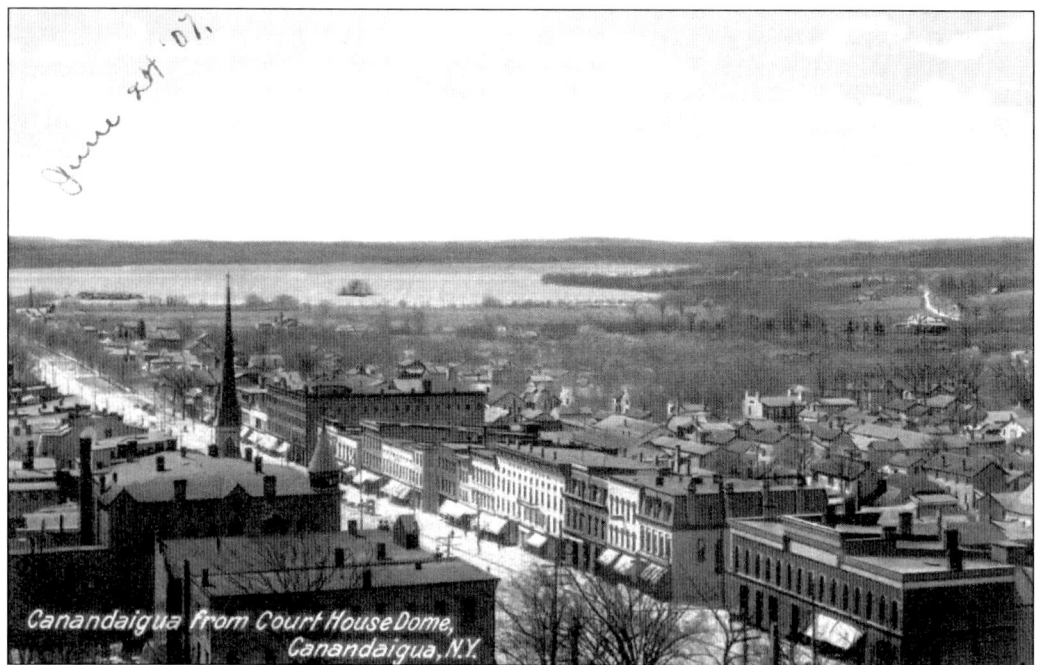

Canandaigua, "the chosen place" in Seneca, is a thriving city and county seat, but the lake still dominates the town. The broad main street shown here was the major route west before the New York Thruway was built.

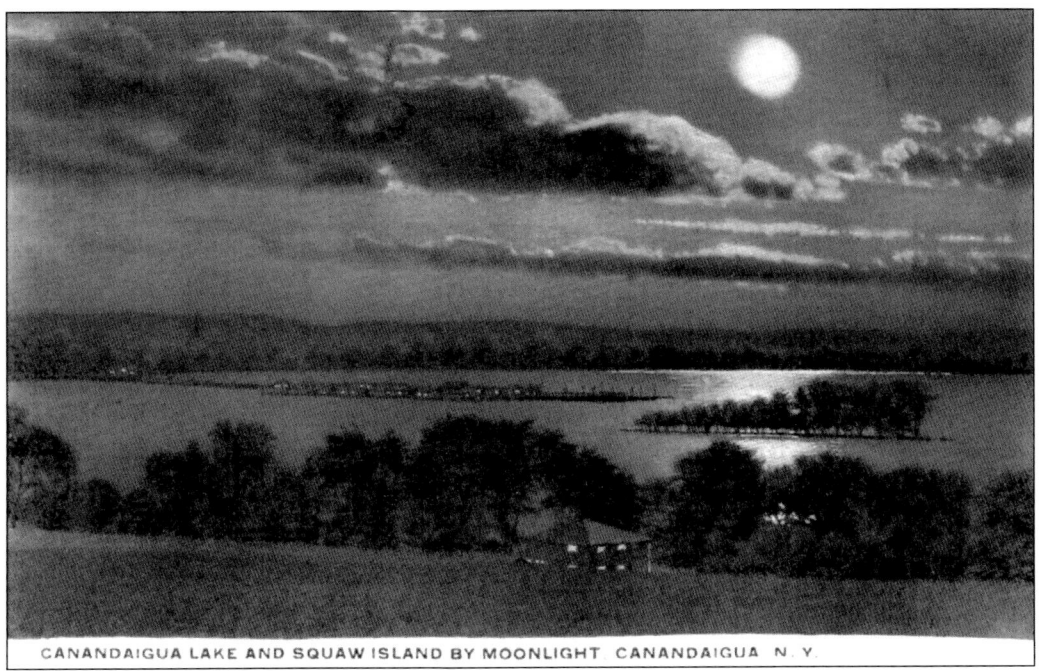

CANANDAIGUA LAKE AND SQUAW ISLAND BY MOONLIGHT. CANANDAIGUA, N.Y.

Squaw Island is so named from the belief that Seneca women and children from Kanadaque took refuge there during Sullivan's Revolutionary War invasion. Gen. George Washington sent Generals James Clinton and John Sullivan on an expedition to punish the Iroquois for helping the British.

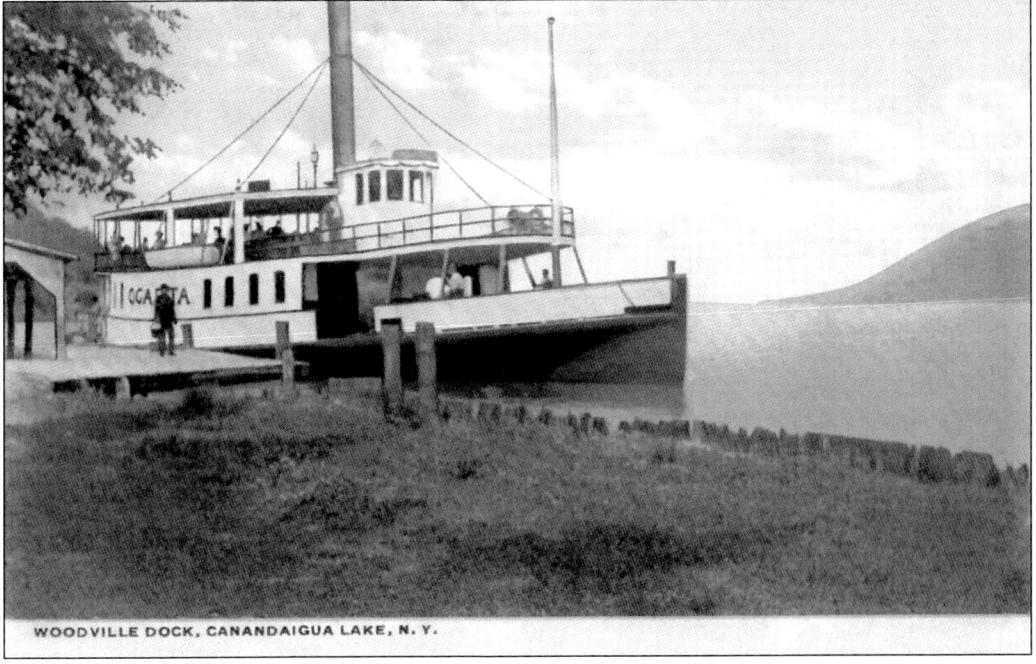

WOODVILLE DOCK, CANANDAIGUA LAKE, N.Y.

Woodville, at the very head of the lake, was one of some 60 landings. Apples were a prime product here. The steamer, with its name partially obscured, is the 1889 *Ogarita*, supposedly called "O'Garrity" by her Irish crew.

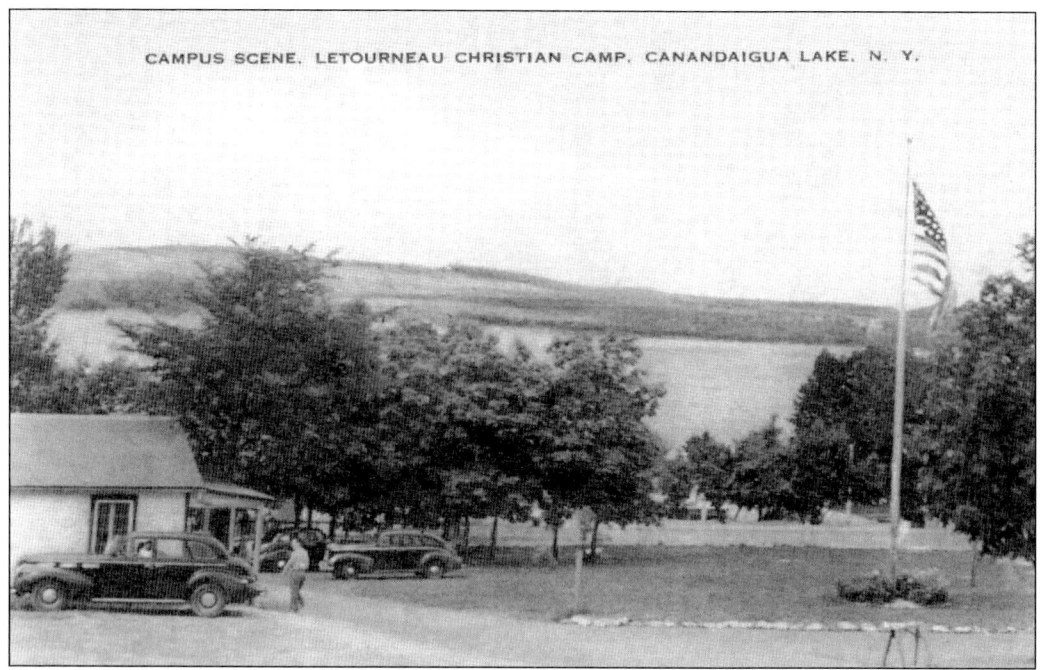

As these old-time automobiles show, LeTourneau Christian Conference Center (on the east shore) has been around for a long time. It housed child refugees in World War II and still performs its ministry today.

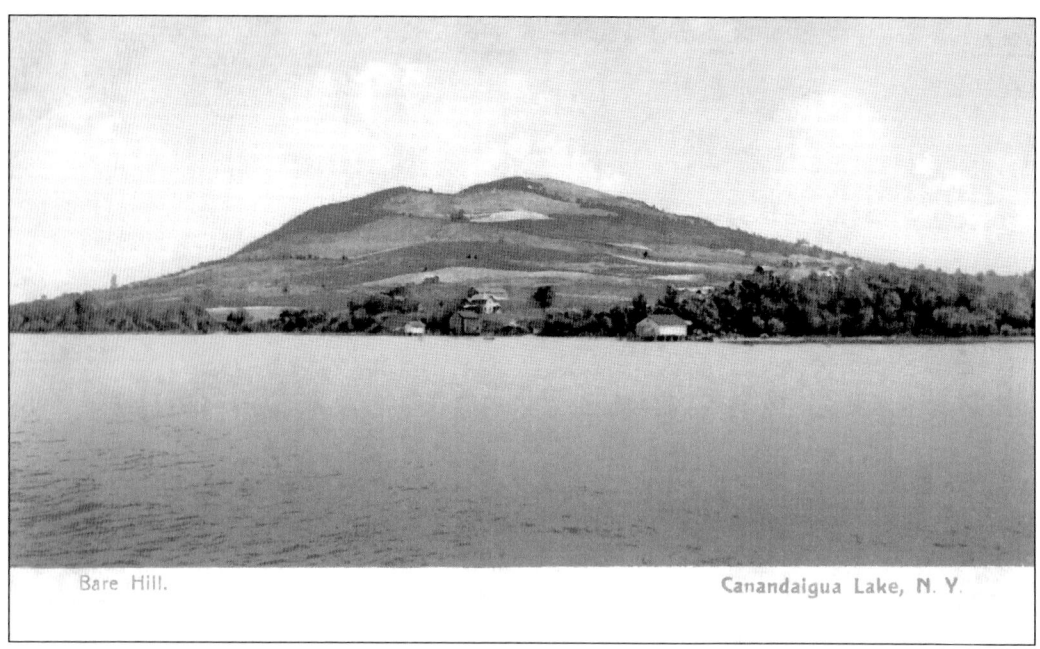

Bare Hill, on the east side of Canandaigua Lake, lives in Native American legend as the birthplace of the Seneca people. The hill people, Nundawao, originated here and gave the area and the lake its name, Kanandague, meaning "chosen place."

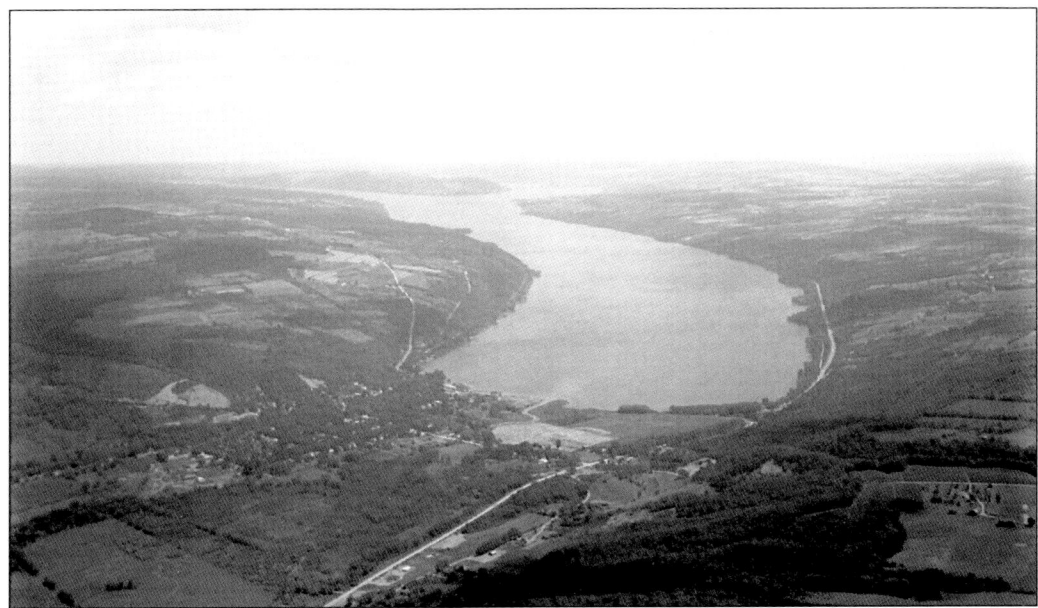

Keuka's bluff divides the East and West Branches of that lake from each other and from the main body of the lake. The bluff is now wooded, but over half of Yates County's land was being used for agriculture as late as 1998. The Seneca name Keuka means "crooked lake," and it carried that name well into the 19th century.

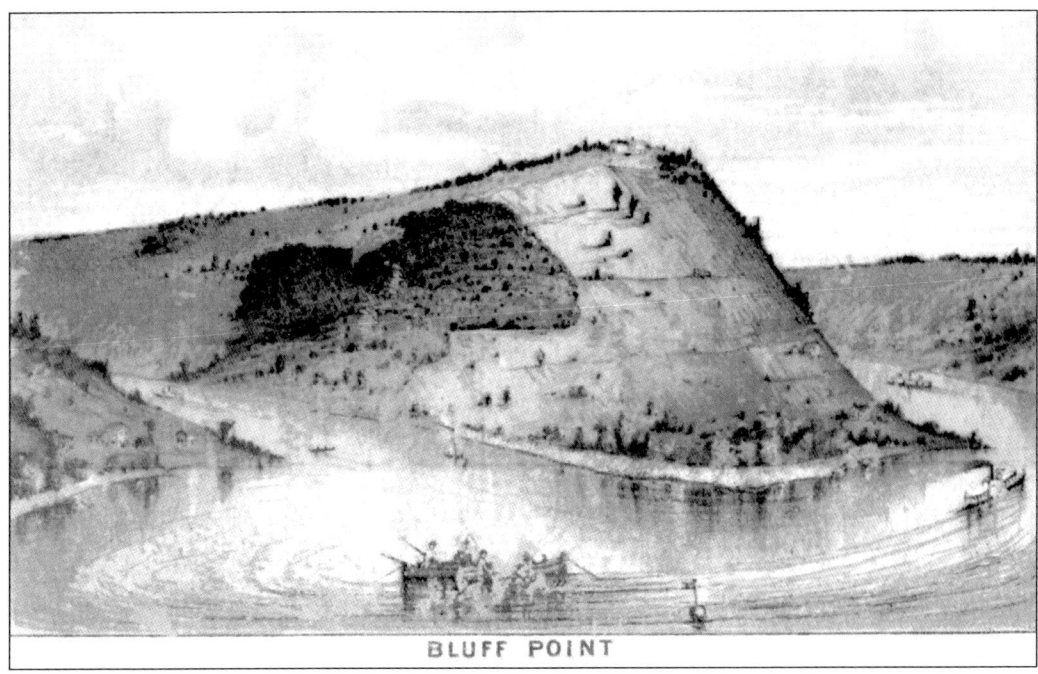

An image from a 19th-century tourism brochure rather exaggerates the height of the bluff. Even at that time, tourism was a major enterprise in the Finger Lakes.

Keuka Lake, N.Y. from Hammondsport.

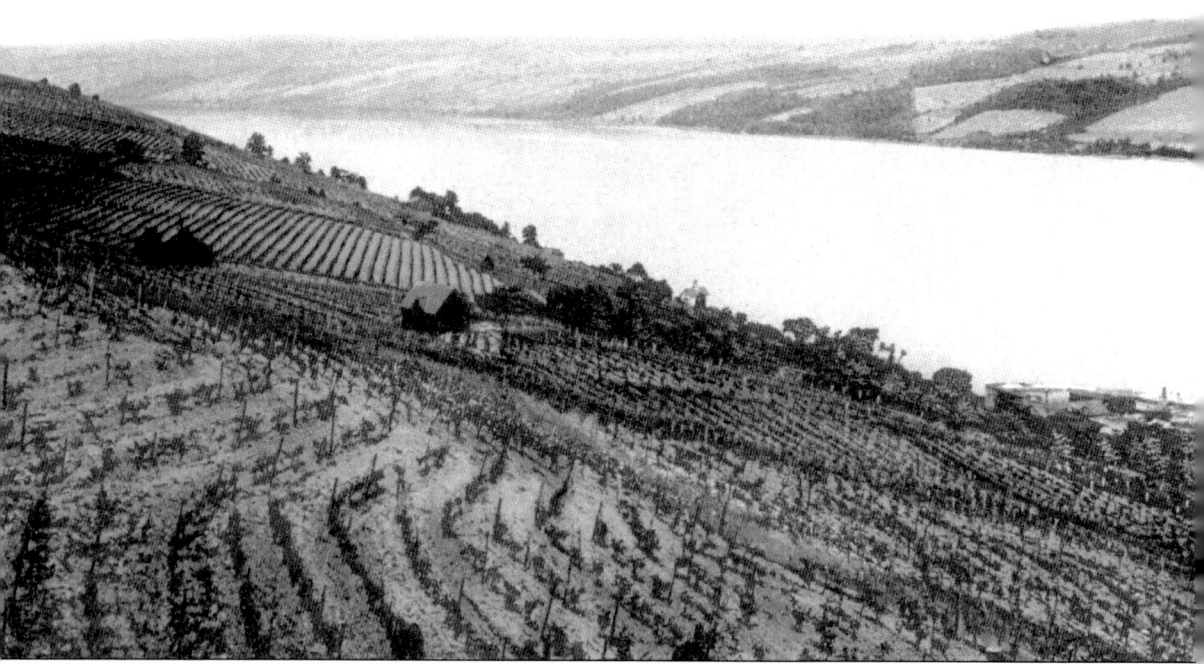

This unusual double card still does not do justice to the sweep of Keuka Lake, but it does give a feel for the extensive agriculture of the day. These double cards required extra postage and

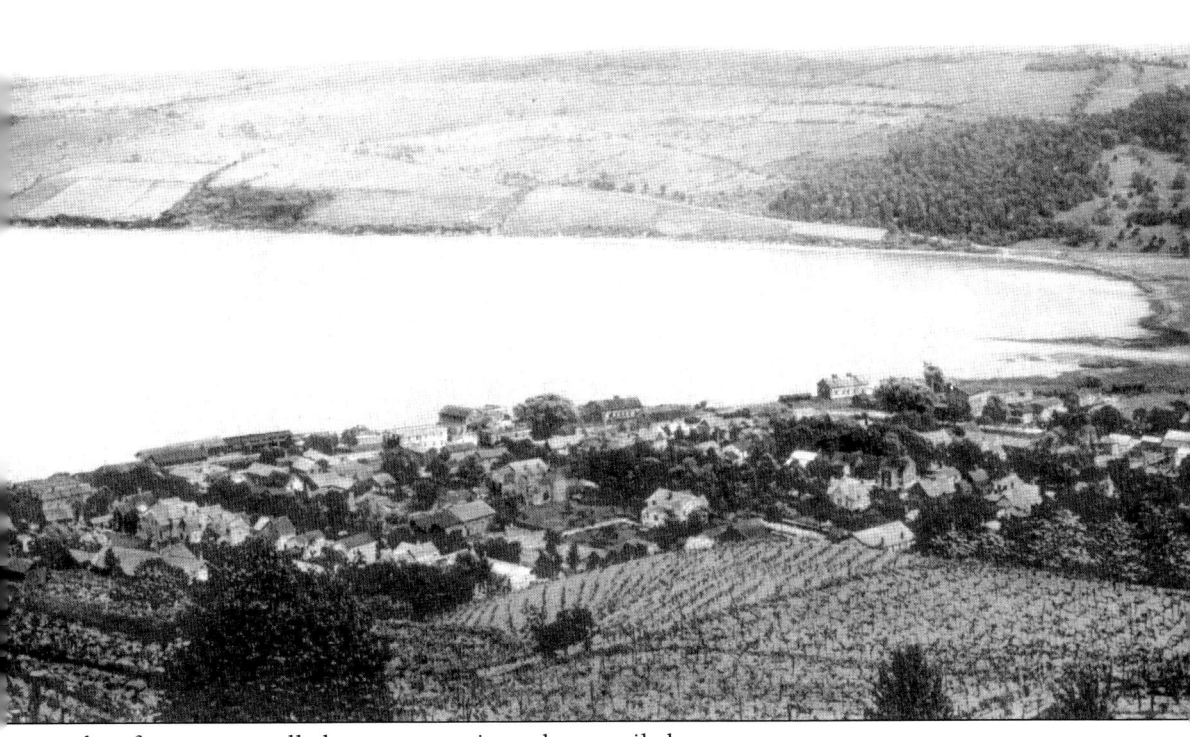

therefore were usually kept as souvenirs and not mailed.

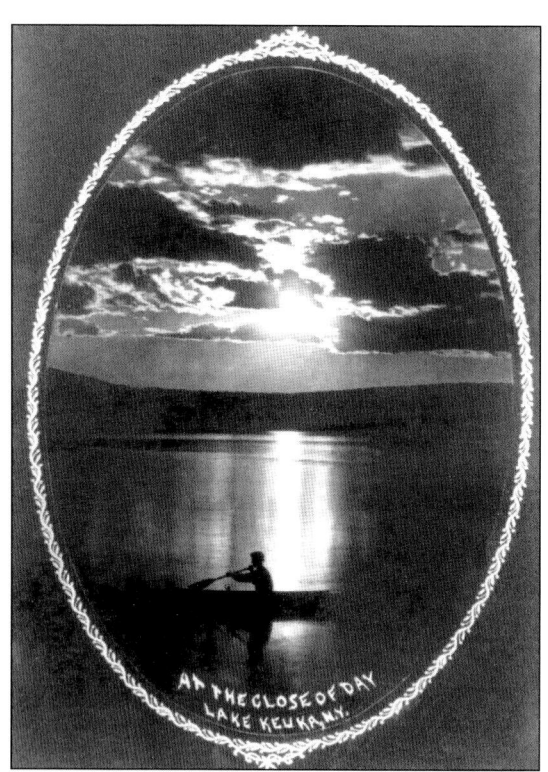

It may be the close of day, but it is clearly a day well spent.

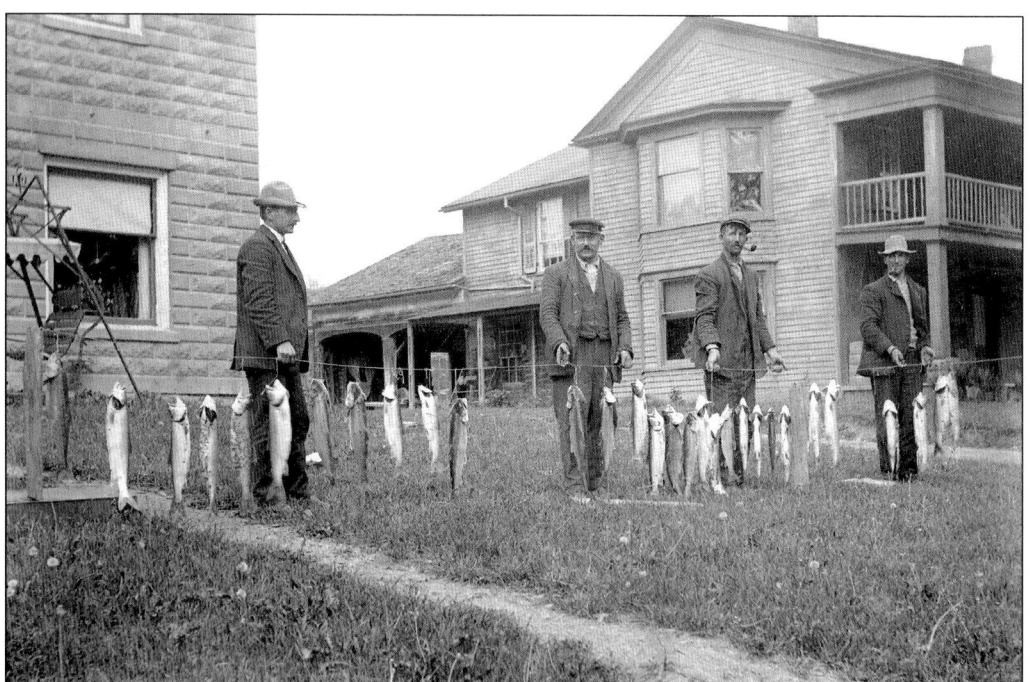

Back in the early 1900s, anglers were known to take 100 trout a day in Keuka's branches. The lake became so overfished that there was no trout fishing season for some years. They are once again plentiful.

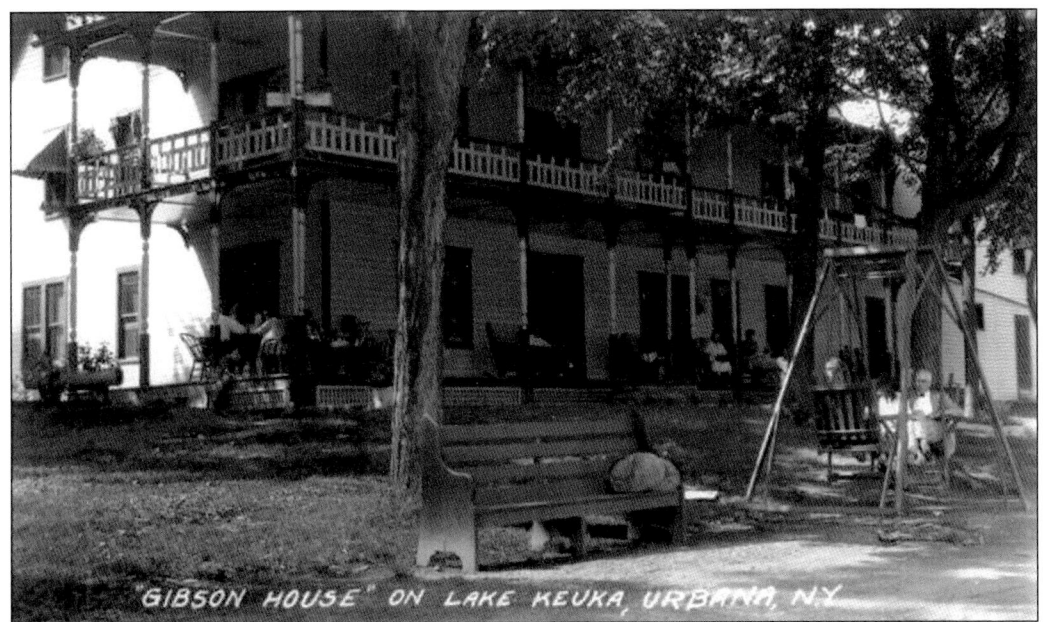

Gibson House hotel enjoyed a fine view of the lake and the bluff. It was even better known for its kitchen. Sadly, the hotel is gone, but the view remains.

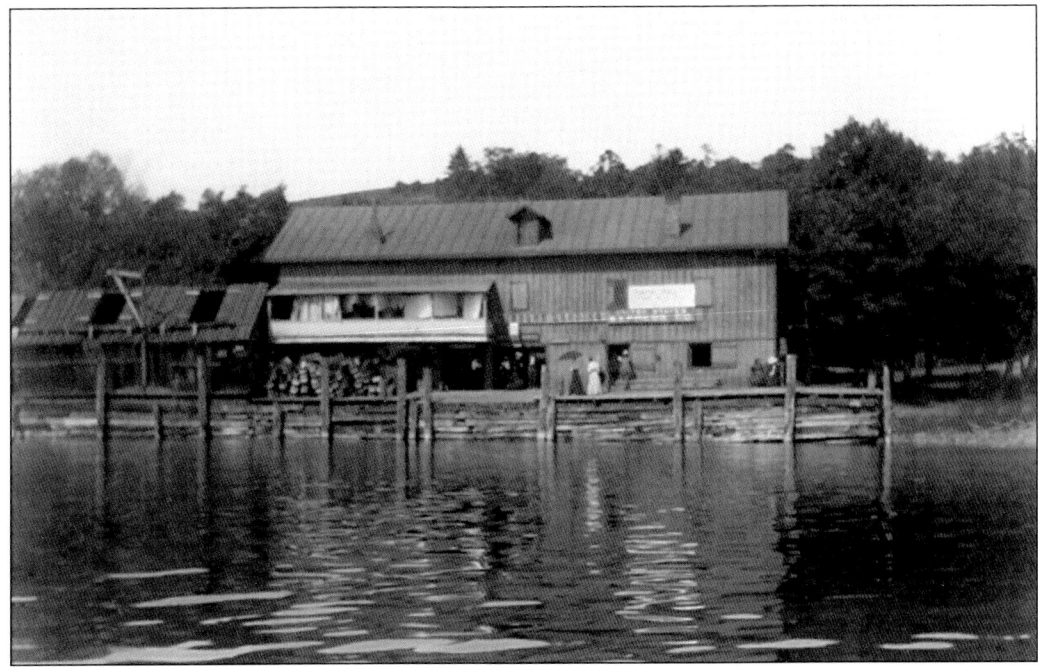

The landing itself did not present a very picturesque sight. It was one of the scheduled stops for all steamboats. Dances were sometimes held here, making it a social center also. In an earlier day, lake ferries had put in at this spot.

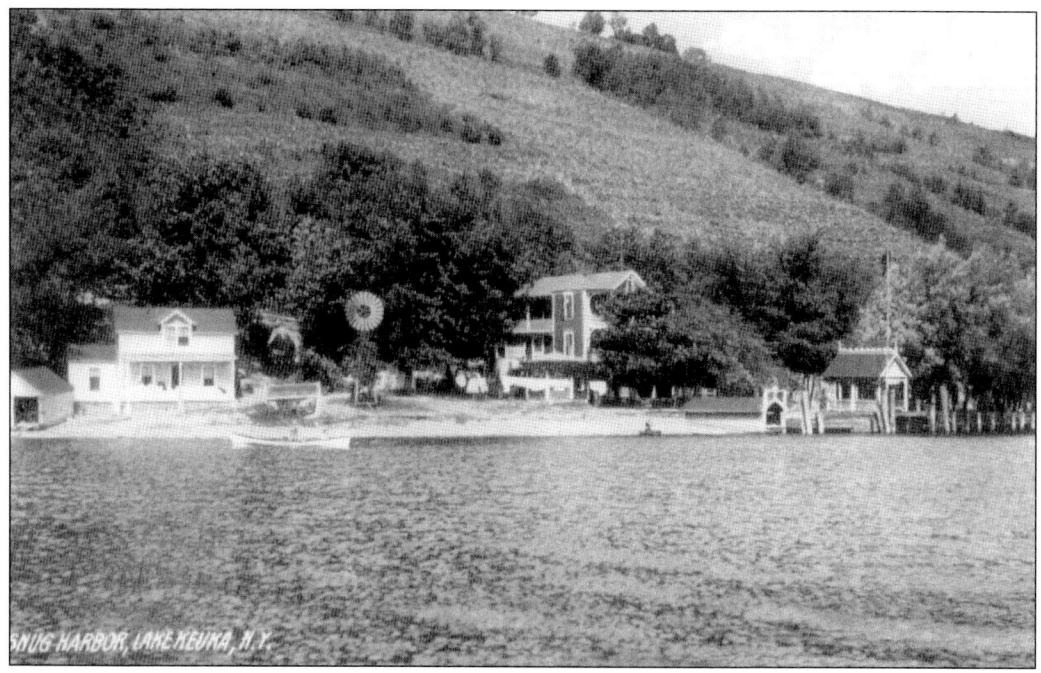

Snug Harbor was the name given by the owners of a cottage there. A popular restaurant now greets drivers and boaters at Snug Harbor.

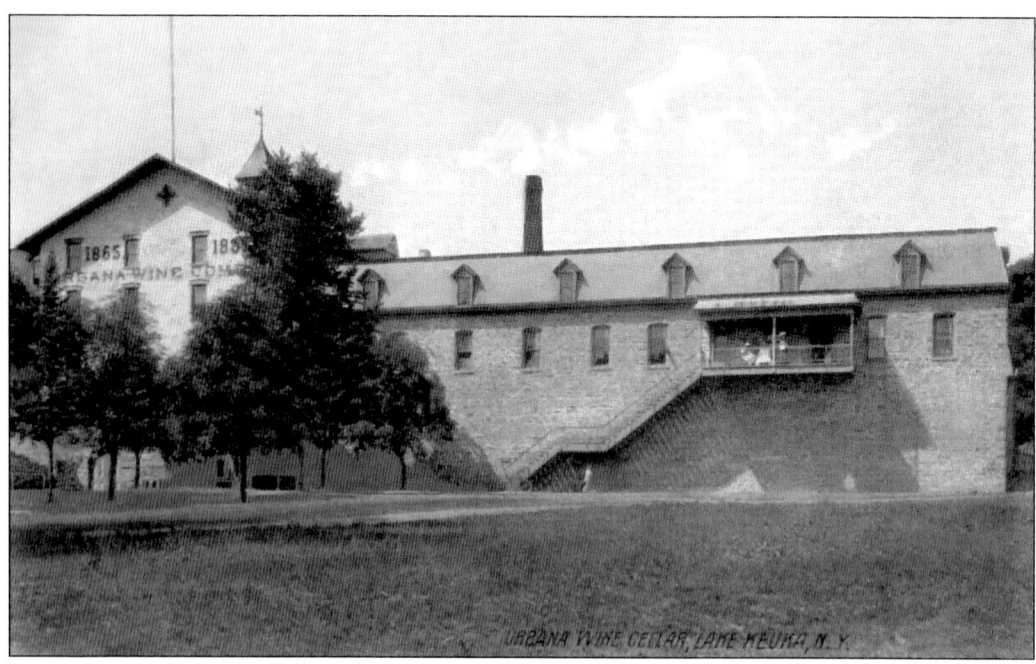

The dramatic stone building of Urbana Winery may be used for storage nowadays, but it still looms impressively over the lake. When the Gold Seal winery was in operation, tours ended with wine sampling on the porch seen in this image.

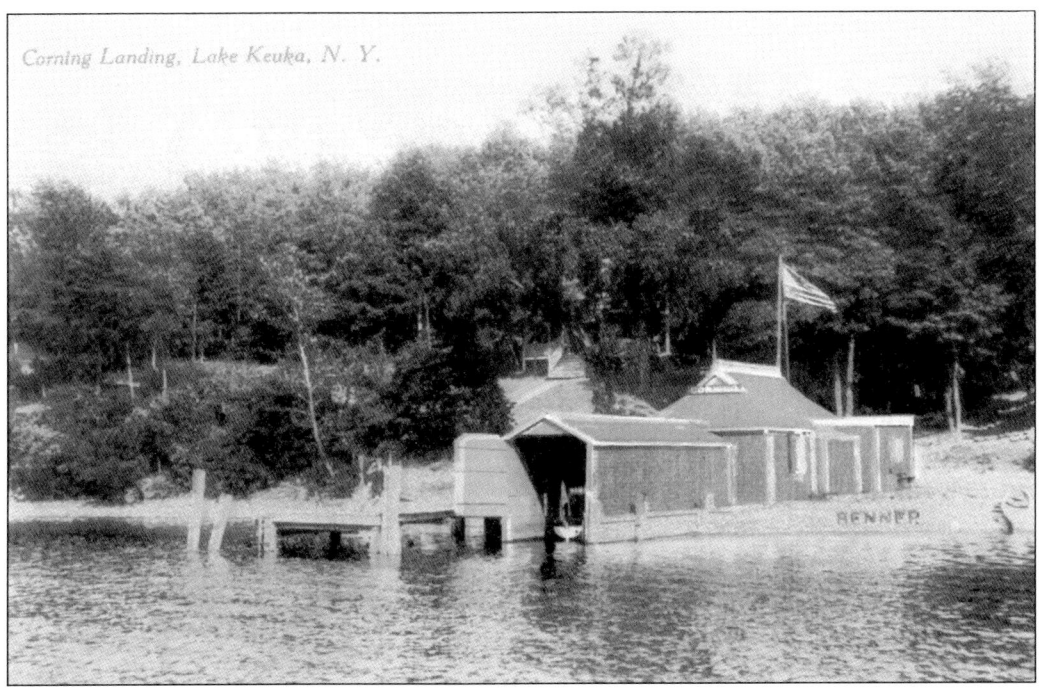

A colony of summer-home owners from Corning gave one spot the name it still bears on Keuka Lake. Many of the cottages from the time of this image are still there.

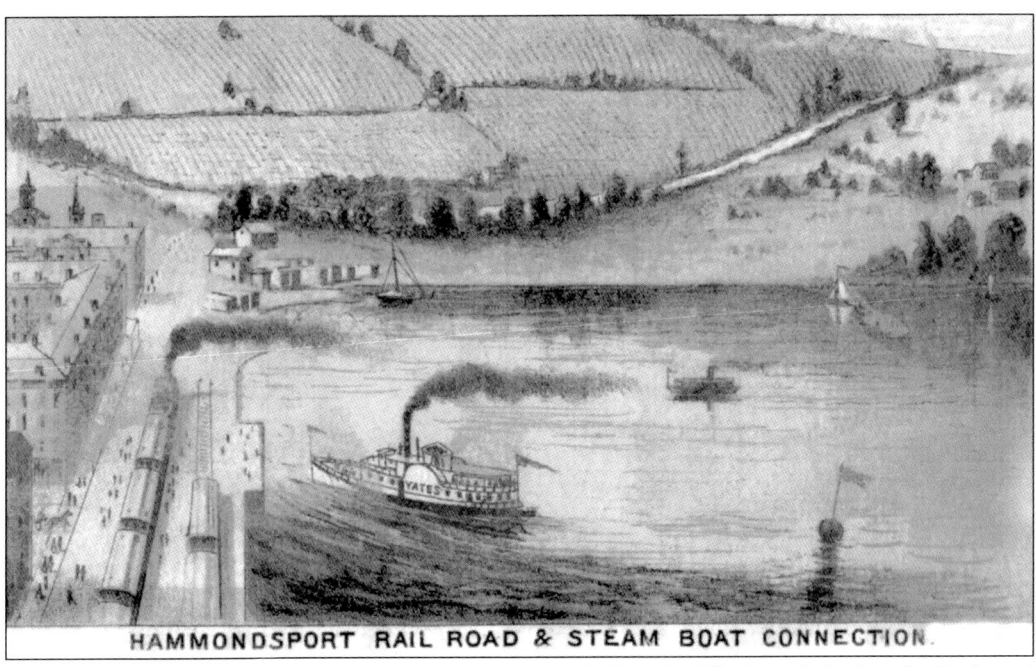

The since-vanished hotels on Water Street are a little bit glorified, and the lovely Bath and Hammondsport depot is frustratingly obscured by smoke, but Hammondsport was indeed a port once, with steamers like the *Yates* making several scheduled stops a day.

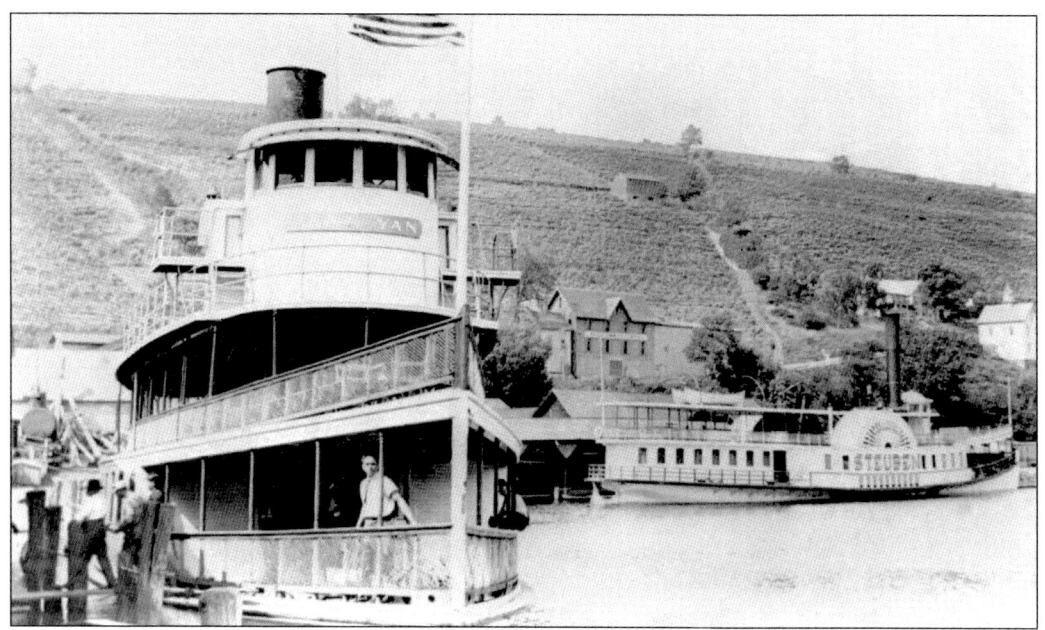

The *Penn Yan* is shown here docking at Hammondsport. Originally christened *Mary Bell*, the *Penn Yan* was marketed as an elegant excursion boat, even sporting colored electric lights. She made her final scheduled run in 1922, making her the last steamboat in operation on Keuka, although she had been refitted with gasoline engines by then. The second steamship moored at the right is the *Steuben* (formerly *William L. Halsey*).

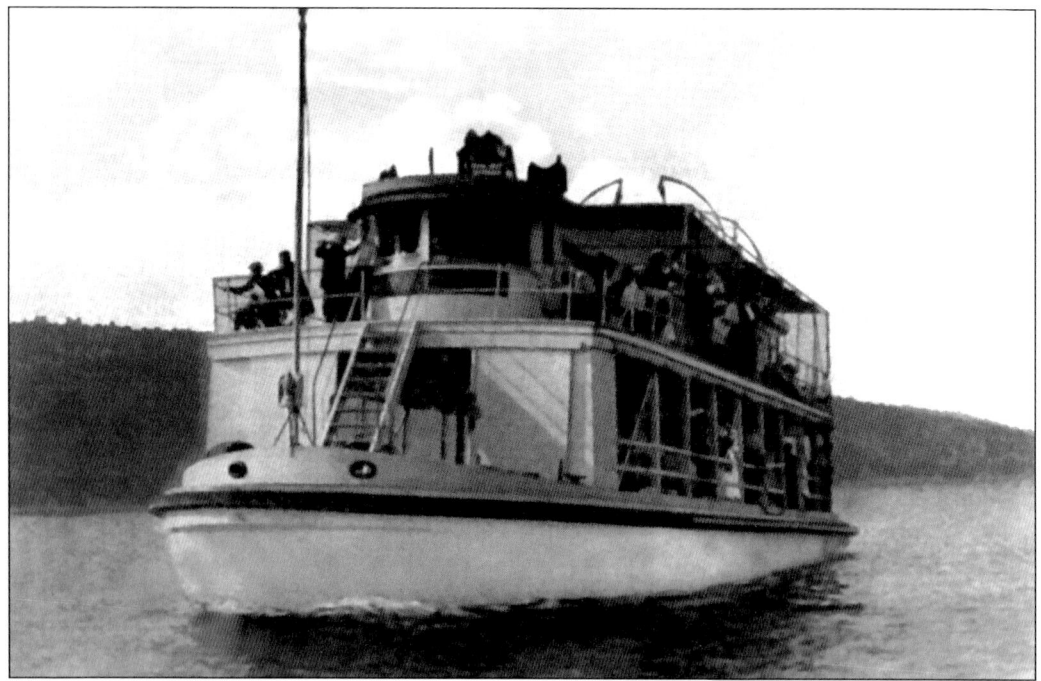

The Lake Keuka Navigation Company operated the twin *City of Rochester* and *City of Elmira* as gasoline freight barges on Keuka Lake, although obviously passengers found their way aboard too. *Rochester*'s metal pennant is now in the Curtiss Museum.

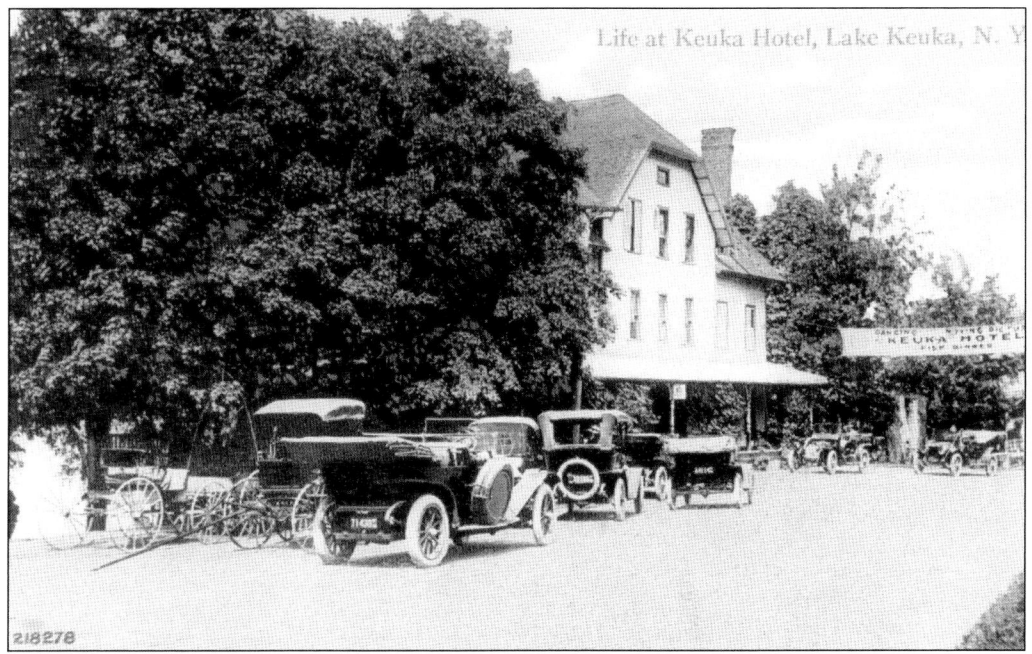

For 80 years the Keuka Hotel was a popular lakeshore destination in Wayne. It was a busy day when this image was made, with fish dinners, and dance, and moving pictures. With no theaters close by, they could apparently draw a crowd to watch movies.

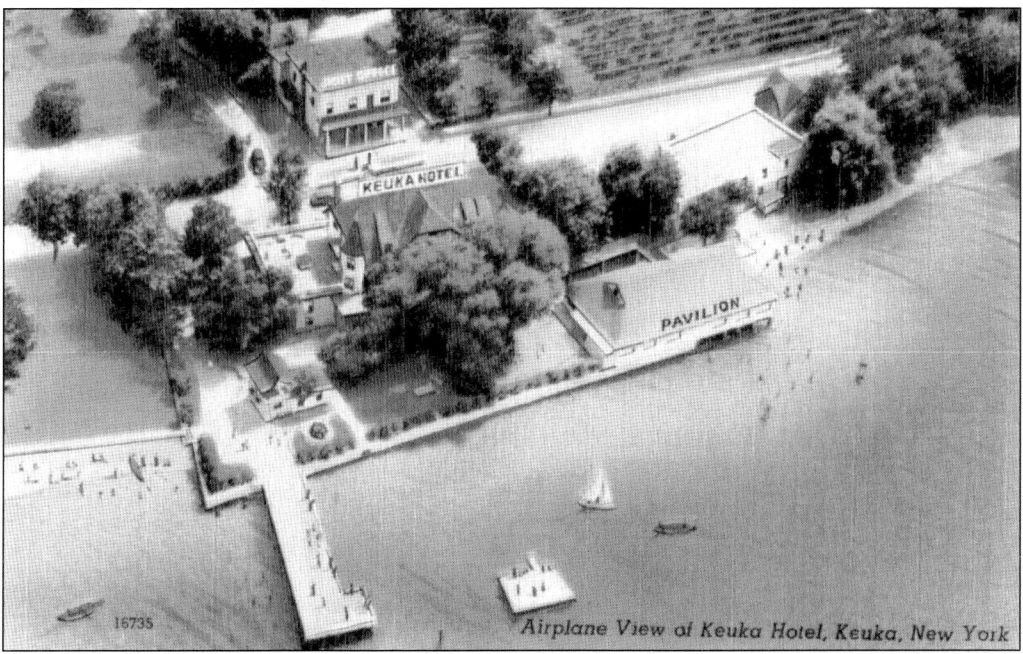

Although labeled "Airplane View," this is a drawing with which the artist took some liberties in the location of roads and the exclusion of buildings not part of the hotel property. The building marked pavilion had previously been perpendicular to the shore and was a dance hall. After it was moved it was converted to a roller rink. Teenagers made the lakeside pavilion a popular roller-skating spot for many years, and the hotel's Rainbow Room was popular with adults.

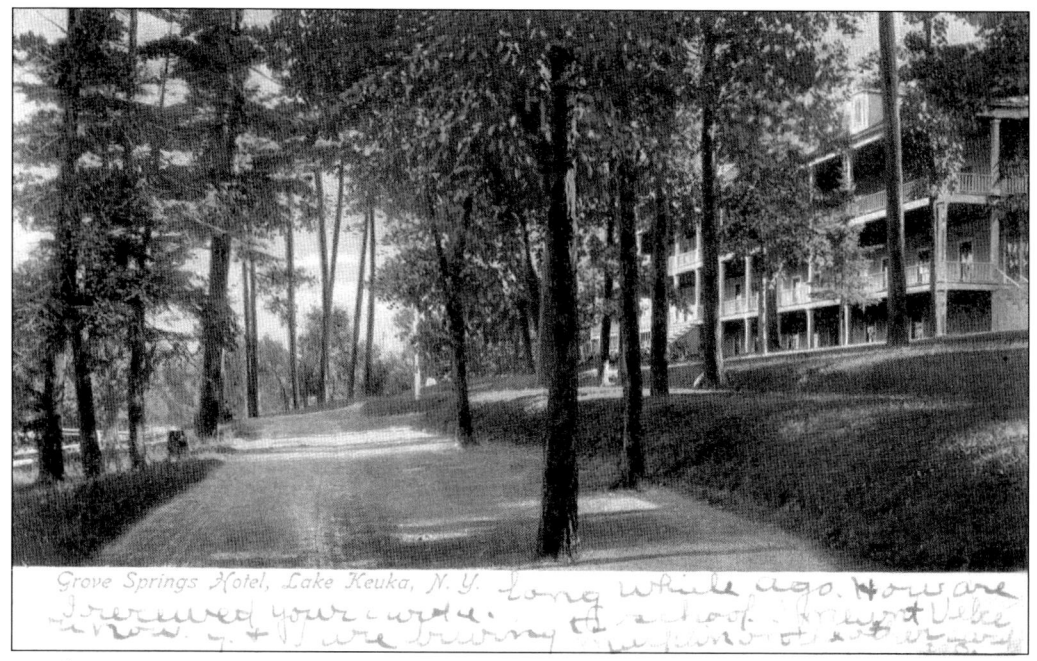

Nearby Grove Springs Hotel was an impressive tree-shaded edifice. In those days with limited personal transportation, vacationing families would often stay for weeks, or even an entire summer, at resorts. The facilities hosted round-the-clock activities for all ages.

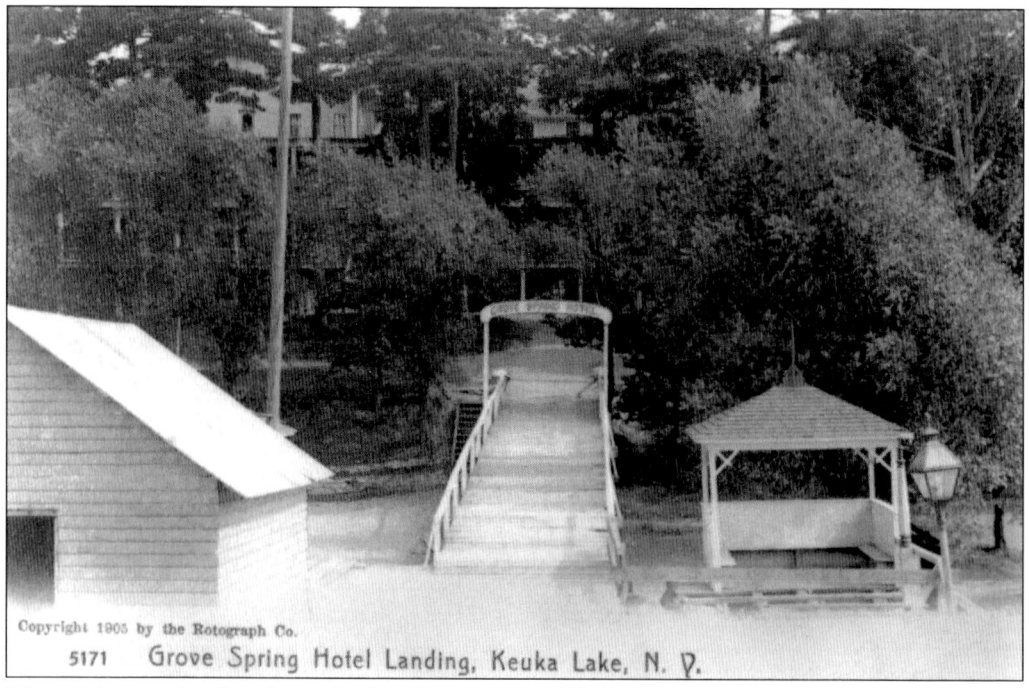

Most visitors arrived at Grove Springs by steamer, and their introduction to the place had to be suitably engaging. This dock was a scheduled stop for all the steamboats.

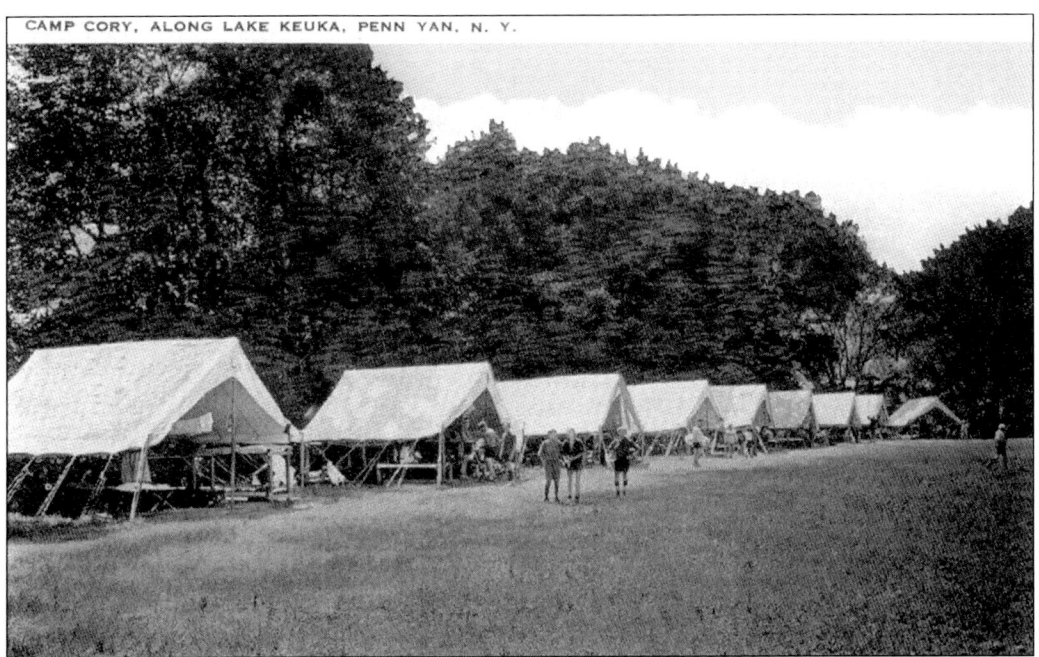

The Finger Lakes region, with its blend of water, hills, and forest, has long been a popular camping destination. The Boy Scouts had this spot on Keuka's East Branch; it is now a YMCA camp.

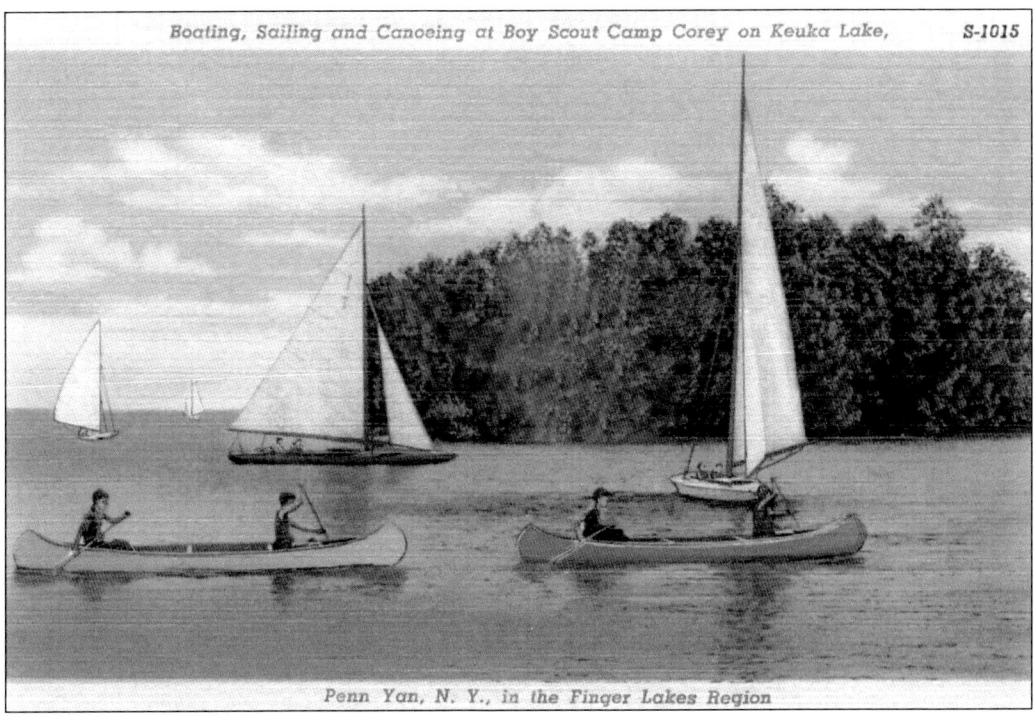

Rochester YMCA Camp Cory has a large fleet of "K" sailboats, which were designed and built near Keuka. Sailboats of all types can be found on the lake, and as people become more energy conscious, they will probably be more plentiful.

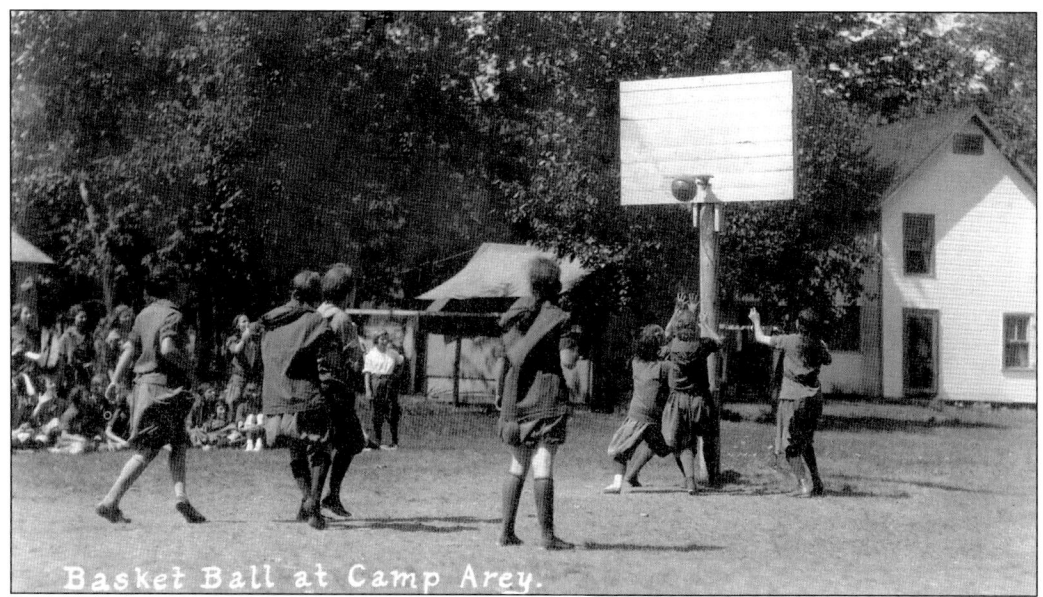

Also on Keuka was Camp Arey, later Science Camp. Notice those old-time basketball uniforms, including bloomers and high socks. John D. Rockefeller once owned Camp Arey, and his wheelchair is still there waiting for him, although there is no record of his ever paying a visit.

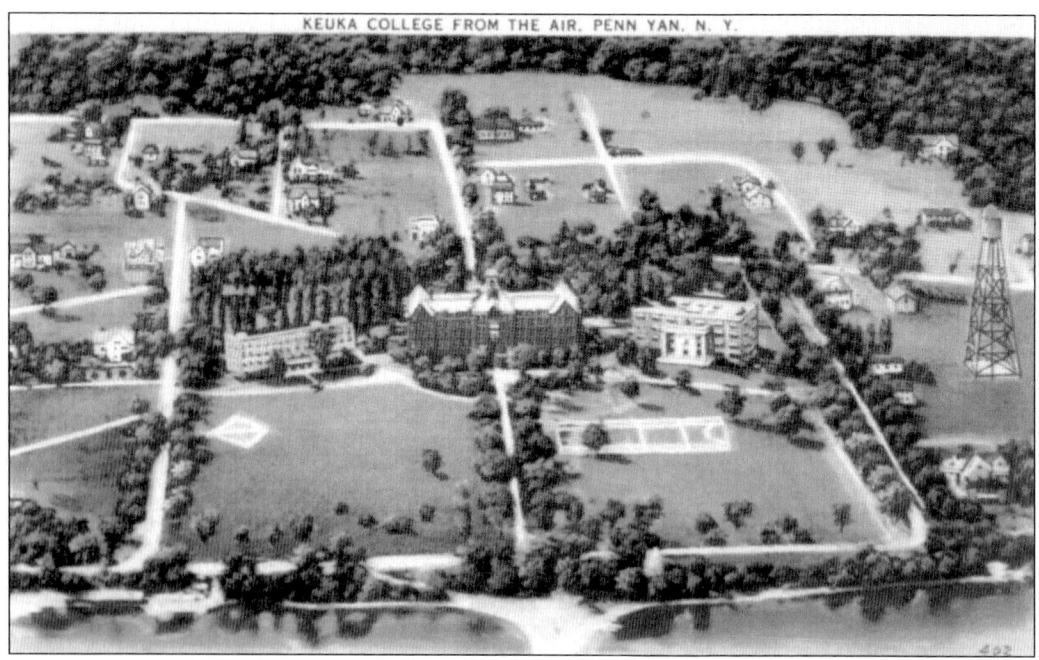

Keuka College has been educating students since 1896. Originally coeducational, Keuka became a women's college in 1920 following a five-year hiatus; coeducation returned in 1985. Keuka, which enrolls 1,000 students or more, has a historic association with the American Baptist Church. Twenty-first-century programs include regular teaching semesters throughout China.

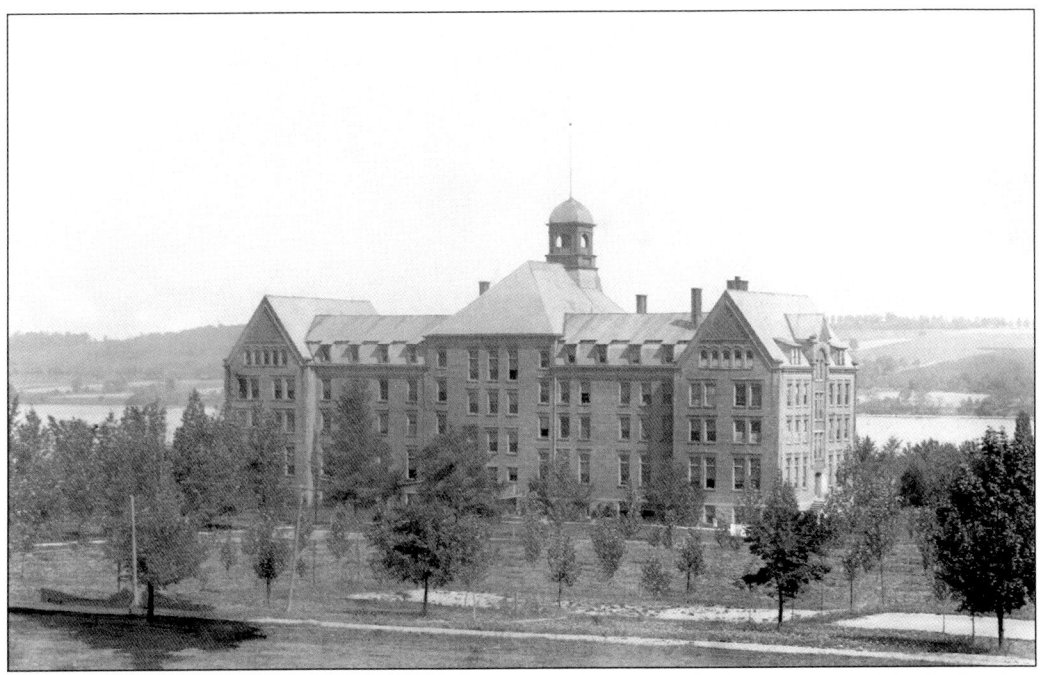

Ball Hall remains the architectural center of Keuka College. The facility was named for the brother canning-jar magnates of Muncie, Indiana, who offered a challenge grant for its construction. Their uncle Rev. George Harvey Ball founded the college.

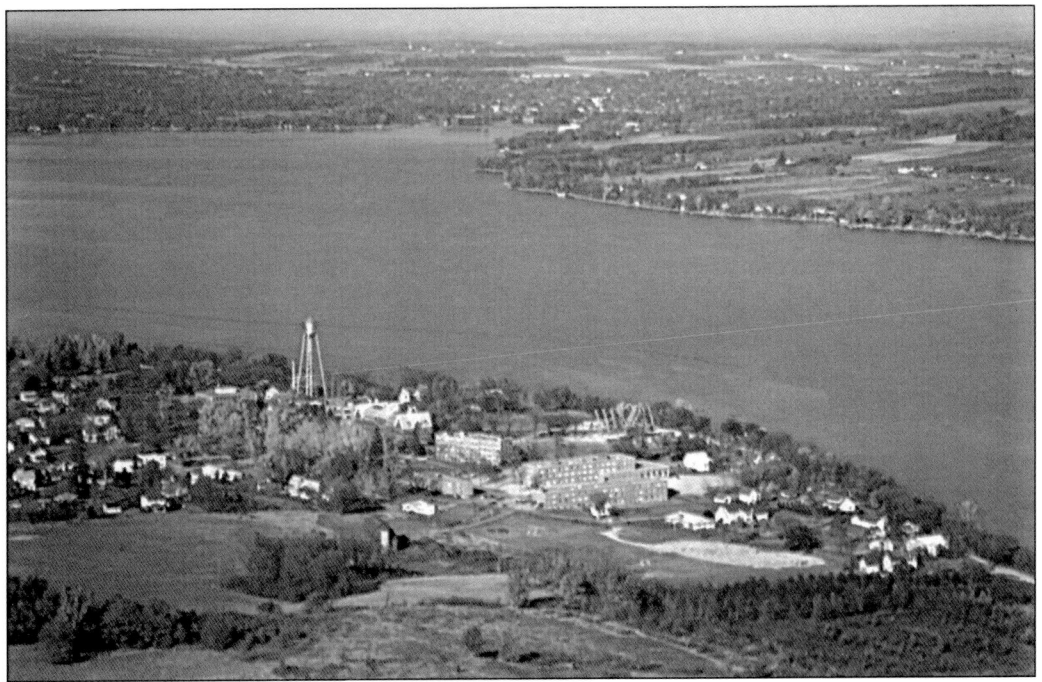

In this aerial view of Keuka College, Norton Chapel can be seen under construction near the lake. A very popular marriage location for college grads, it is often booked for multiple weddings on a summer Saturday.

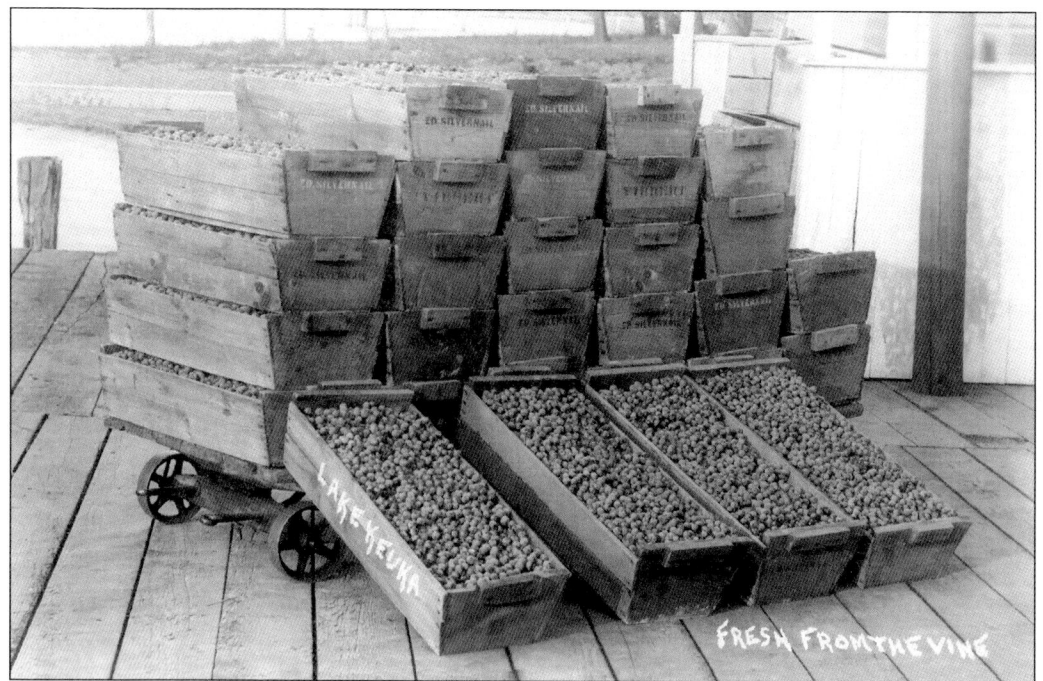

These grapes are indeed "fresh from the vine"; they are still in their picking flats, probably en route to the packer. Millions of baskets of eating grapes were shipped out of the Finger Lakes annually in the early years of the 20th century.

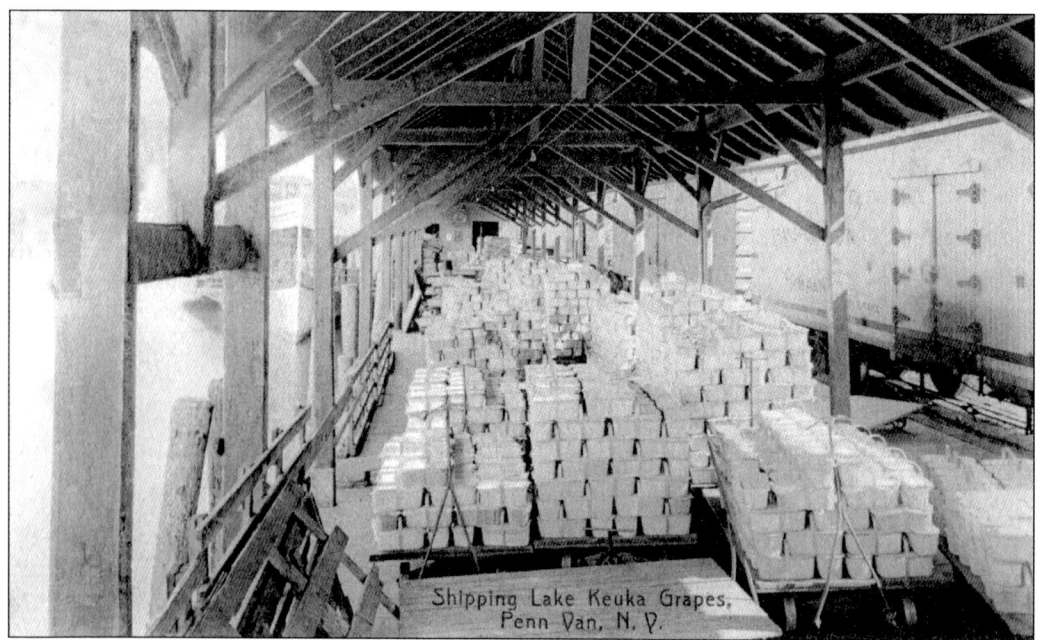

Now properly packed in their pony baskets, these grapes have just come off the steamer *Cricket* (in background) to be transferred to the New York Central Railroad. Keuka College students working off their tuition made thousands of such baskets in an on-campus factory.

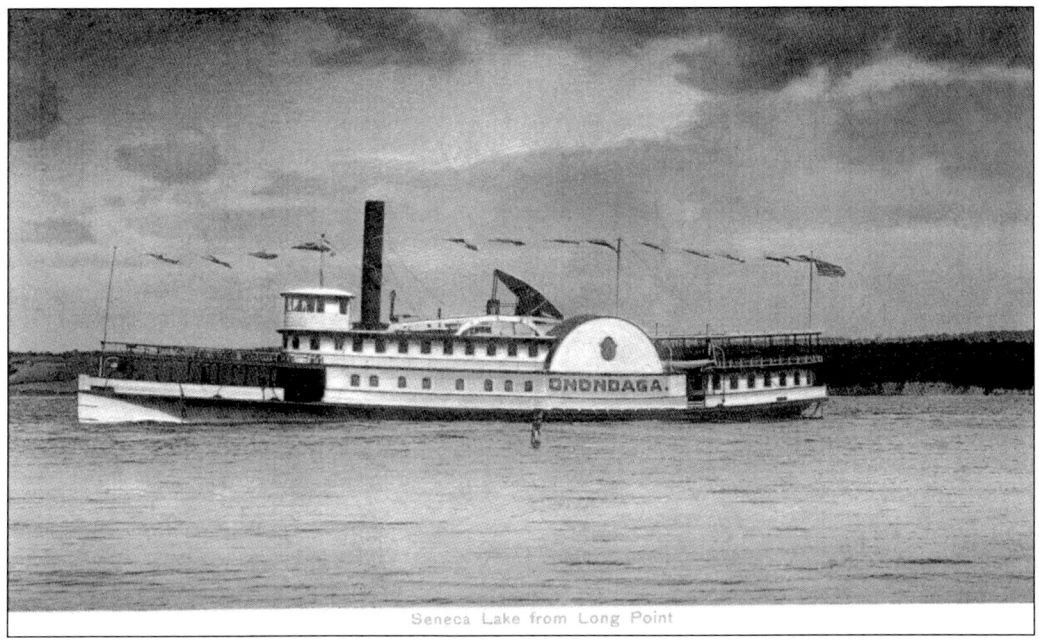

The largest of the Finger Lakes is 36-mile-long Seneca, so it is not surprising that steamboat traffic flourished, especially with the New York Central and Lehigh Valley Railroads, and Cayuga-Seneca Canal stops on the north end at Geneva, and a major tourist attraction on the south end at Watkins. Long Point, south of Dresden, is now a Salvation Army camp.

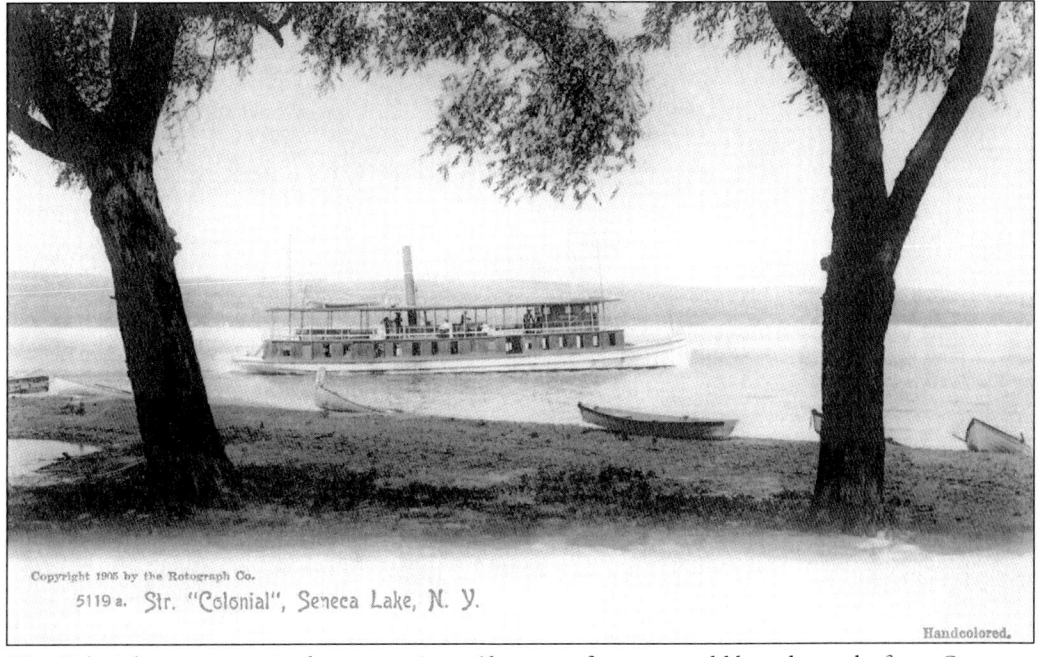

*The Colonial* was more suited to excursions. She was a four-year-old boat brought from Oswego. Rated to carry 400 passengers, she operated from 1900 until 1914.

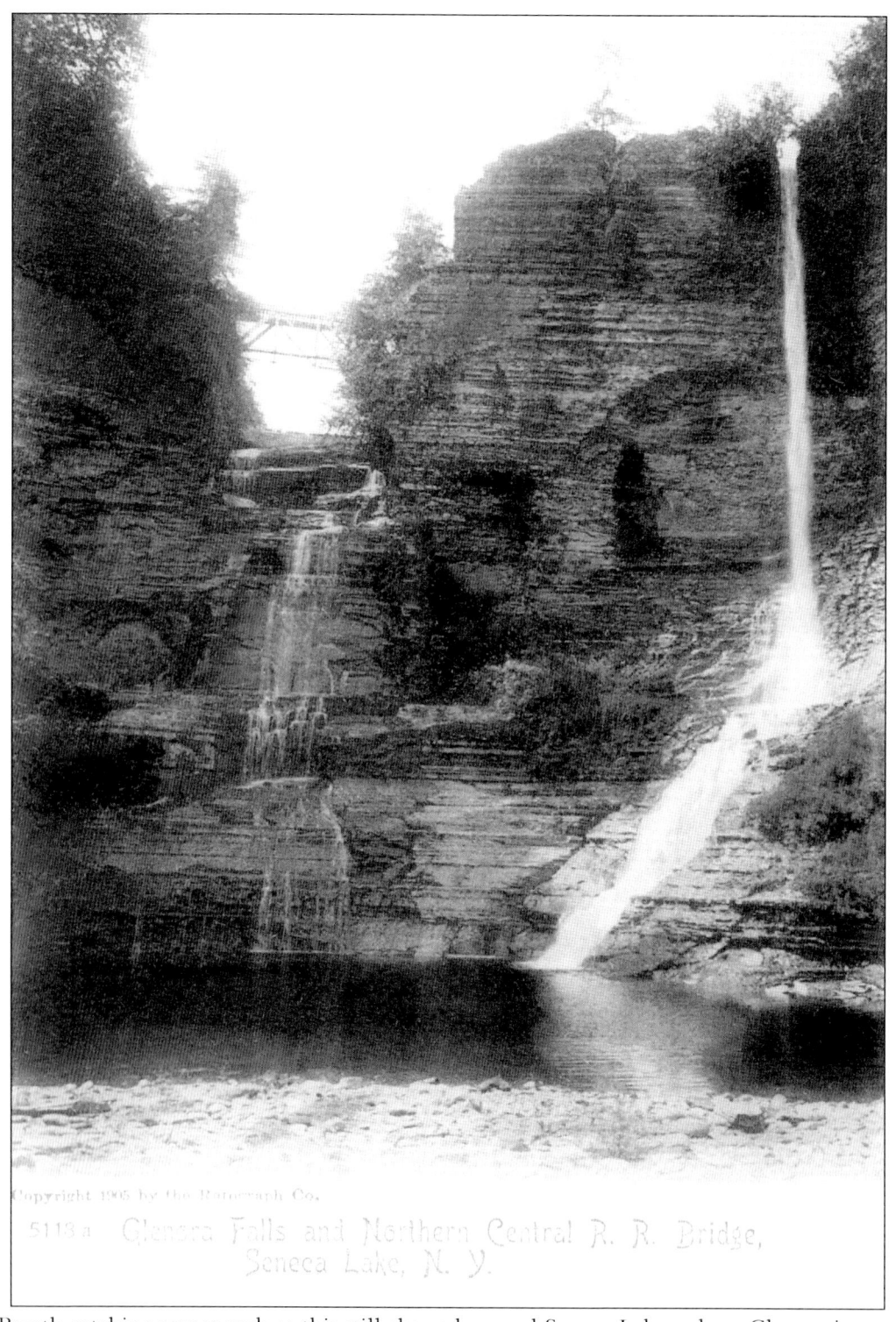

Breath-catching scenes such as this still abound around Seneca Lake, where Glenora is now home to a popular winery and inn.

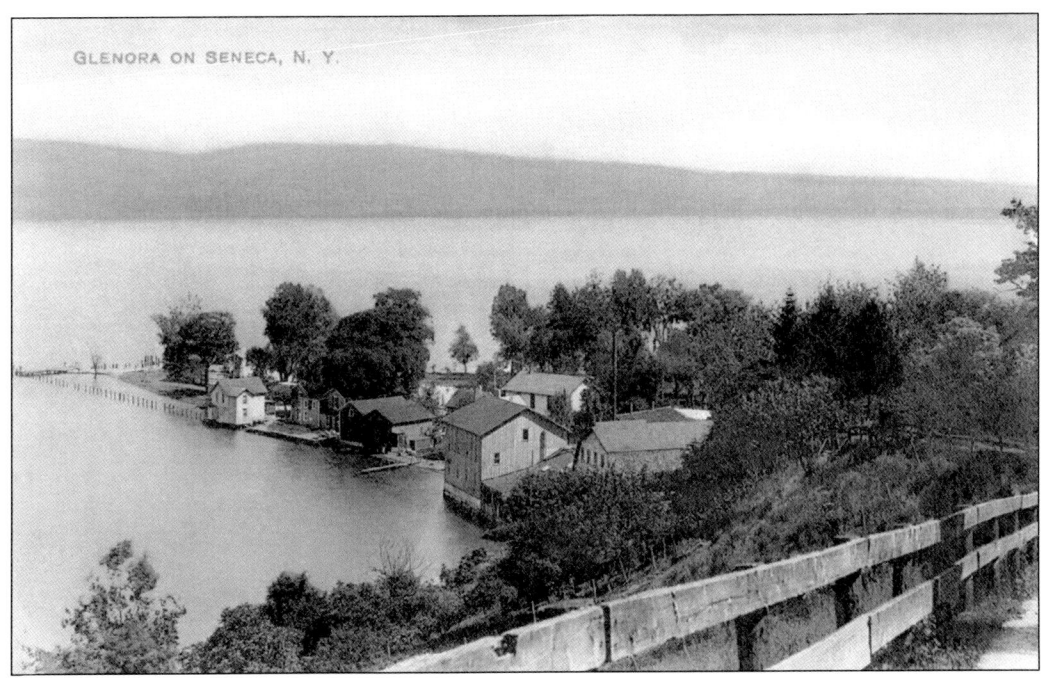

The landing at Glenora looks much the same today. The road down still winds, but it is paved and the fence is stronger.

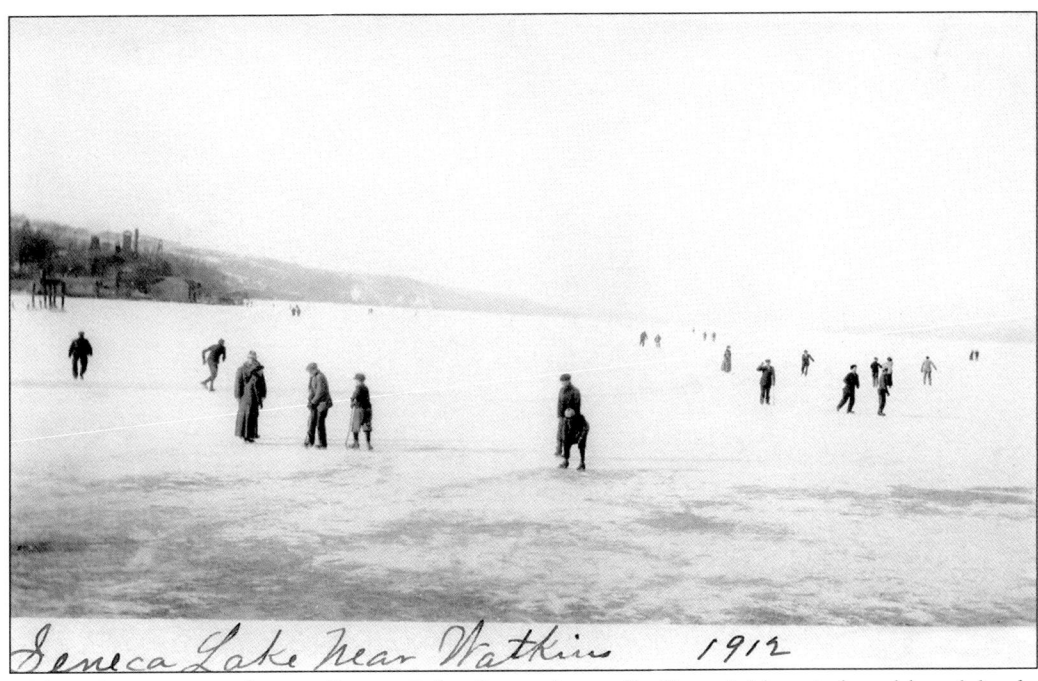

Although not quite as long as Cayuga Lake, Seneca beats all of its neighbors in breadth and depth, forming a prodigious body of water containing over four trillion gallons. Old-timers reportedly filled their car radiators from Seneca on the grounds that the lake never froze; actually it does from time to time, and so presumably did the radiators.

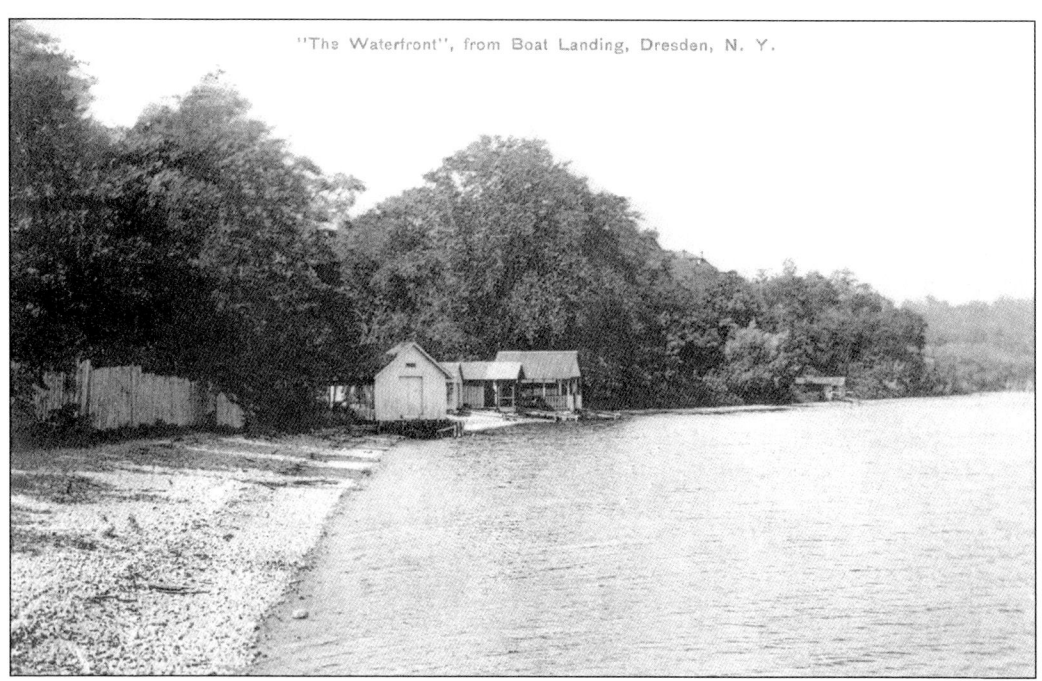

Seneca Lake was a vital link in New York's chain of inland waterways. Besides the Cayuga and Seneca Canal (which joined with the Erie Canal), feeder canals connected Seneca at Dresden with Keuka Lake and with the Chemung River at Watkins.

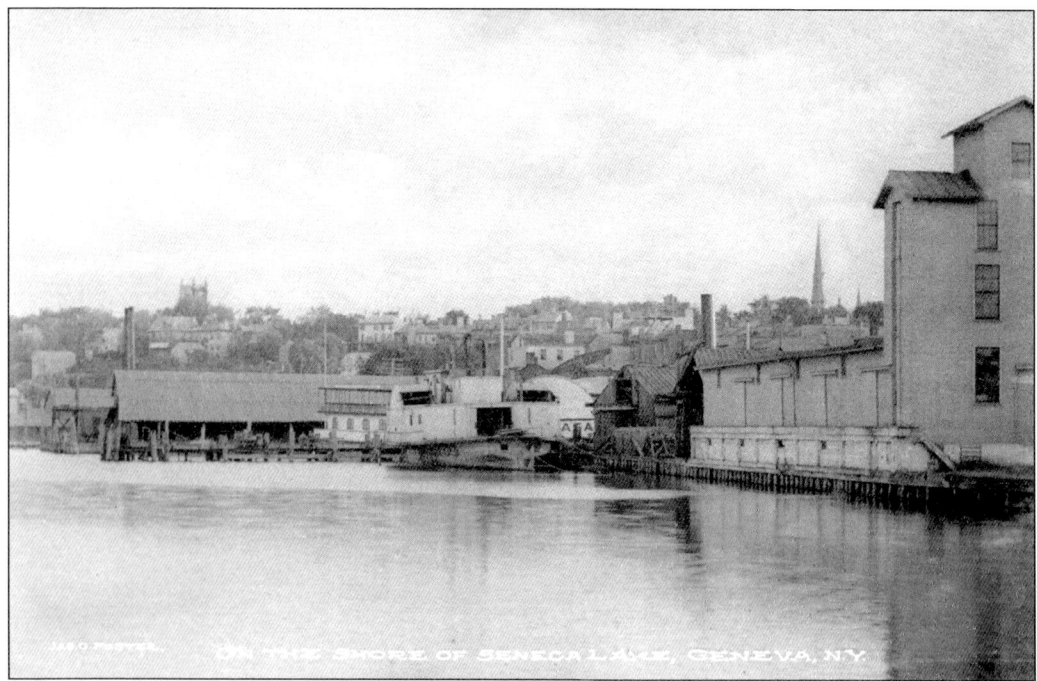

Thanks to these and other interconnecting waterways, such lake towns as Geneva (along with Hammondsport, Penn Yan, and Ithaca) were significant ports. Most of them also became important rail stops.

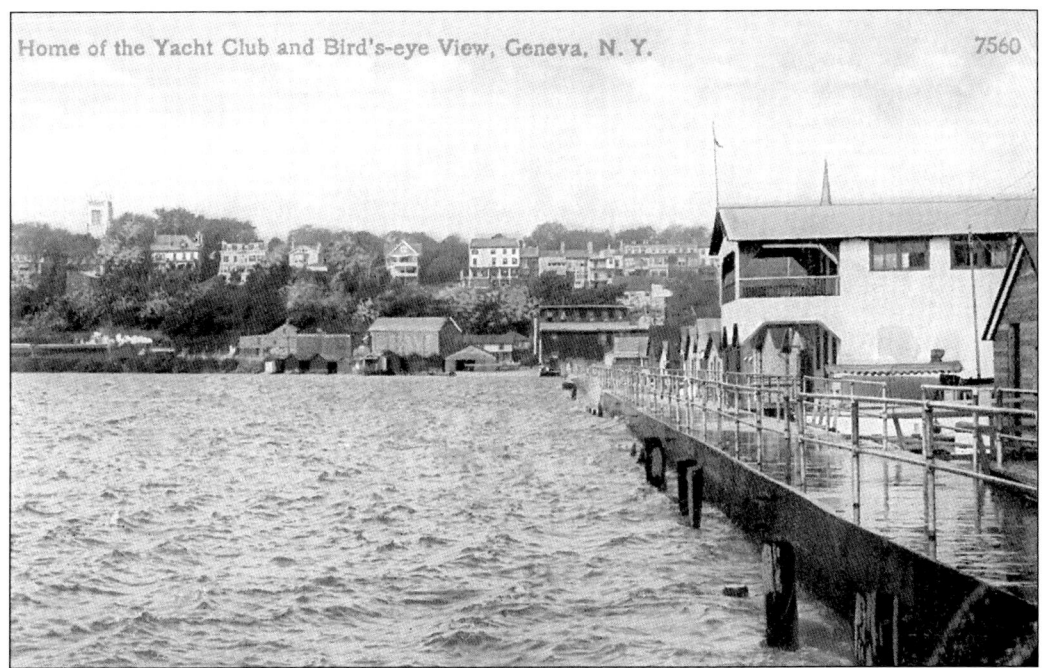

In another period, that same spot was home to the yacht club. Today most of the houses and churches in the background are still there, only the waterfront has changed.

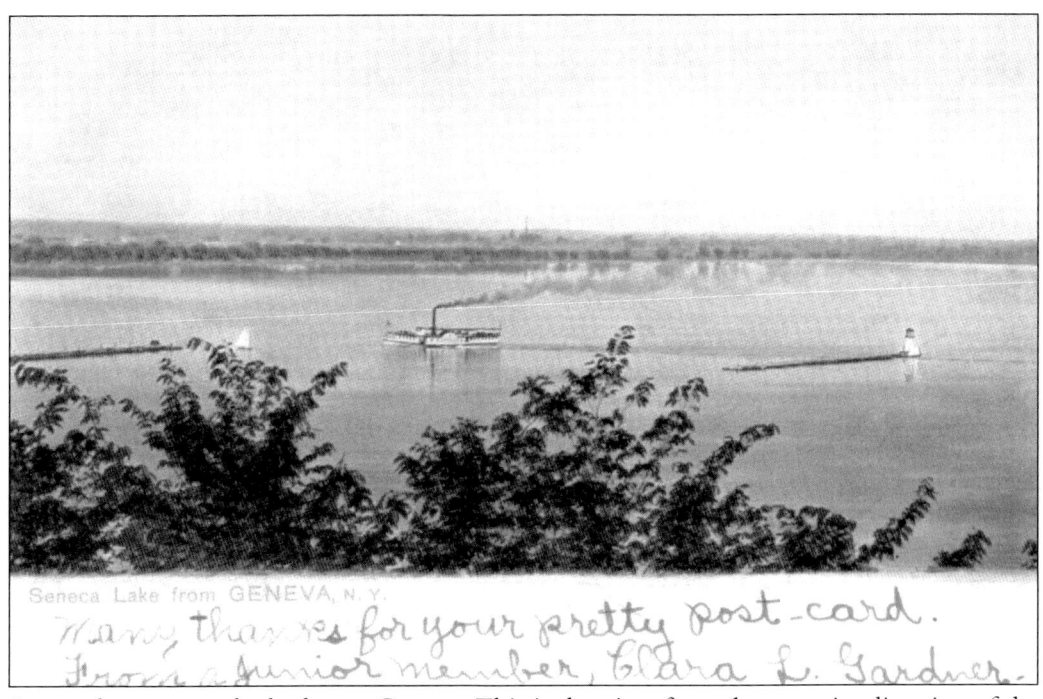

A steamboat enters the harbor at Geneva. This is the view from the opposite direction of the harbor as the image above. Seneca in the Iroquois language means "place of the stone."

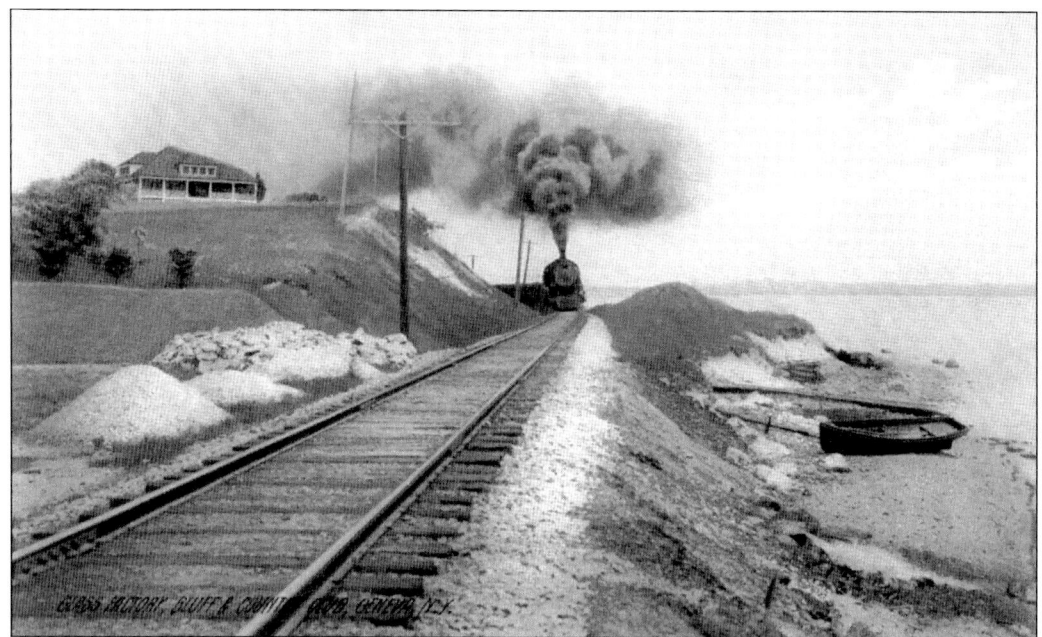

The New York Central Railroad, now replaced by Finger Lakes Railway, traveled the length of Seneca Lake on the west side. Today it would be practically impossible to build a railroad along such a beautiful lake, but 100 years ago the railroads were welcomed and lake frontage was considered little better than worthless. How times change!

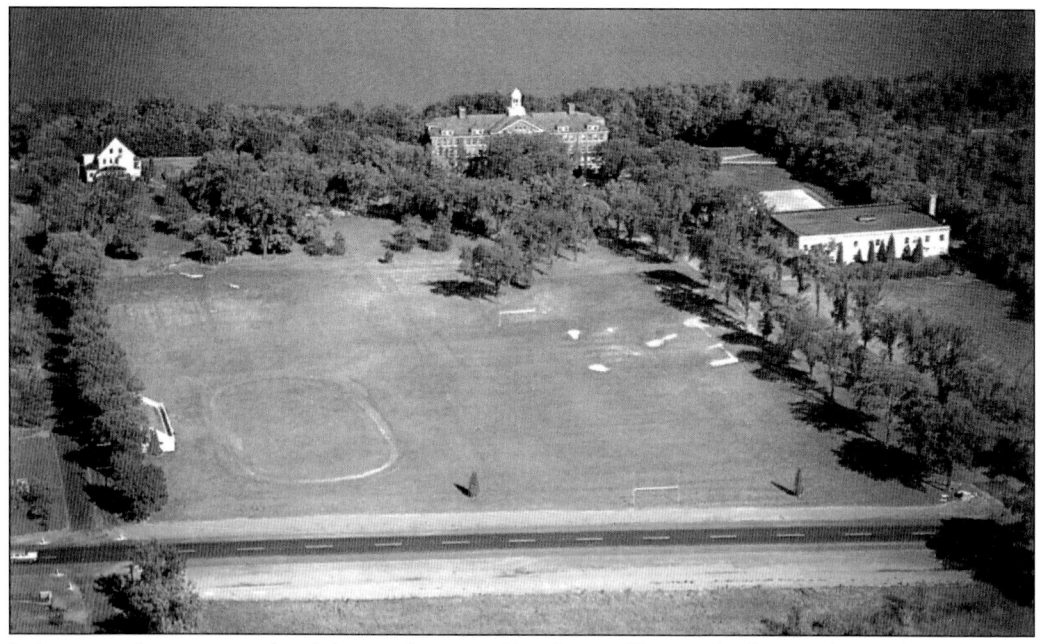

Lakemont, then a prep school, is now home to Freedom Village, which is a religion-based school for troubled teenagers. The large building (top center) has since burned.

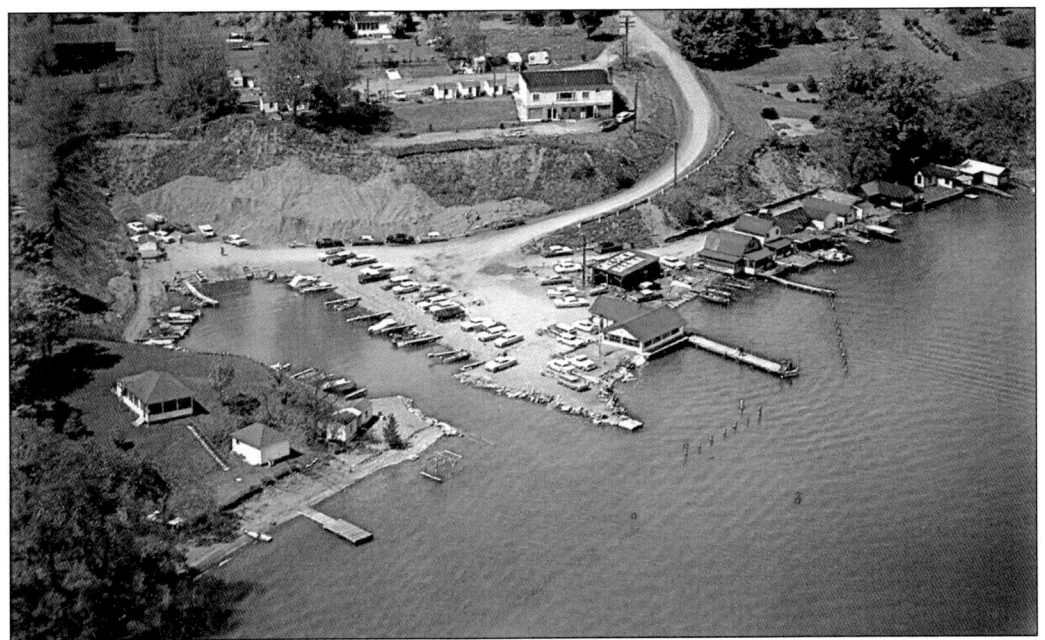

Dresden Bay and Marina advertised itself as the only all-weather harbor on Seneca's west side. The Crooked Lake Canal, which connected Keuka Lake to Seneca, was abandoned in the 1870s. Had it continued, Dresden as its eastern terminus would have been one of Seneca's important ports.

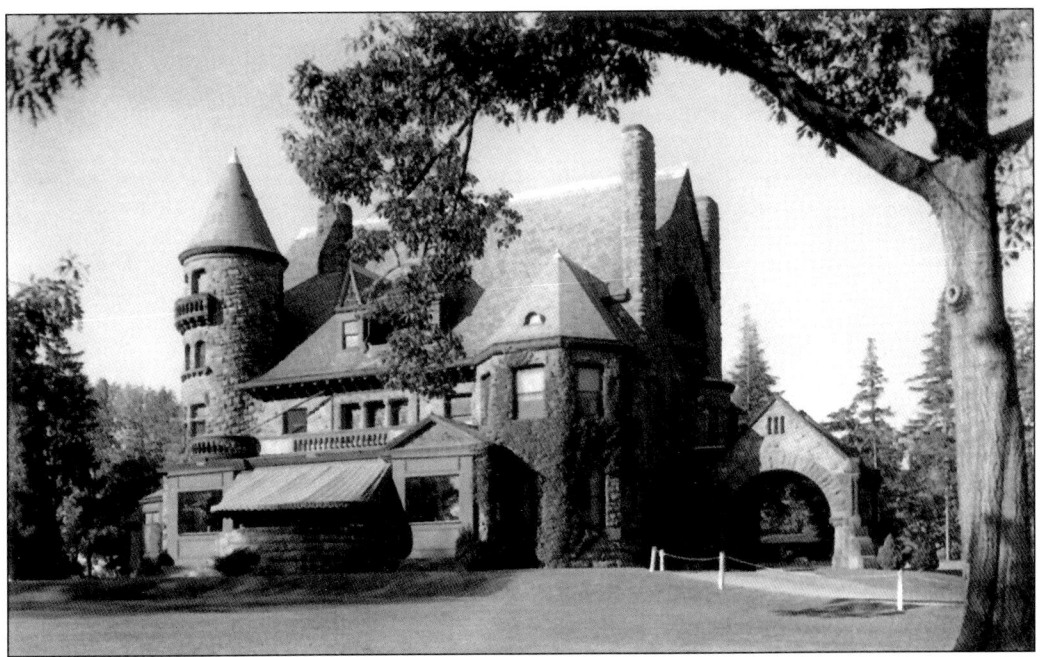

Belhurst Castle (1885) is still a popular destination on Seneca. It was recently expanded beyond the building shown here, adding more hotel rooms and a winery.

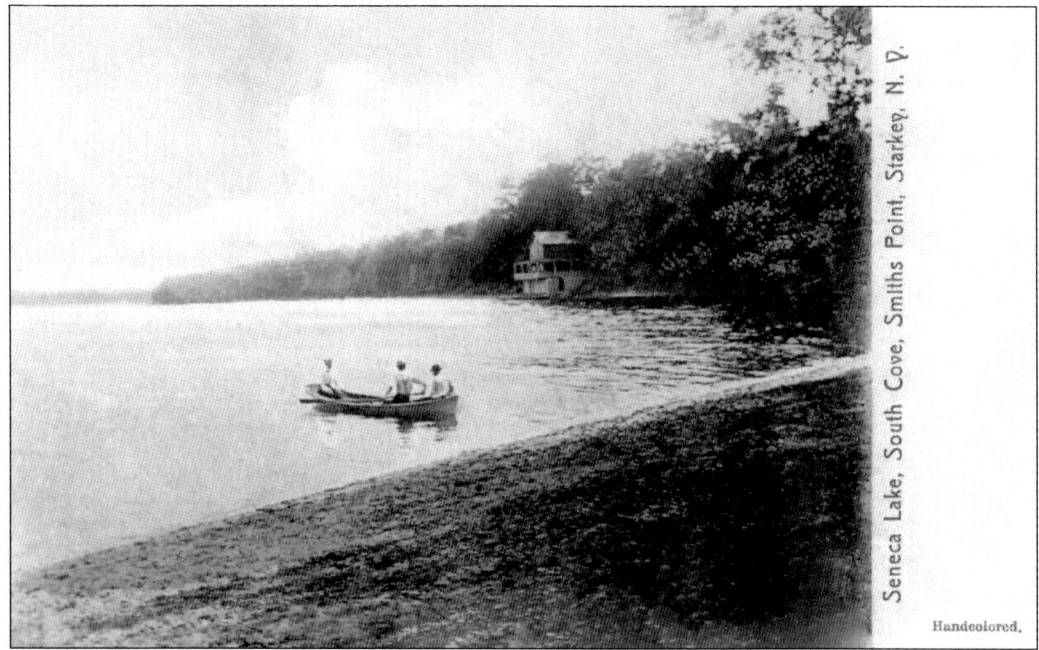

Notice that these boaters are overdressed. A hundred years ago this practice was common as well as dangerous. Is the extra person in the boat a chaperone?

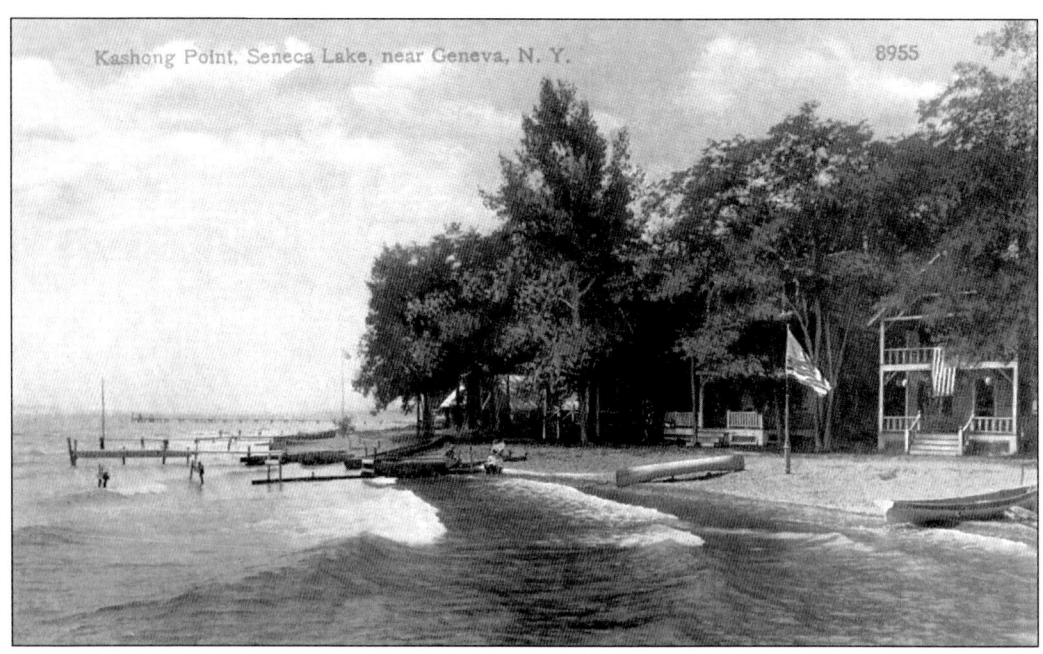

The only Revolutionary War military engagement in Yates County occurred here in 1779 when troops under Gen. John Sullivan destroyed crops and burned Seneca longhouses.

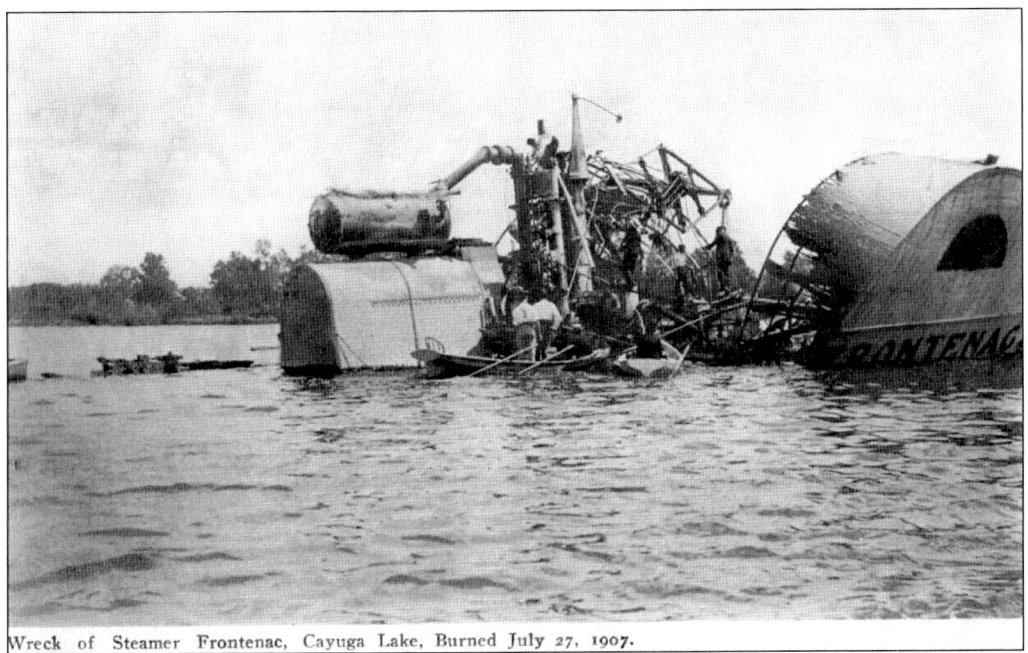

Wreck of Steamer Frontenac, Cayuga Lake, Burned July 27, 1907.

Over on Cayuga Lake the *Frontenac* burned—an all-too-frequent fate of steamboats—on July 27, 1907. Nine women and children died.

These falls tumble down near Frontenac Beach. Notice the well-dressed climbers at lower left. Frontenac Island in Cayuga Lake was a dwelling place for Paleo-Indian Lamokan people.

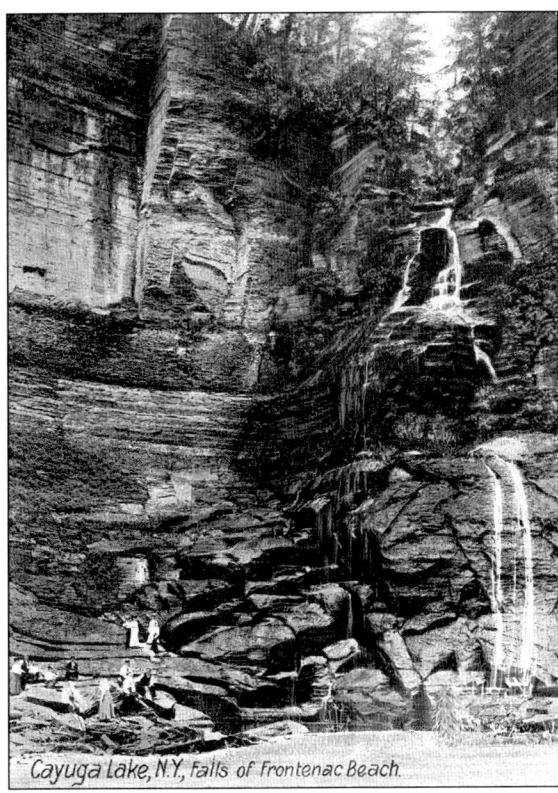

Cayuga Lake, N.Y., Falls of Frontenac Beach.

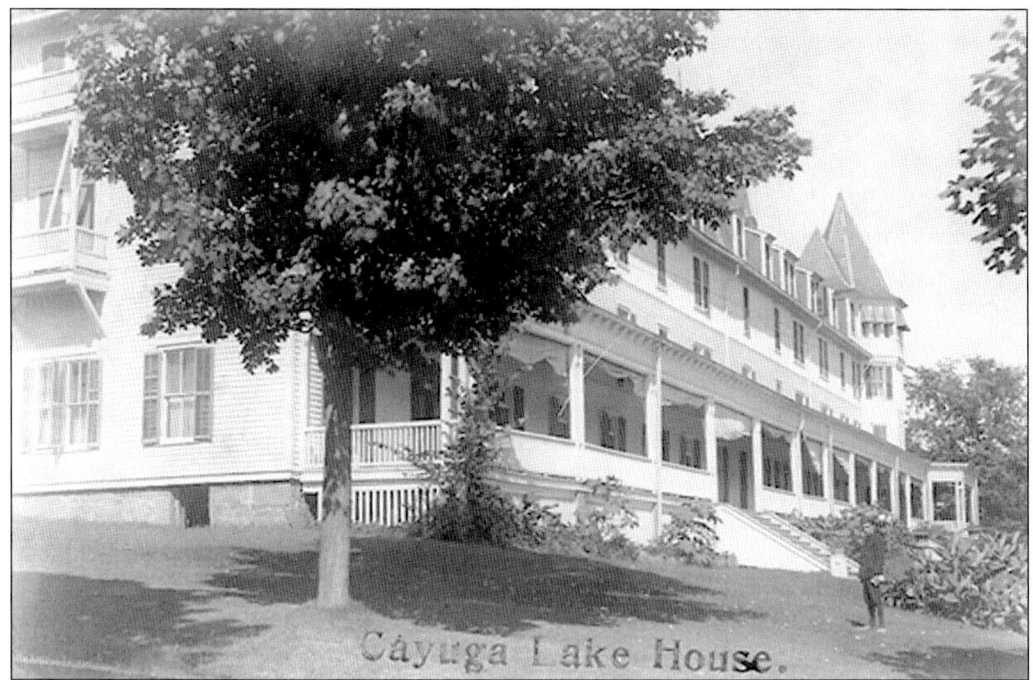

The grand hotels were grand indeed. Imagine whiling away a summer afternoon on that long front porch.

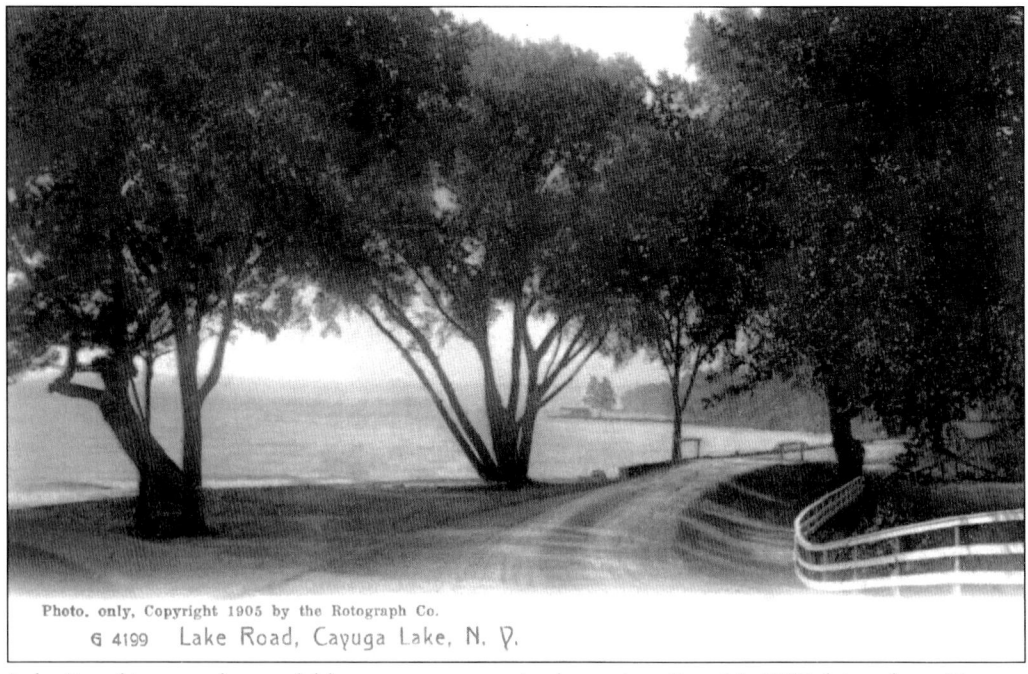

Lake Road is an understandably common name in the region. But this 1905 drive along Cayuga seems uncommonly lovely.

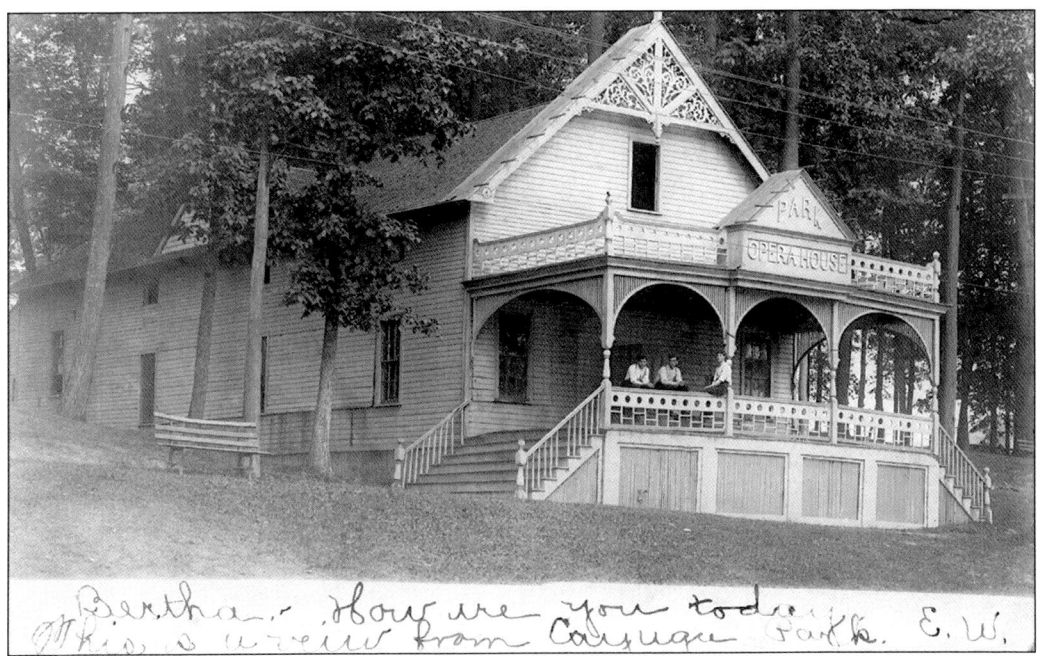

Opera houses likewise were once common. They hosted all sorts of entertainment, but only a few of these were actually operas.

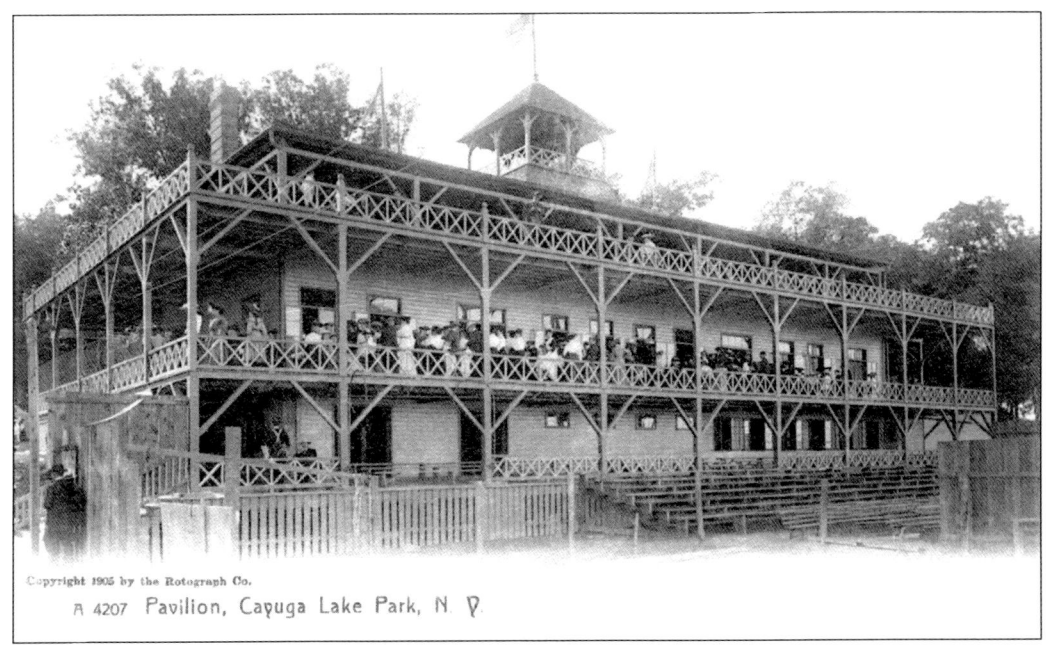

It would be interesting to know why folks on the second level are lining up. The line may be long, but it is hard to beat the setting.

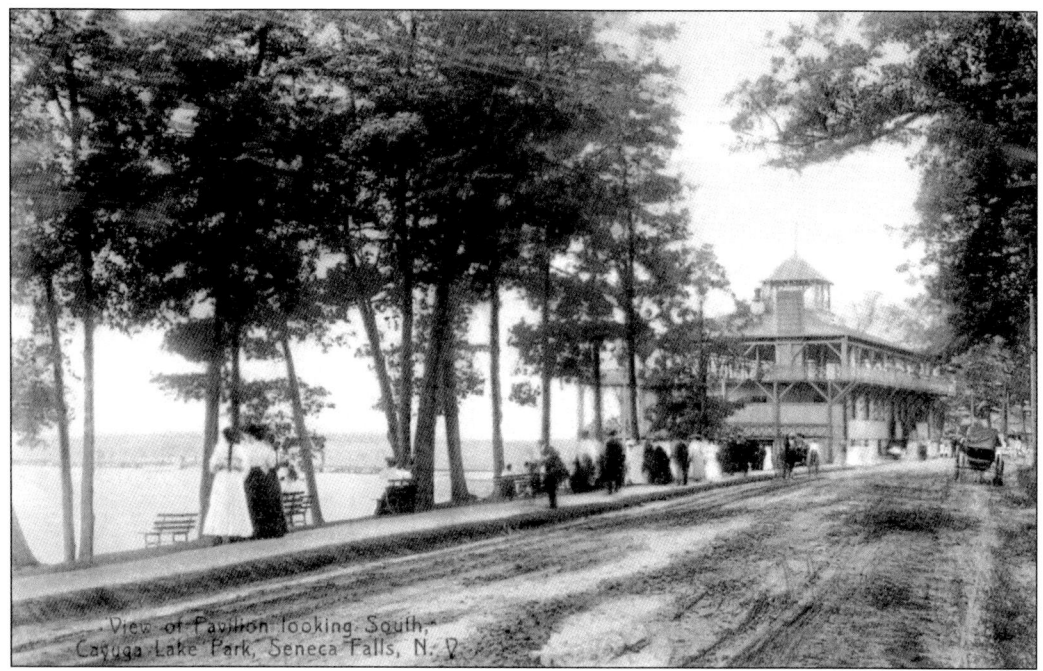

Here is another view of the pavilion at the park near Seneca Falls on the lake. Cayuga meant "boat landing" in the Native American tongue.

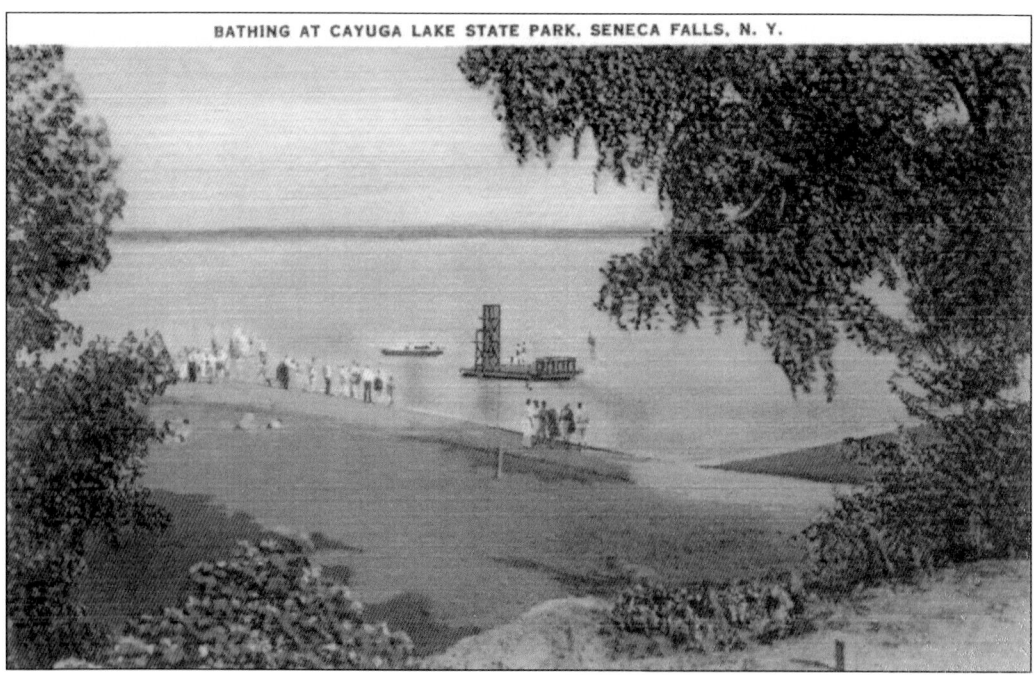

Cayuga Lake State Park is still a popular spot near Seneca Falls. It is unknown what was going on when this image was created, but most of the people in the park are watching rather than swimming.

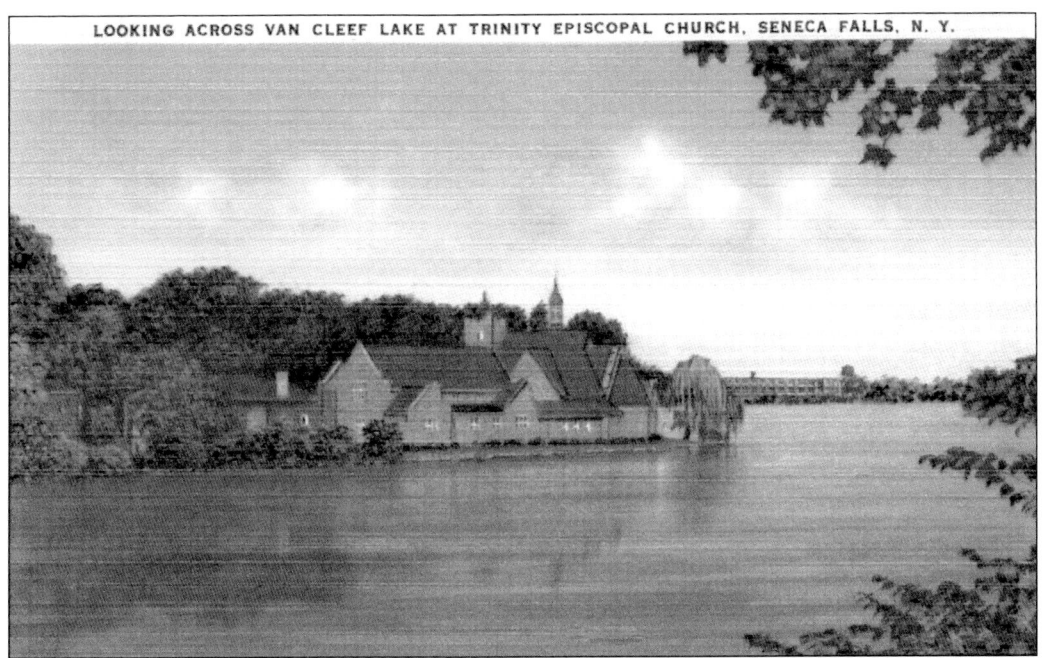

Even the small lakes in the region are lovely. Van Cleeve was formed in the process of creating and expanding the canal.

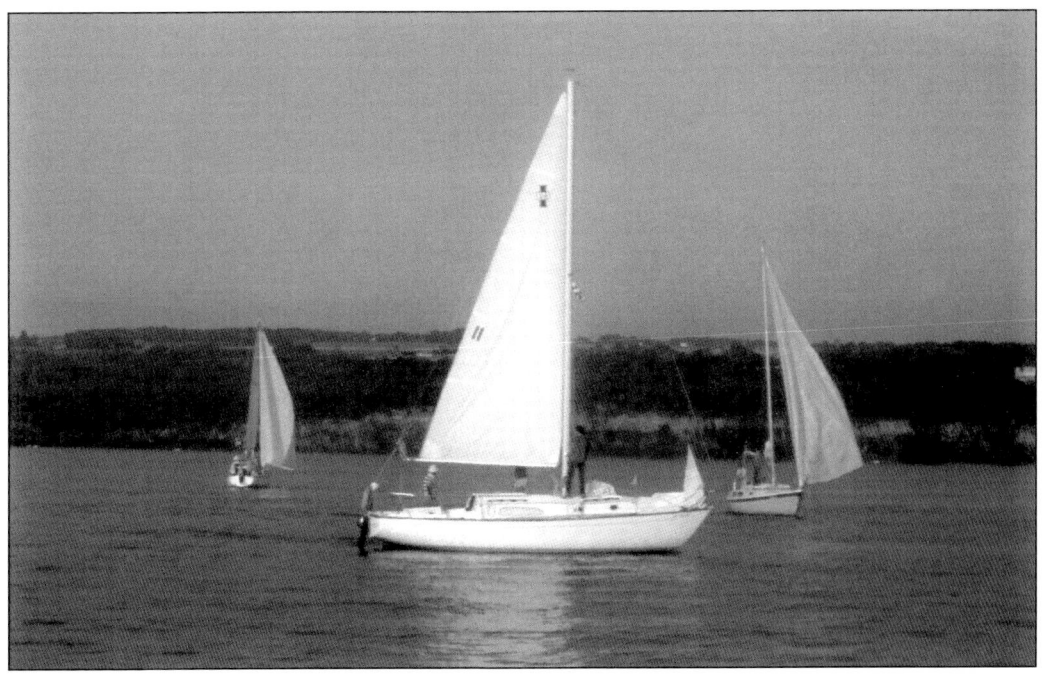

As with all the Finger Lakes, sailing is popular, as can be seen in many of the images. On Seneca and Cayuga (pictured here) the boats tend to be larger since boaters on these two lakes, because of access to the canal system, can get off the lake and literally go anywhere in the world. (Photograph by H. H. Lyon.)

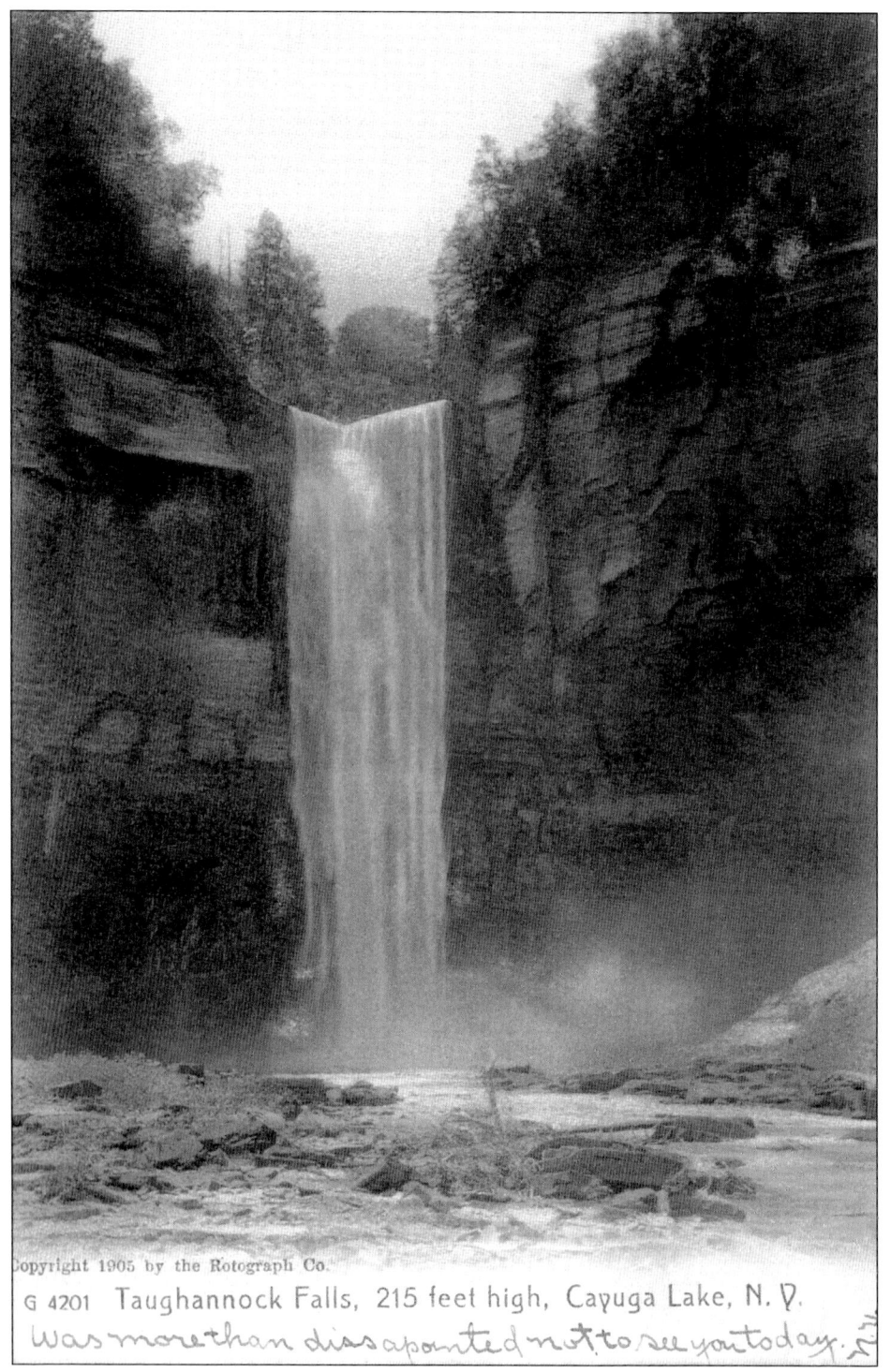

Taughannock (near Ulysses) is the highest free-falling waterfall east of the Rockies, beating Niagara by 33 feet. The name comes from a Delaware word meaning "great waterfall in the forest."

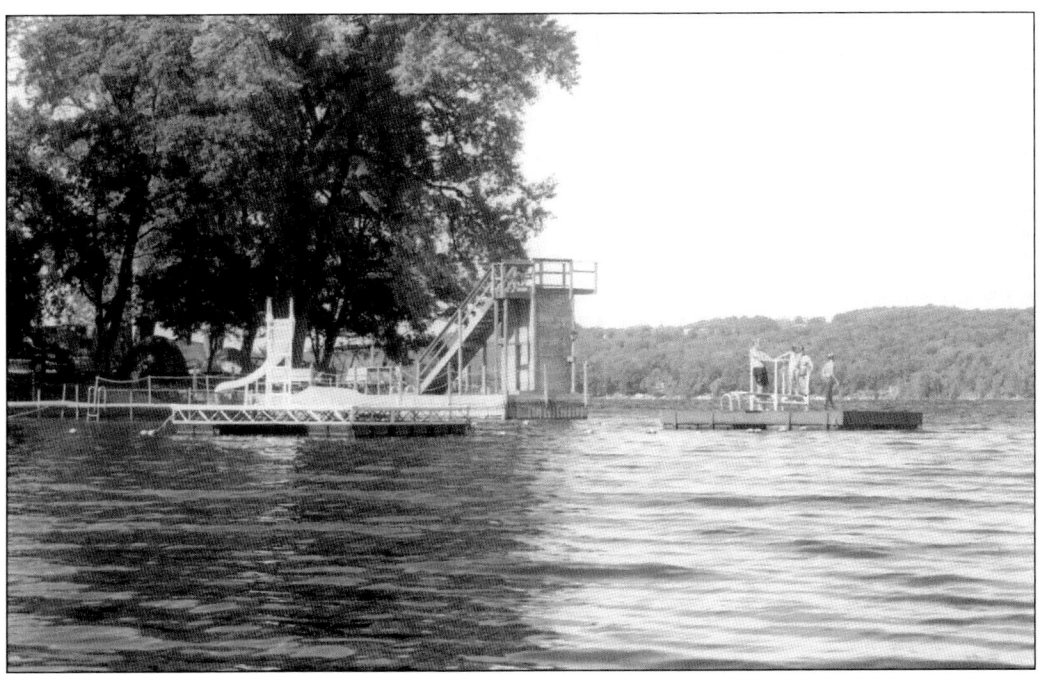

Owasco and other Finger Lakes remain magnets for recreation, as here in a Mennonite retreat at Camp Casowasco near Moravia. Pres. Millard Fillmore was born on the other side of Moravia, in what is now the town of Summerhill. (Photograph by Joshua B. House.)

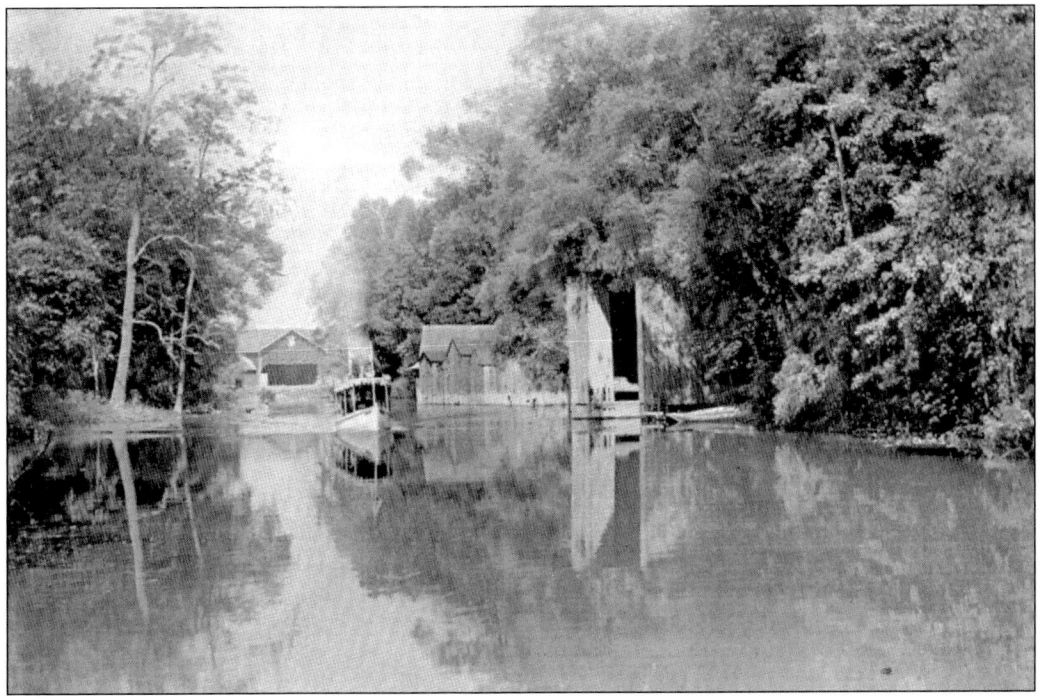

Owasco Lake drains out near Auburn, an Underground Railroad center that was home to Harriet Tubman and William H. Seward. The Cayuga Nation maintained its town of Wasco, "river crossing," near the outlet.

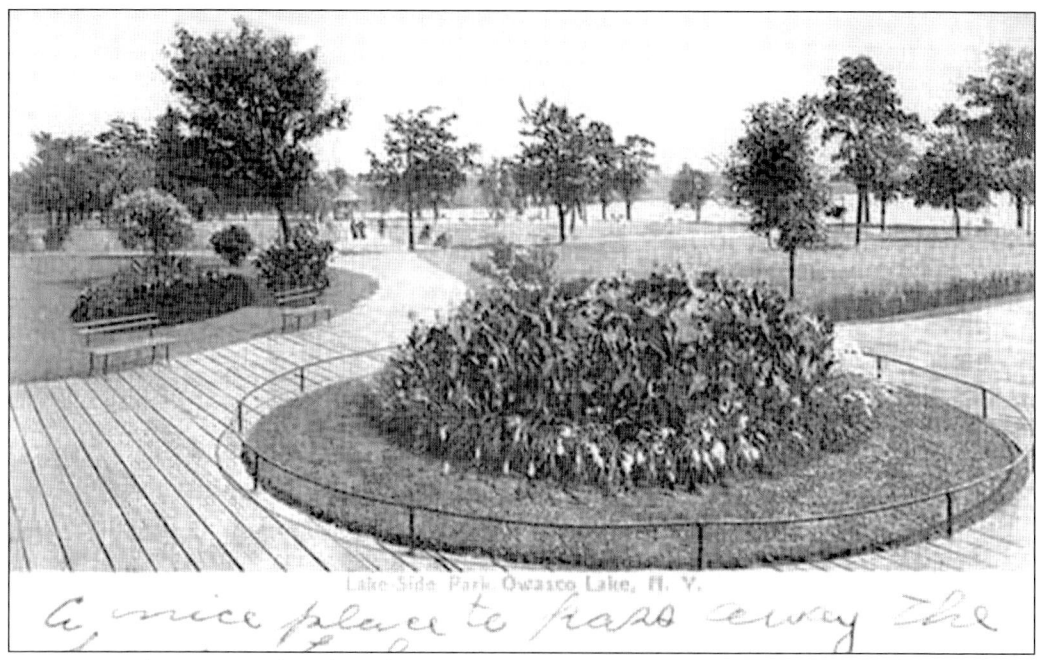

Emerson Park is now Auburn's park on Owasco Lake. It is the site of the annual Tomato Fest. The park includes a swimming beach, a boat launch, a playground, and picnic facilities.

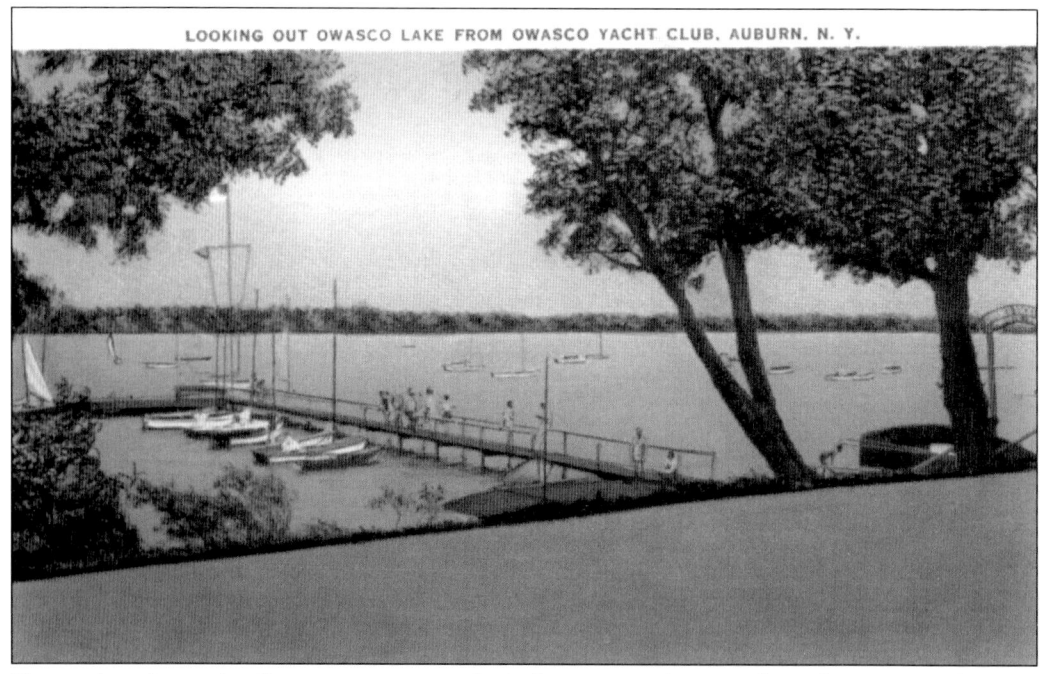

Harnessing the outlet for waterpower made Auburn an early manufacturing center. Owasco Lake drains north through Auburn into the Seneca River.

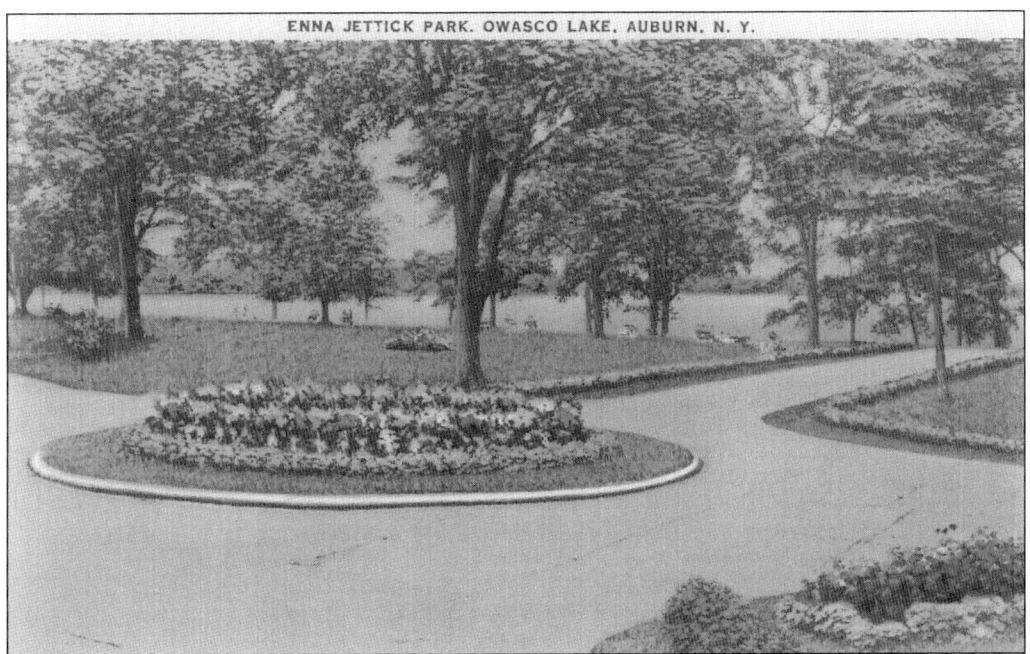

Enna Jettick was one of the shoe manufacturers that were in Auburn. Like many of Auburn's industries, they are now gone.

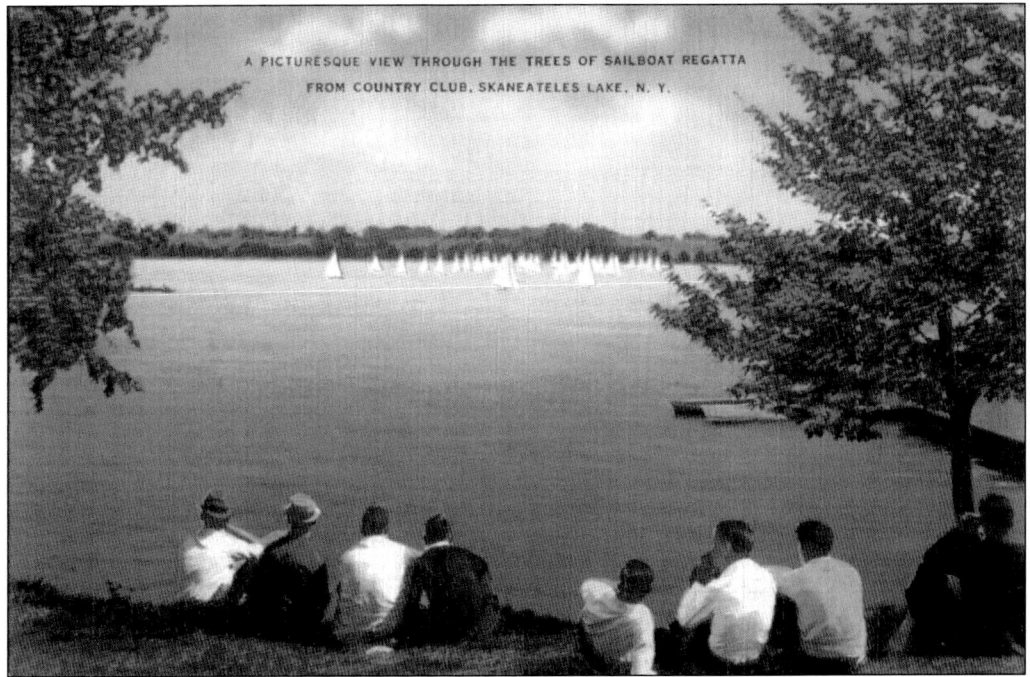

The spectators on the shore of Skaneateles Lake are watching the races at the country club. Sailors at these clubs are very competitive, within the club and at regattas with other clubs.

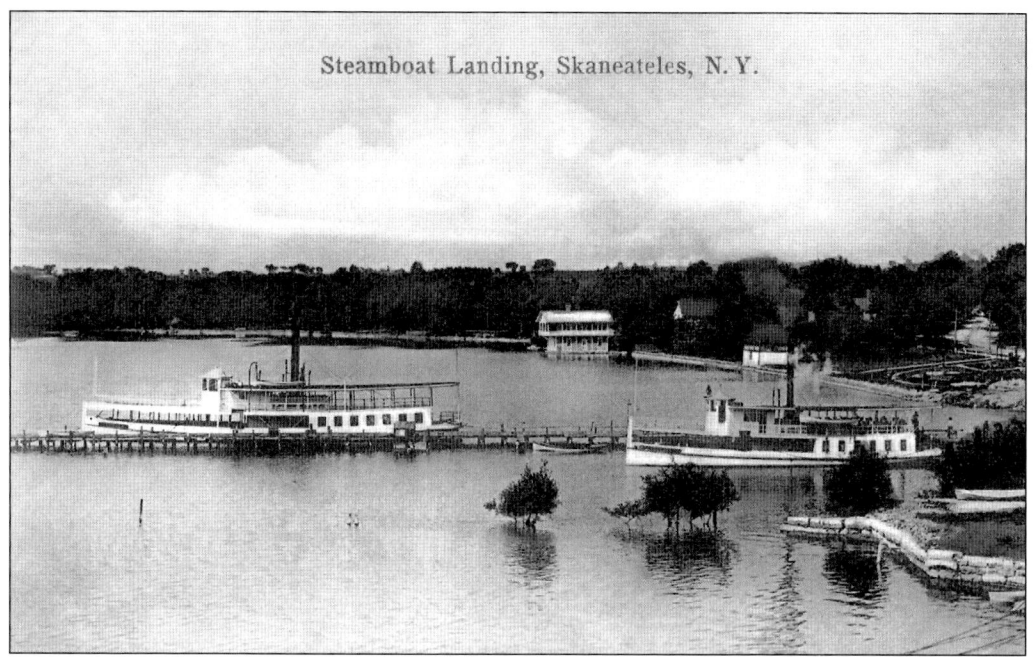

These steamers may be long gone, but one of the nation's few remaining mail boats still makes its rounds on Skaneateles. Boats were manufactured in the town of Skaneateles for over 75 years, and the utopian Skaneateles Community struggled through a brief disappointing life in the 1840s. Winston Churchill's American grandfather clerked store and read law here.

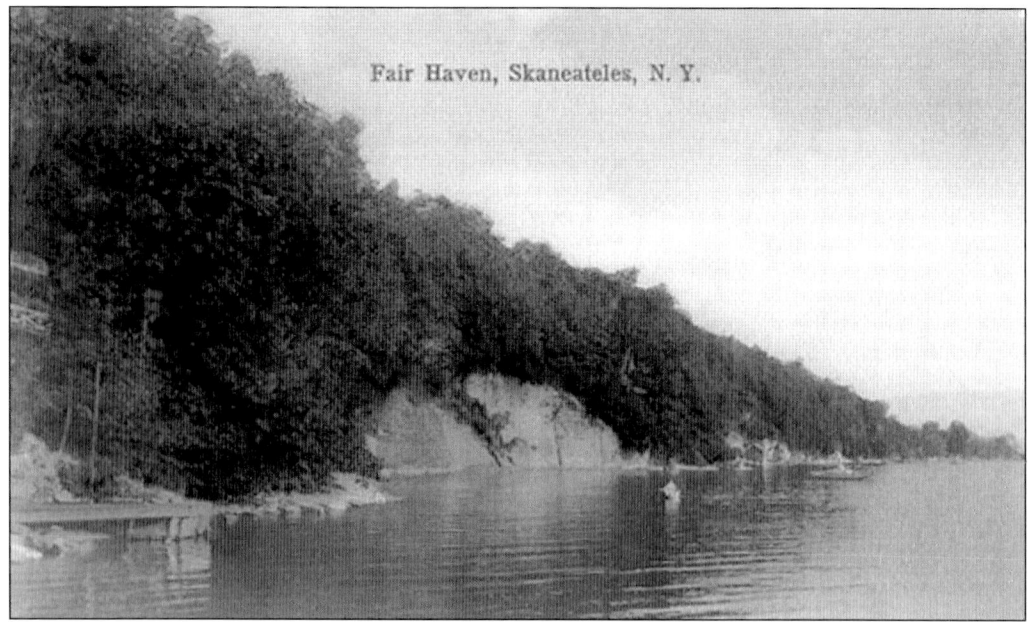

Syracuse and other communities draw their drinking water from Skaneateles Lake, which is so pure that it does not require filtration. Over 1,000 residences line its 14-mile length. Skaneateles means "long lake" in the Iroquios language.

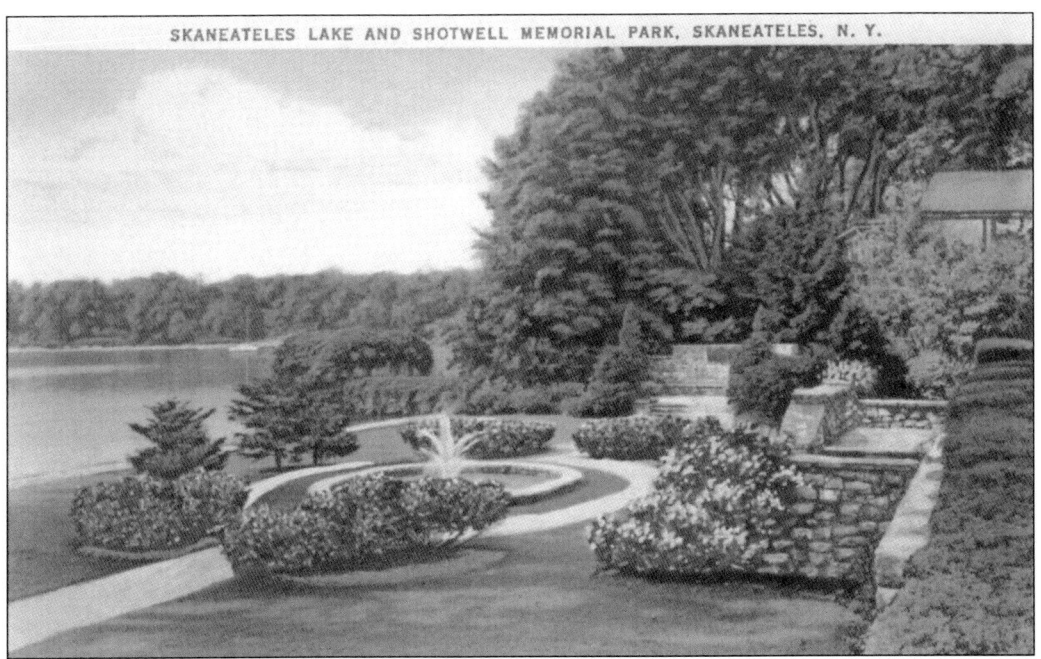

The village of Skaneateles is perfectly situated on the end of the lake, such that the lake is part of the community and many of its activities.

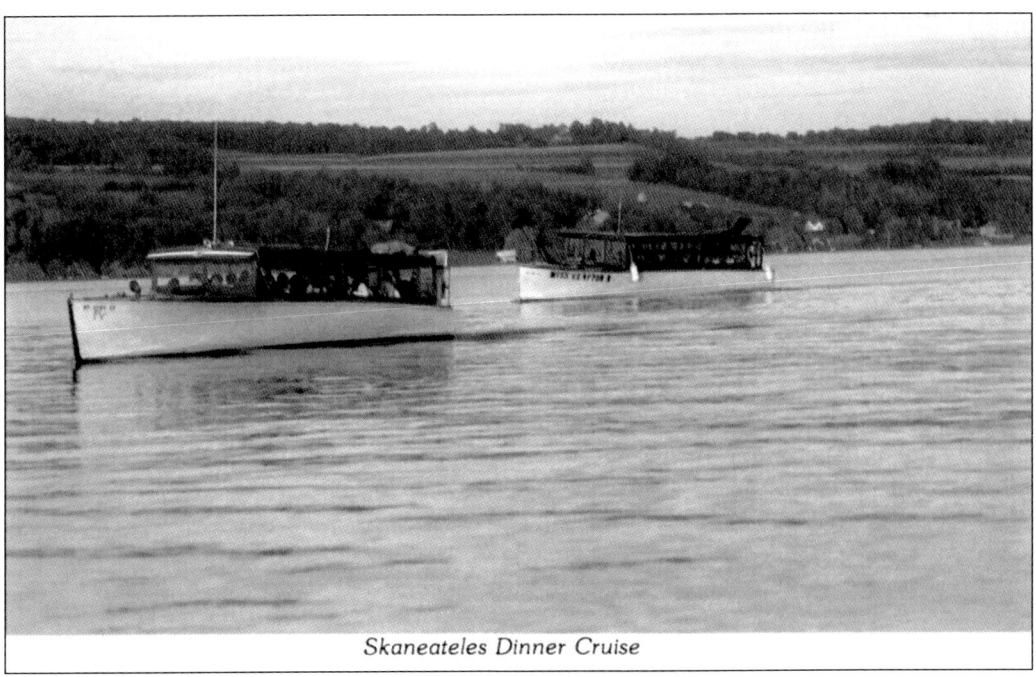

Dinner cruises were and are popular on Skaneateles Lake, as on most of the other Finger Lakes. It is extremely relaxing to enjoy a meal while cruising along one of the lakes.

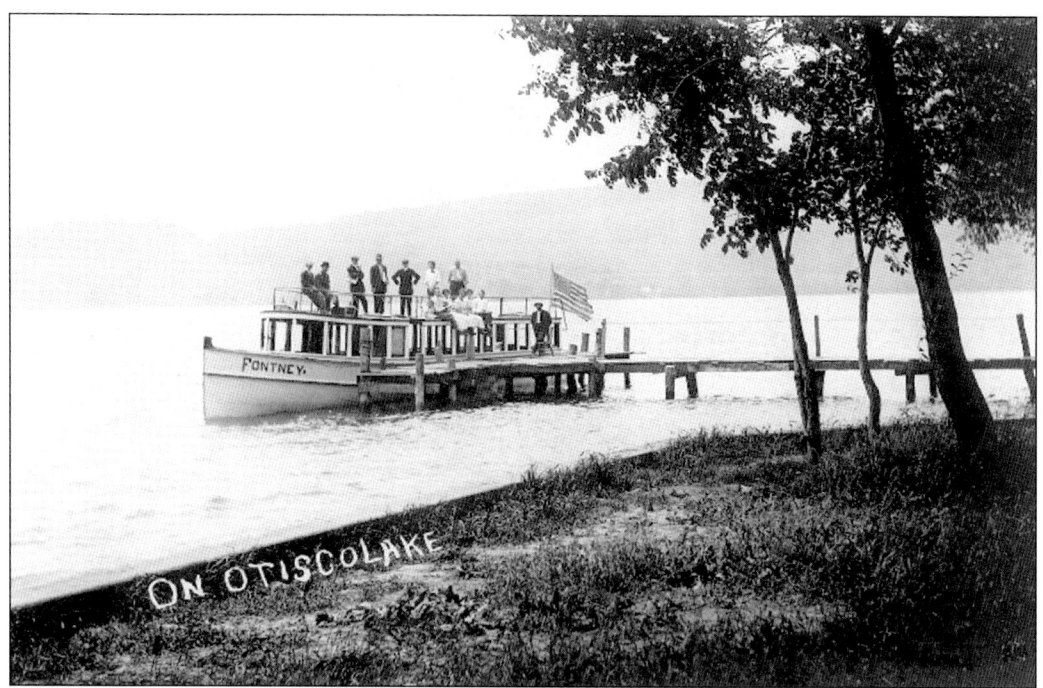

The ferry *Fontney* supposedly carried 130 passengers, although few modern travelers would want to risk it. *Fontney* (1907–1913) connected with the Marcellus and Otisco Lake Railroad (1907–1935). The Marcellus Historical Society has a life preserver from the *Fontney*.

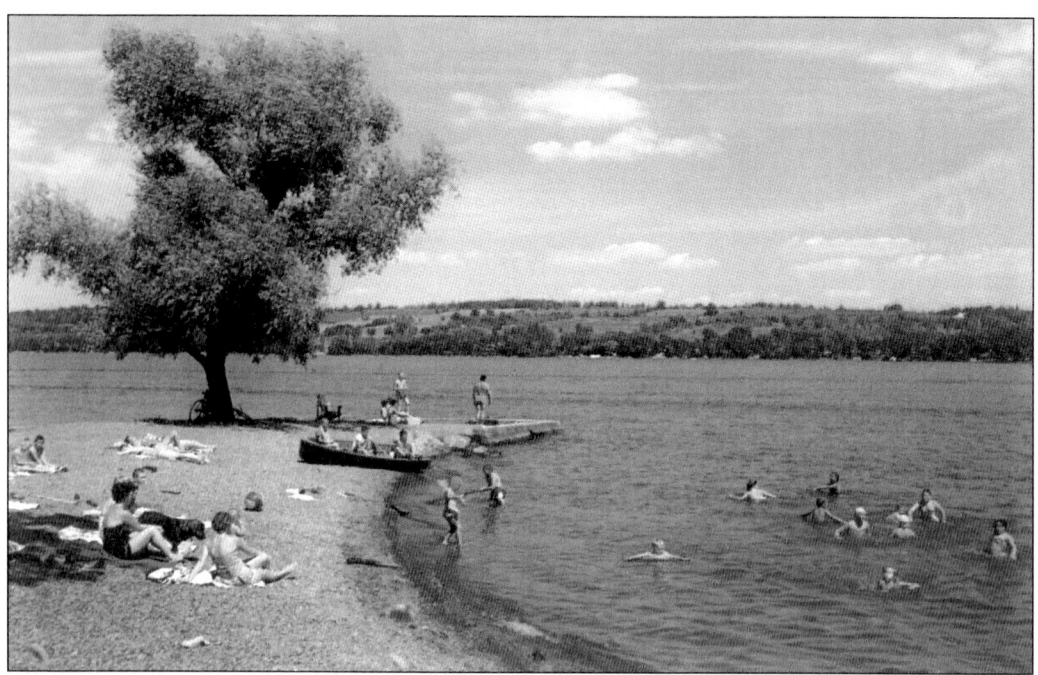

Wherever water laps the shore in the Finger Lakes, New Yorkers and their visitors are enjoying themselves.

# Two

# ABOVE THE LAKES

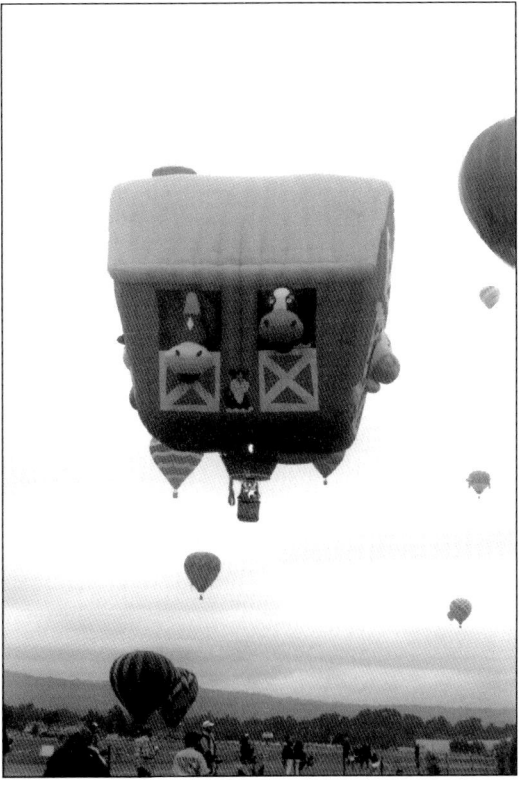

In the 19th century, New Yorkers rose into the sky in hot-air balloons, seeing the Finger Lakes as no one but winged creatures had ever done before. Then came airplanes. For 15 years, manufacturers and experimenters flourished throughout the region. Now gliders sail from Elmira's Harris Hill, the "Soaring Capital of America." And each September, in Dansville, the skies are filled once again with hot-air balloons. (Photograph by Joshua B. House.)

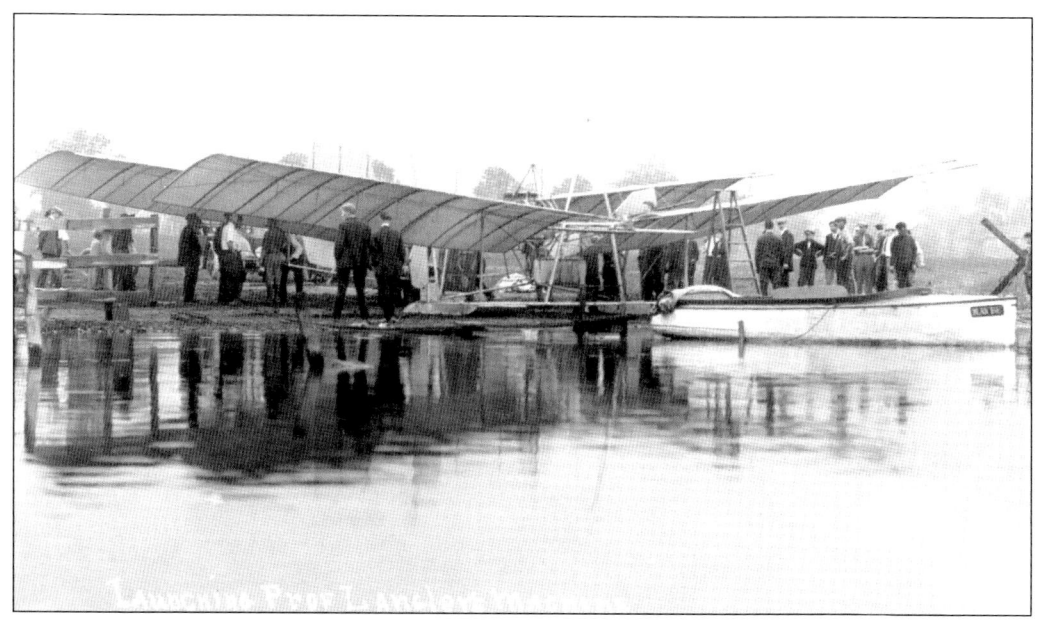

In 1914 at Hammondsport, Glenn Curtiss succeeded in flying Samuel Pierpont Langley's thitherto-unsuccessful 1903 aerodrome. *May Be*, in the right foreground, was a privately owned launch. E. P. Bauter wrote on the reverse of this card, "I saw it raise from the water the first time Curtiss tried it out." He also assured his correspondent, "We will go at the grapes tomorrow."

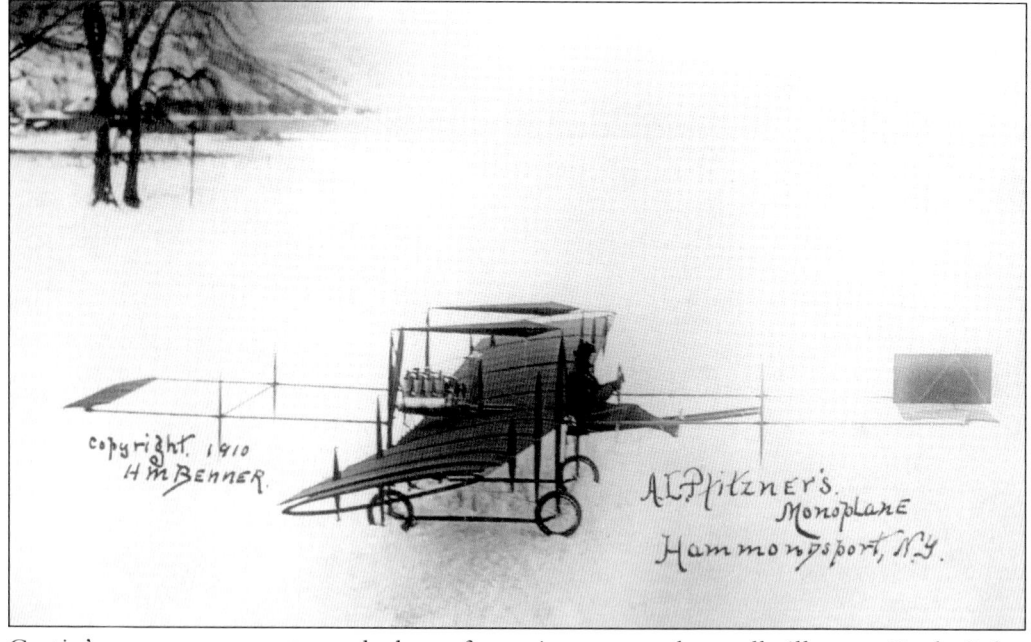

Curtiss's many successes attracted a host of experimenters to the small village on Keuka Lake; A. L. Pfitzner was notably unsuccessful. Photographer Harry Benner did an excellent business for years, recording aviation activity in Hammondsport. He also served in the army aero section's photography unit during the Great War. The message on the card states, "We are having nice sleighing," juxtaposing a very new transportation technology with a very old one.

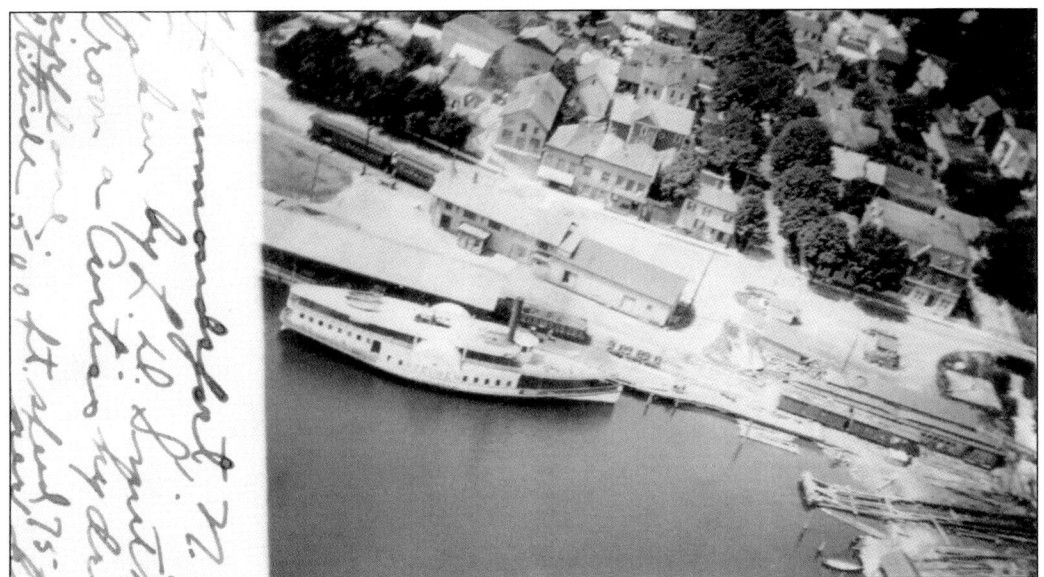

Pioneer aviator Leon D. Smith captured this image of Water and William Streets in Hammondsport with the steamer *Steuben* alongside the Bath and Hammondsport anchorage. "Windy" Smith, feeling responsibility as one of the world's first aviators, later organized an illegal but necessary strike by airmail pilots, who were being killed because of unrealistic performance demands. The government caved in but asserted itself by firing Smith, who took up operating an airfield near Elmira. The waterfront space, including the depot and the area to its left, is now a public park.

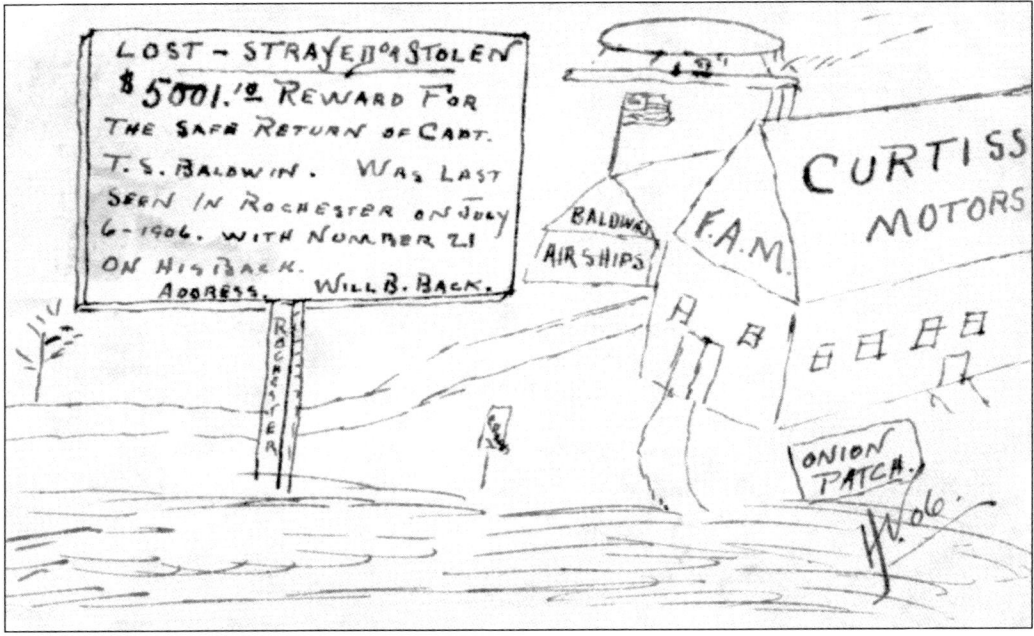

At the time of this hand-drawn card, Glenn Curtiss still had his feet firmly on the ground in his motorcycle business. His friend Tom Baldwin, though, was America's leading maker of airships, or blimps as they are called now. The sketch crudely shows the two plants in Hammondsport, while apparently commemorating a flight in Rochester in which Baldwin was blown astray. "F.A.M." is the Federation of American Motorcyclists.

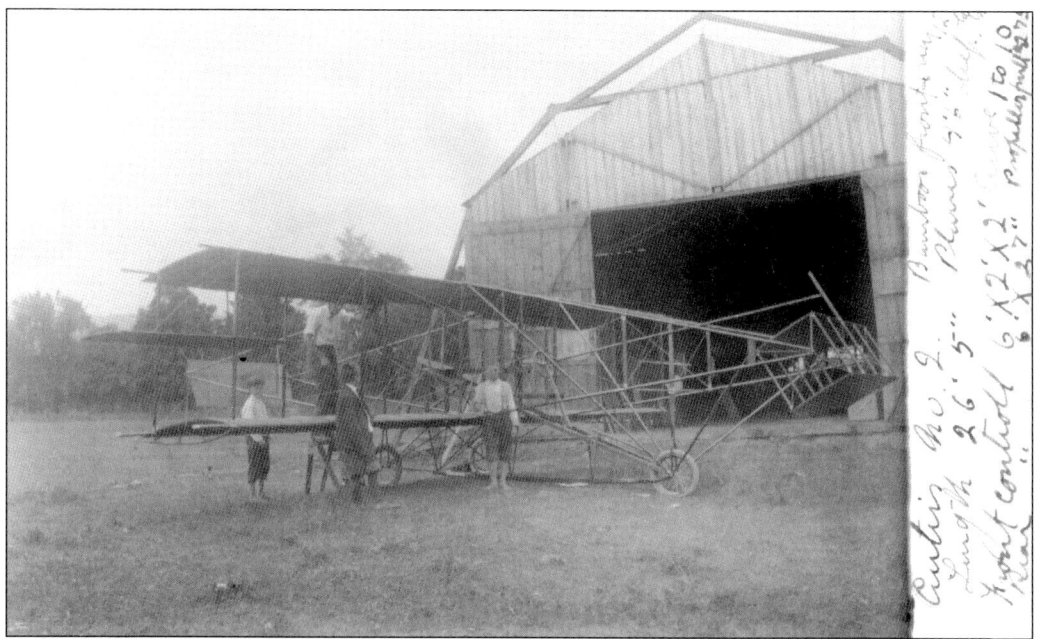

Once Glenn Curtiss entered the aviation field, he quickly established Hammondsport as a major manufacturer. "Curtiss Number 2" is probably the airplane with which he set the world air speed record (a little over 46 miles per hour) at the first international air meet in Reims, France, in 1909.

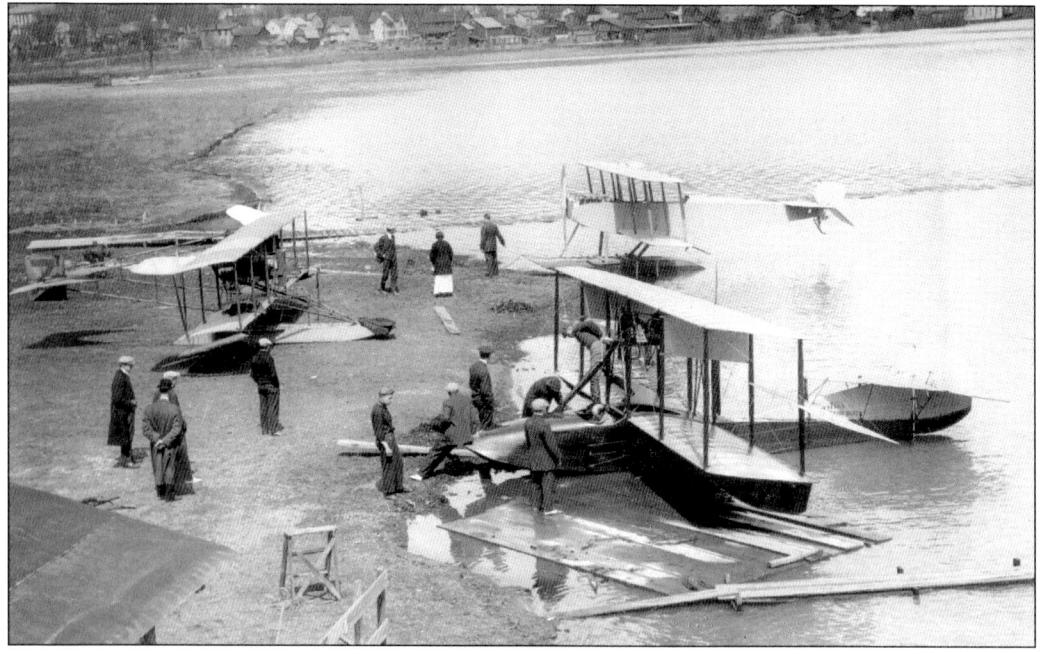

The Curtiss flying school at Keuka Lake became a popular tourist destination. There were very few locations in America were one could see this many airplanes at once.

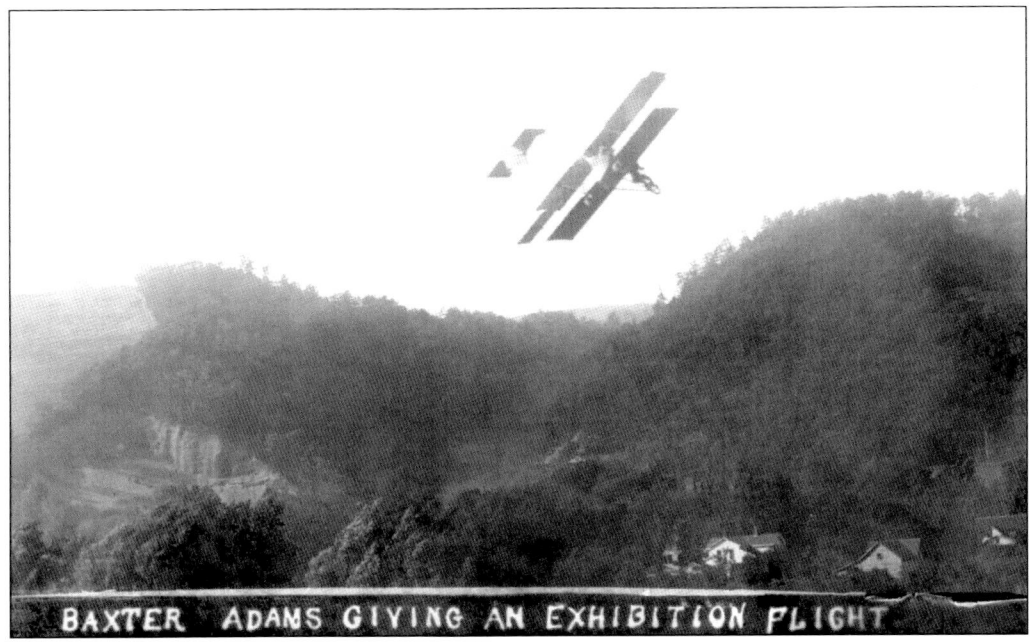

Baxter Adams was a popular star on the air-show circuit back before World War I. That is the Hammondsport Glen in the background.

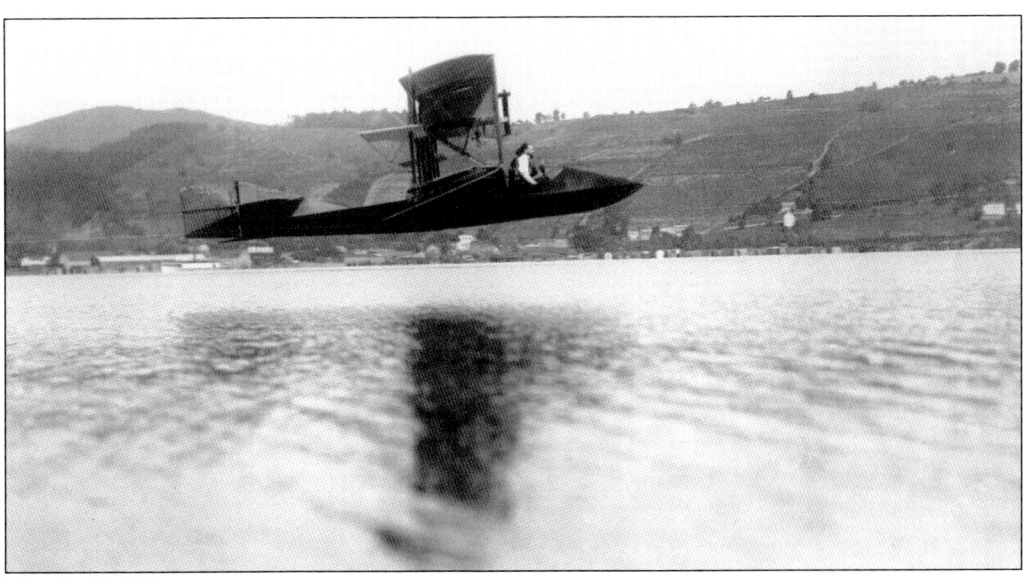

Curtiss created the first flying boat (an aircraft with a hull, capable of cruising on the water's surface) at Keuka Lake in 1912. Speedboats and seaplanes still use the stepped hull that Curtiss originated.

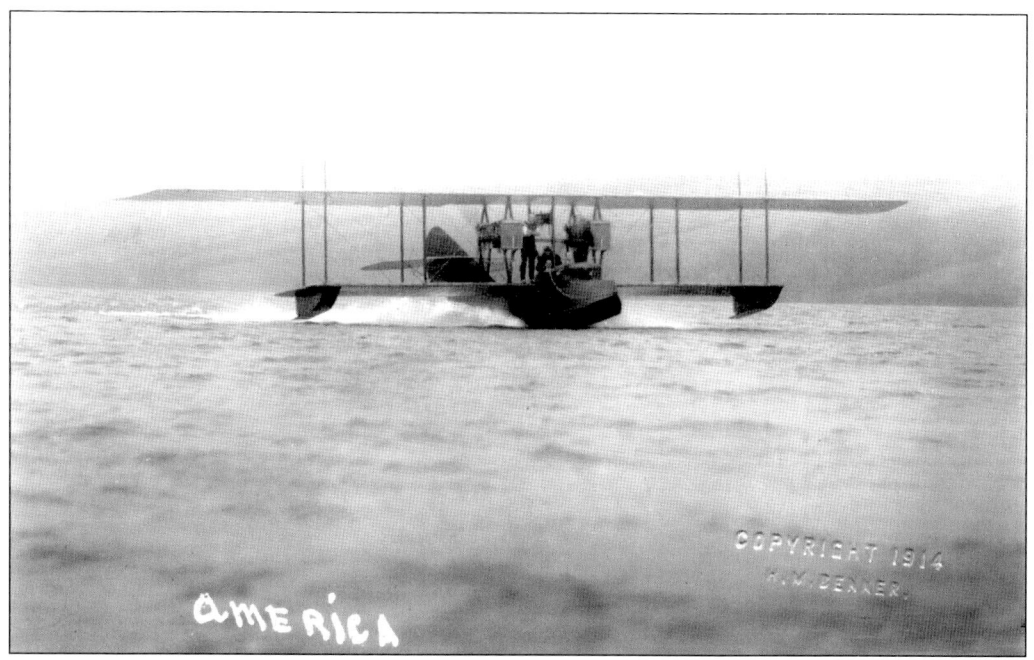

Glenn Curtiss built the *America* to fly the Atlantic in 1914, but World War I canceled the flight. Curtiss Museum volunteers reproduced the aircraft to fly from Keuka Lake some 95 years later.

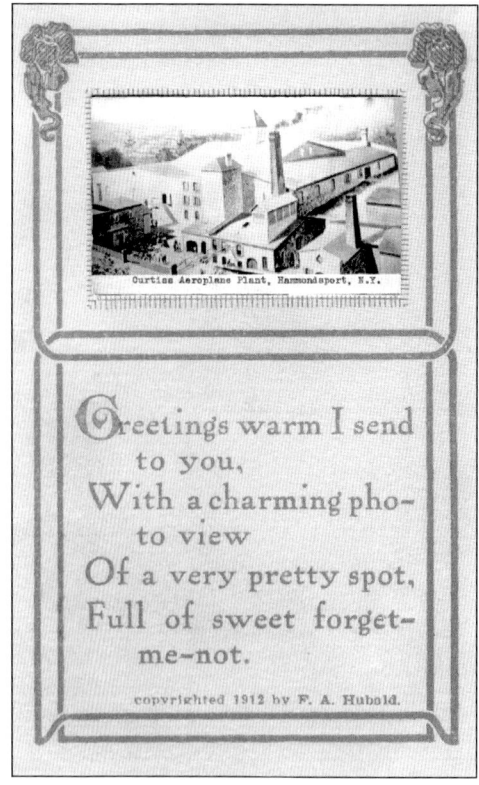

Glenn Curtiss was obviously an optimist. This view of the plant does not strike one as "a very pretty spot," but it still looks better than the real thing did!

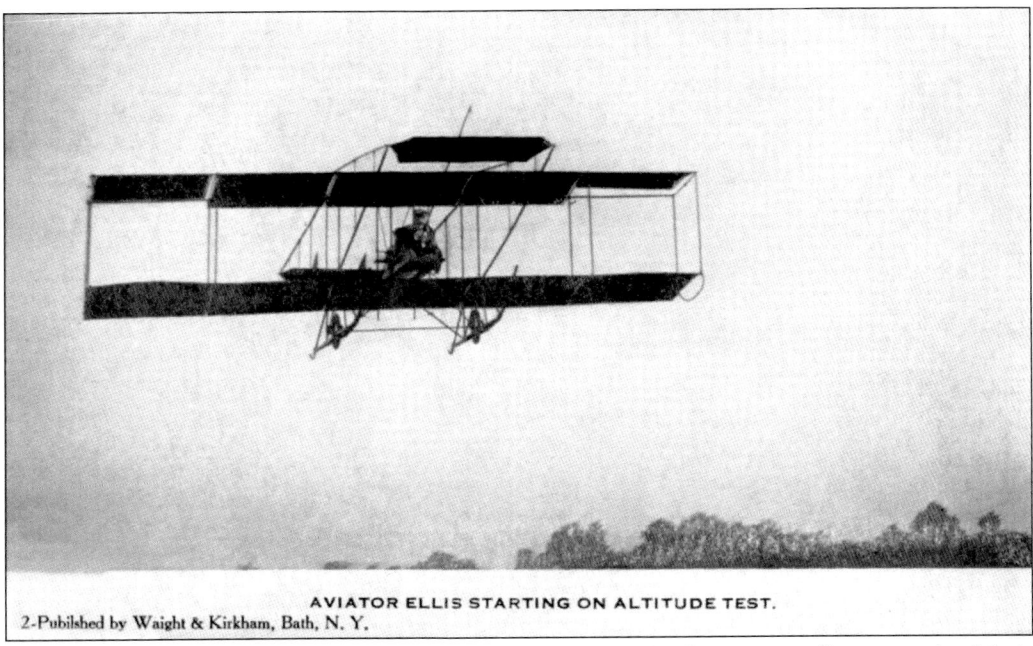

Bath, Naples, and Rochester honor Fred Eells (not Ellis) as the first man to fly over each of their communities. For a time Eells and Charles B. Kirkham designed and built their own airplanes in Bath, similar to those Curtiss was making in Hammondsport. Eells lies buried in Bath's Nondaga Cemetery.

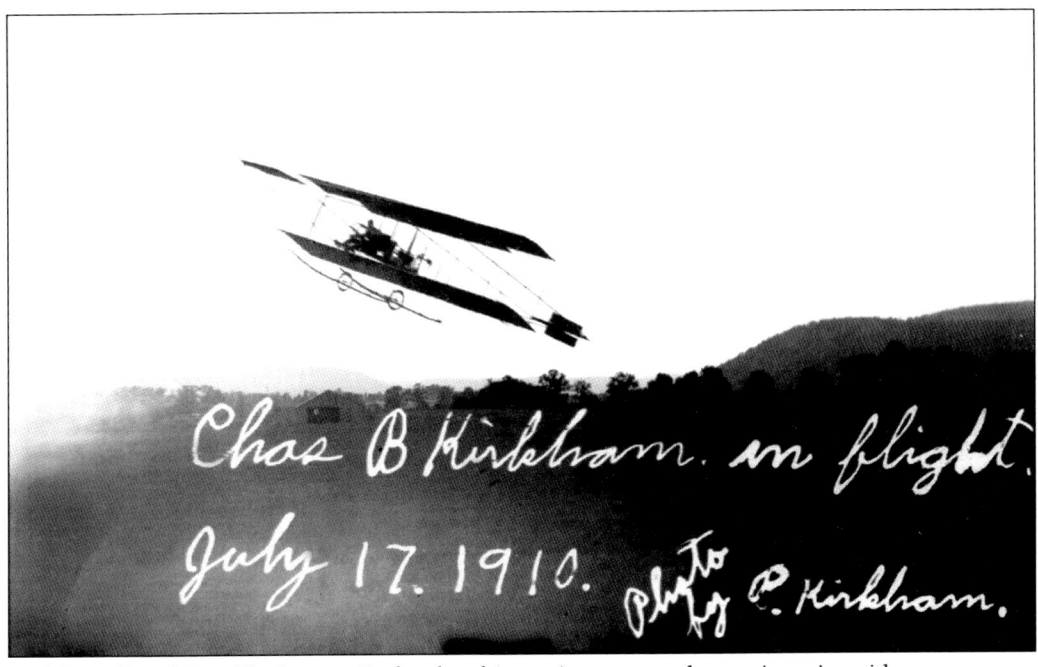

Kirkham flew himself—here at Bath—but his genius was on the engineering side.

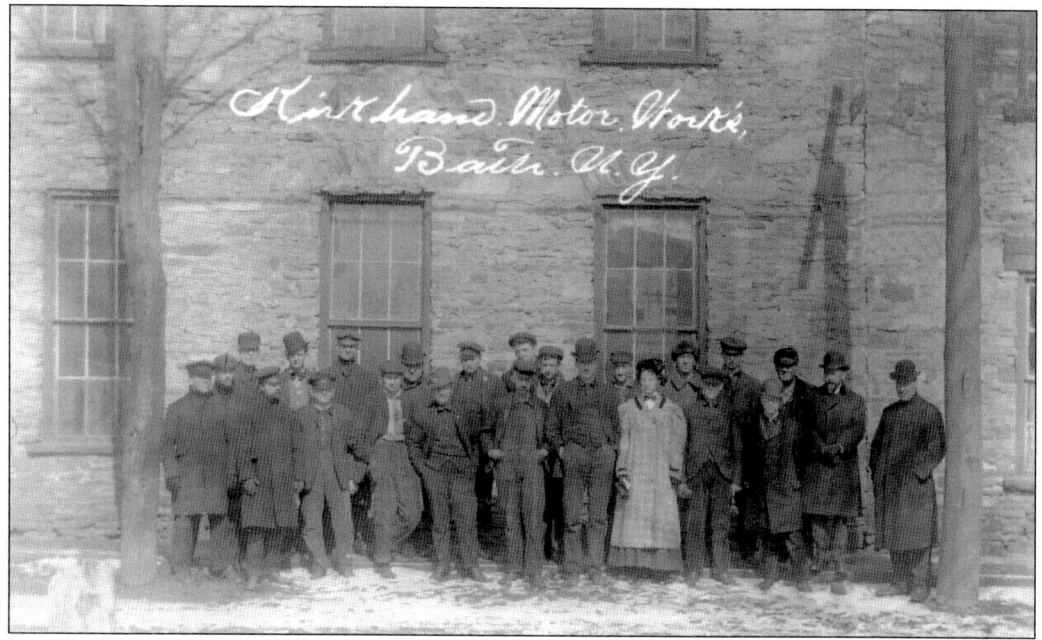
The Kirkham works also made engines for Pullman automobiles and for Alexander Graham Bell.

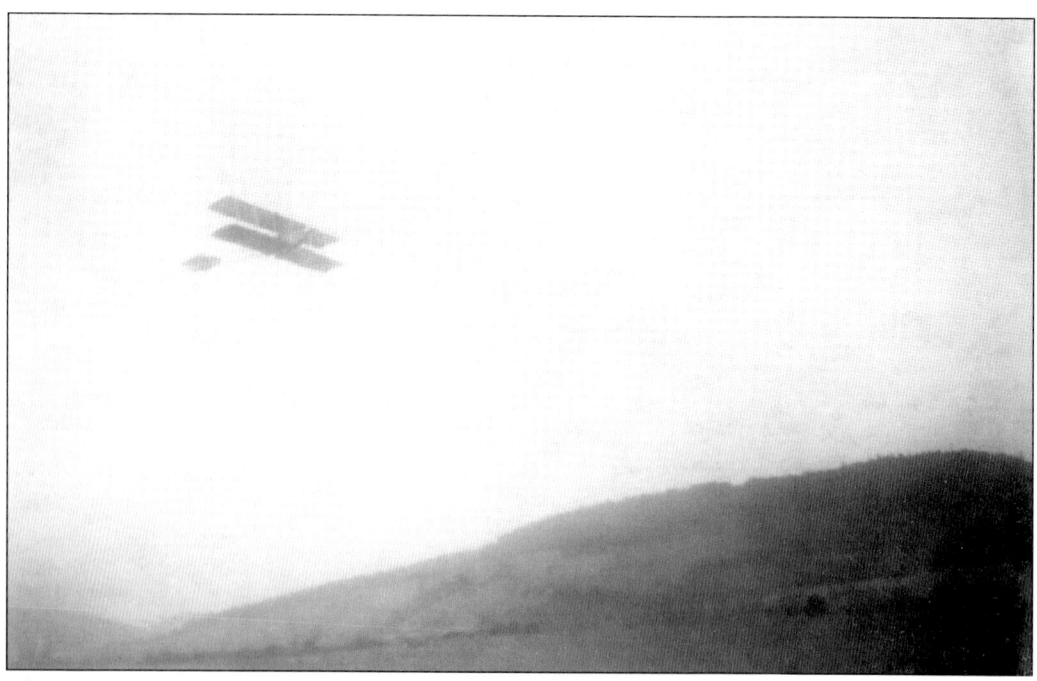
Charles Kirkham in 1912 designed and built an advanced tractor biplane, which former Curtiss pilot Kondo Motohisa tested. Moments after this photograph was taken Kondo, inexperienced with Kirkham's controls, crashed into a windmill on Eagle Valley Road between Bath and Savona. The pilot was killed; windmill and airplane were both destroyed.

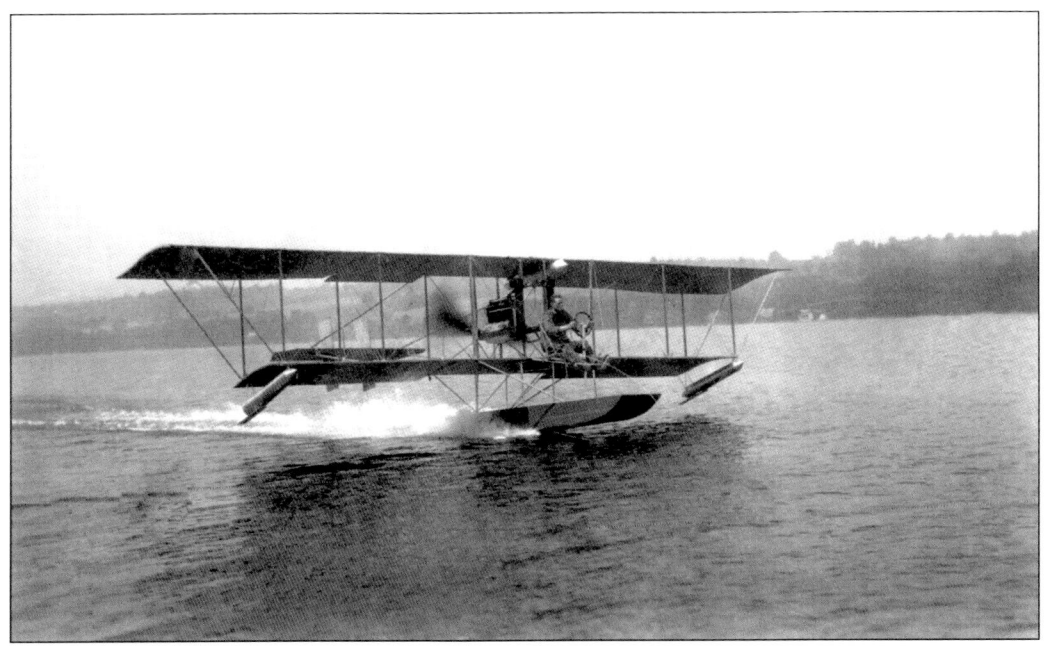

Thomas Brothers made Curtiss-type airplanes in Bath, often using Kirkham engines.

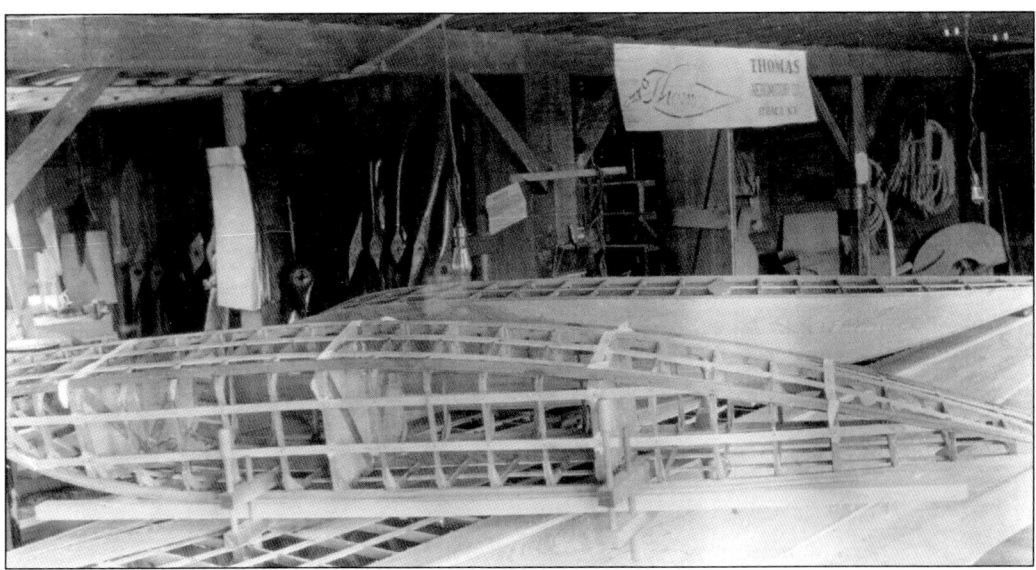

As World War I deepened, Thomas moved to Ithaca and merged with the Morse Chain Company. Thomas-Morse became the U.S. military's fourth-largest producer of airplanes for 1917–1918. The "Tommy Scout" is still fondly remembered. Here workers are making pontoons for seaplanes.

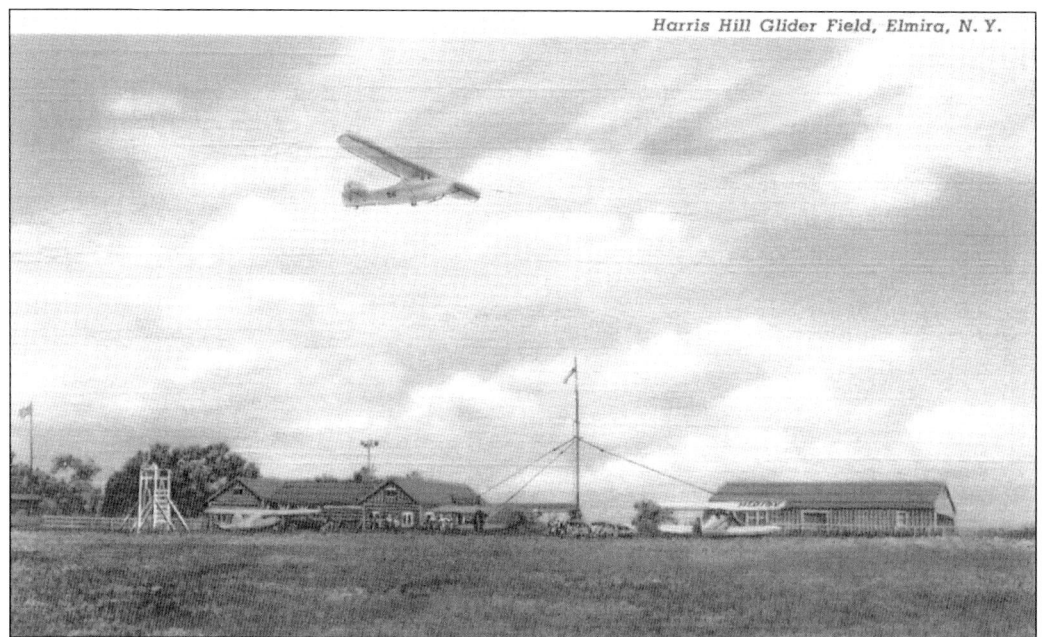

Harris Hill near Elmira is the "Soaring Capital of America," home to the National Soaring Museum, the first national soaring meets, and a World War II school for army glider pilots. Nearby Schweizer Aircraft (founded 1939) made the majority of all sailplanes ever produced in America, and an Elmira high school girl named Eileen Collins did errands here in exchange for flying lessons. Just lately she pilots the space shuttle.

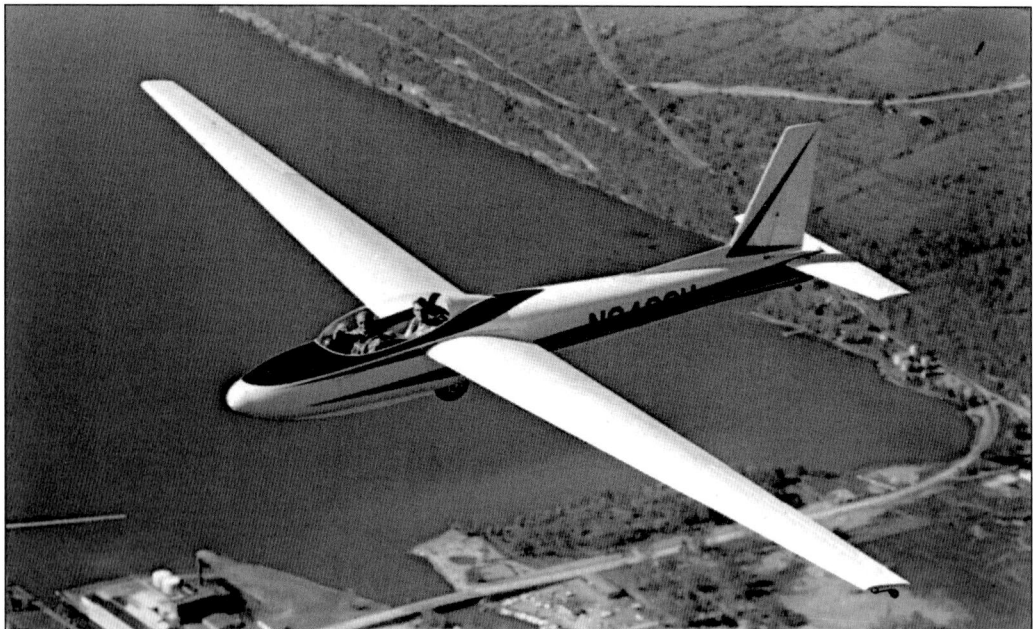

Seneca Lake and Watkins Glen are below as a high-performance 2-32 Schweizer sailplane soars through the Finger Lakes. Schweizer also manufactured the Grumman (later Schweizer) Ag-Cat and the Hughes (later Schweizer) 300C helicopter. Now a division of Sikorsky, Schweizer was until then the longest-lived private aircraft manufacturer in America.

# *Three*

# BETWEEN THE LAKES

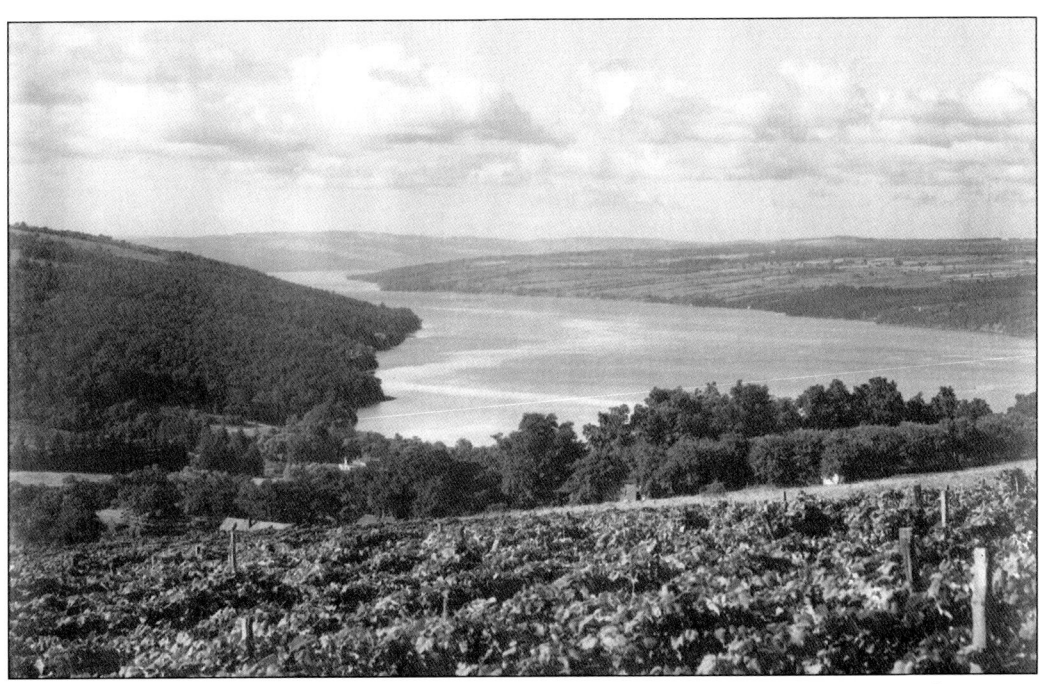

People come from hundreds of miles just for a chance to drive through the Finger Lakes. It is a drive past long green slopes with vineyards tumbling down them, through farms and country lanes, into hamlets and towns, with here and there a great university. Every fall the hillsides sparkle like a sun-drenched kaleidoscope—colors from the sky, in Iroquois legend. Winter lays a blanket on the sleeping farmland, keeping it fresh for the coming year.

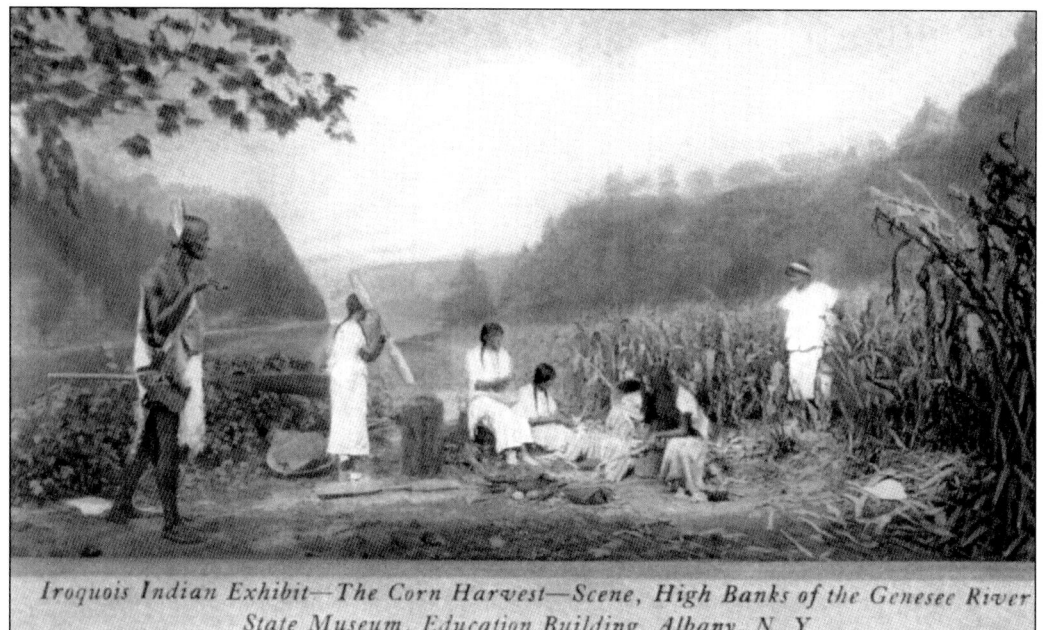

*Iroquois Indian Exhibit—The Corn Harvest—Scene, High Banks of the Genesee River State Museum, Education Building, Albany, N.Y.*

Dominating the Finger Lakes and more at the time of European contact was the five-nation Confederation of the Iroquois (a French word—in their own tongue they were called Haudenosaunee, or "Longhouse people"). This life-size diorama of the Seneca is set below Squakie Hill near Mount Morris.

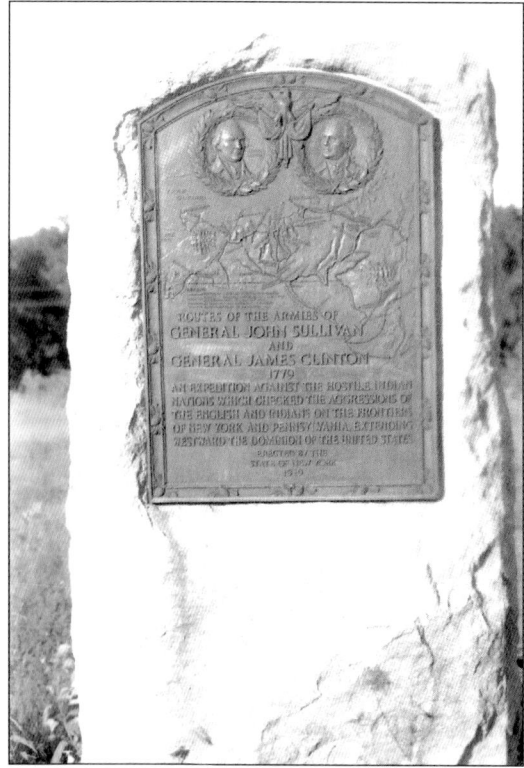

Generals John Sullivan and James Clinton headed up the largest independent command of the Revolutionary War, laying waste the Iroquois towns throughout the Finger Lakes to suppress, according to these markers, "aggressions . . . on the frontiers of New York and Pennsylvania." Perhaps there should be markers noting U.S. aggression on the Iroquois.

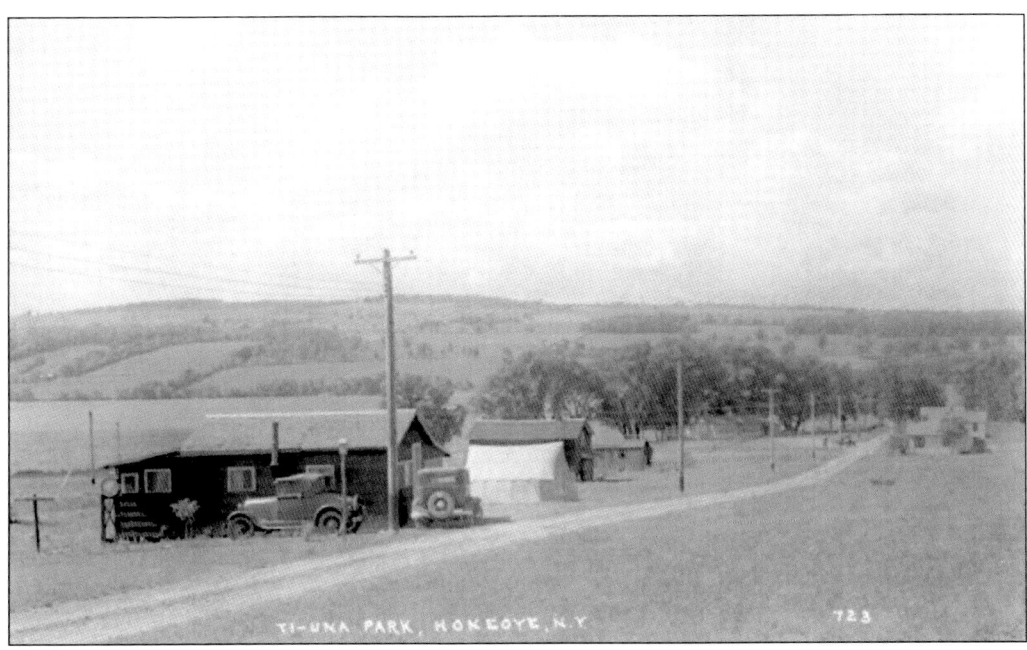

Besides attracting visitors to the lake, the lake's Honeoye Creek outlet powered mills. Ti-una Park does not appear to offer many amenities.

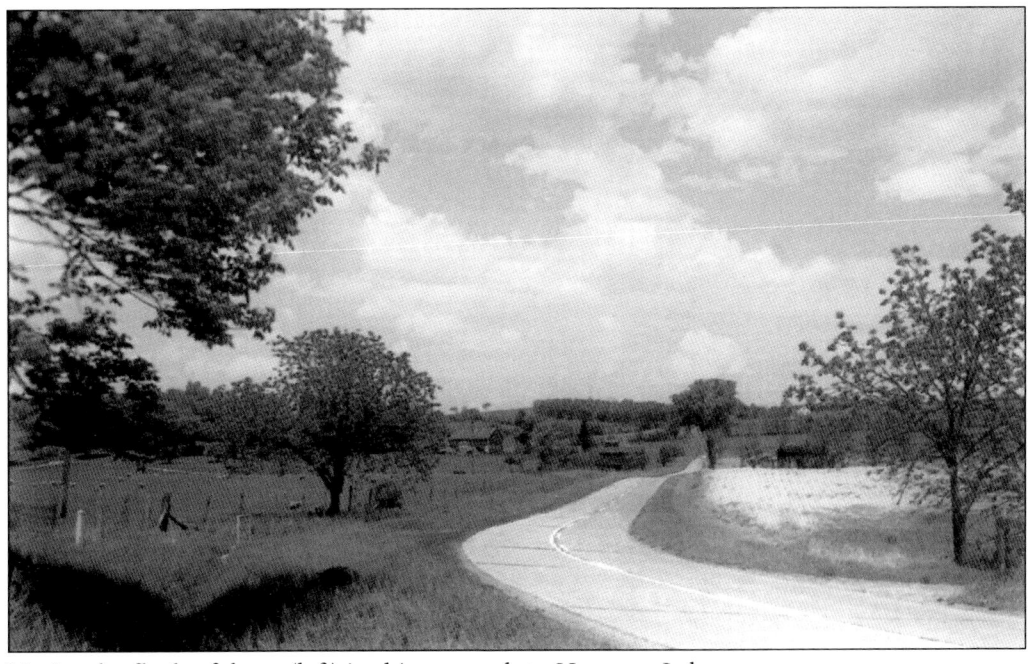

Notice the flock of sheep (left) in this approach to Honeoye Lake.

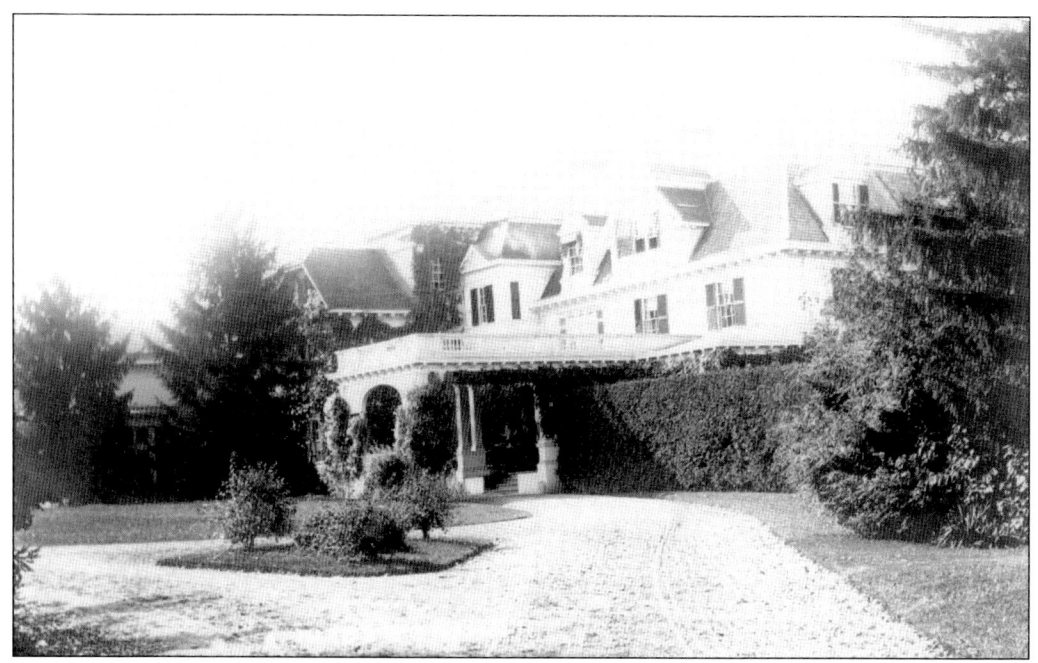

The Wadsworth family—senators, generals, agricultural experimenters, entrepreneurs, and foxhunters—have been prominent in Geneseo since the earliest days of white settlement, in 1790. The ancestral home is still in the family, and still lovely; Frederick Law Olmsted designed the site.

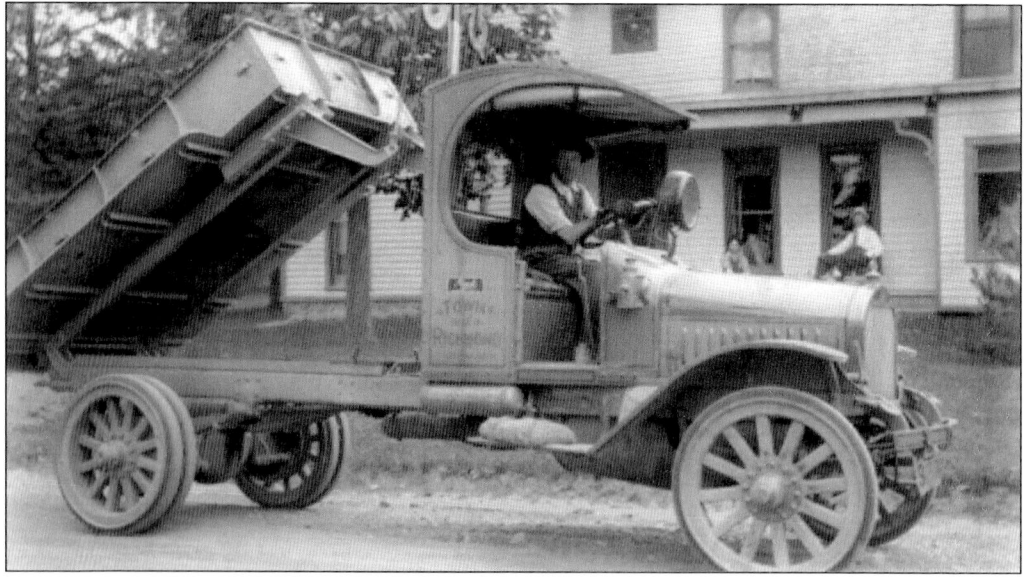

The town of Richmond (which includes most of Honeoye Lake) was the state's leading producer of wool in 1865. There is still much sheep farming, along with other agriculture. Harold B. Logan drives the town's Mack truck.

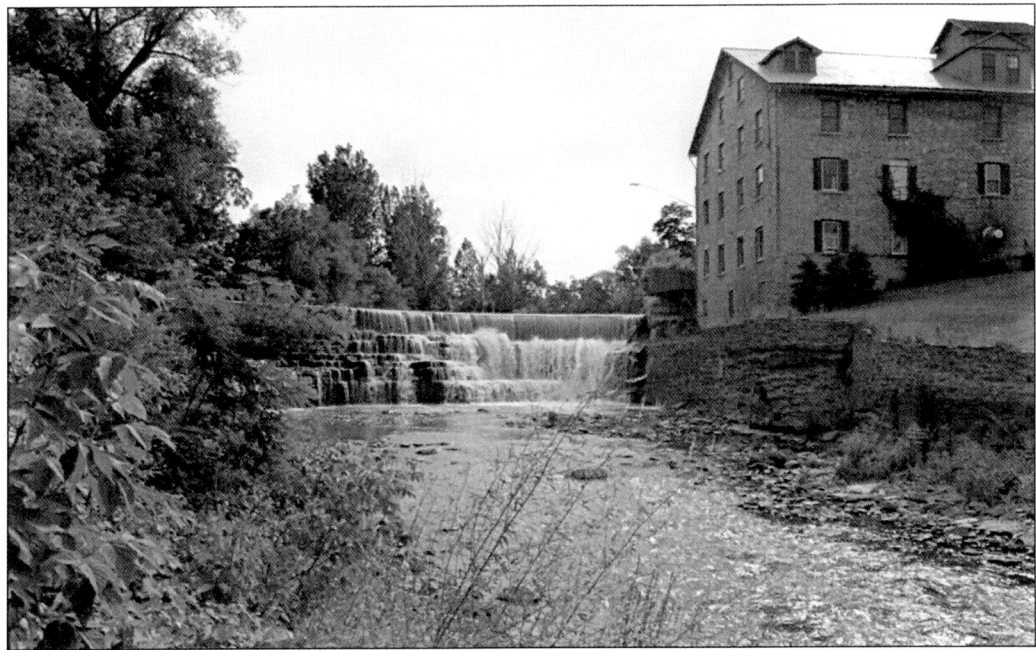

The village of Honeoye Falls was established in 1791, taking advantage of its waterpower to become a flour milling town. This mill is on Honeoye Creek, which is the outlet of Honeoye Lake.

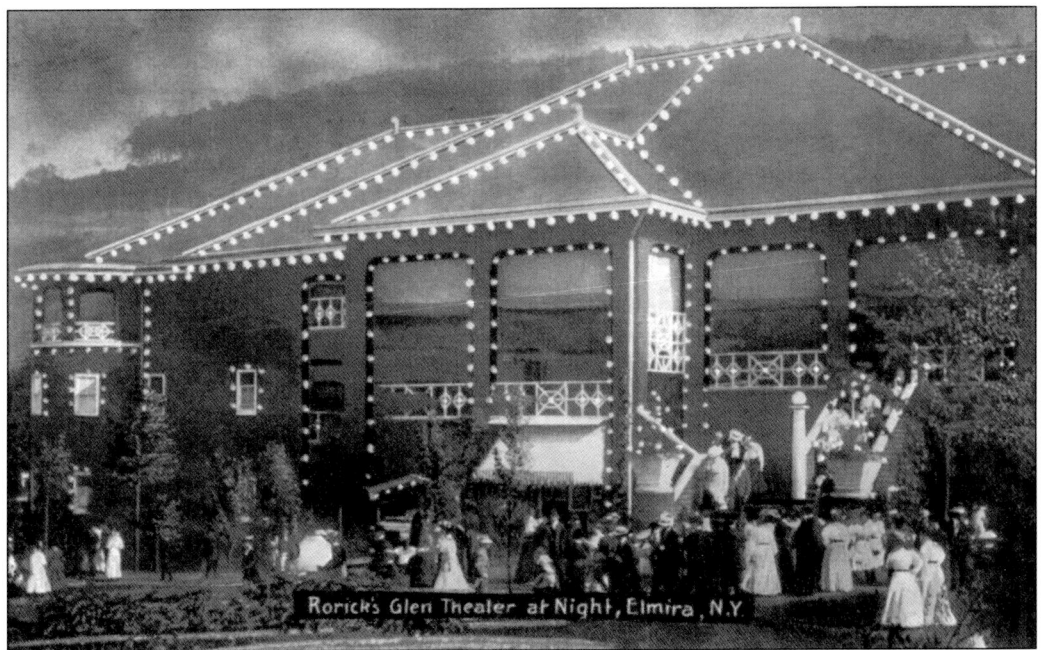

Rorick's Glen, with an amusement park and summer theater, was a popular park on the Chemung River in Elmira. The park is gone, but the Boy Scouts use the area.

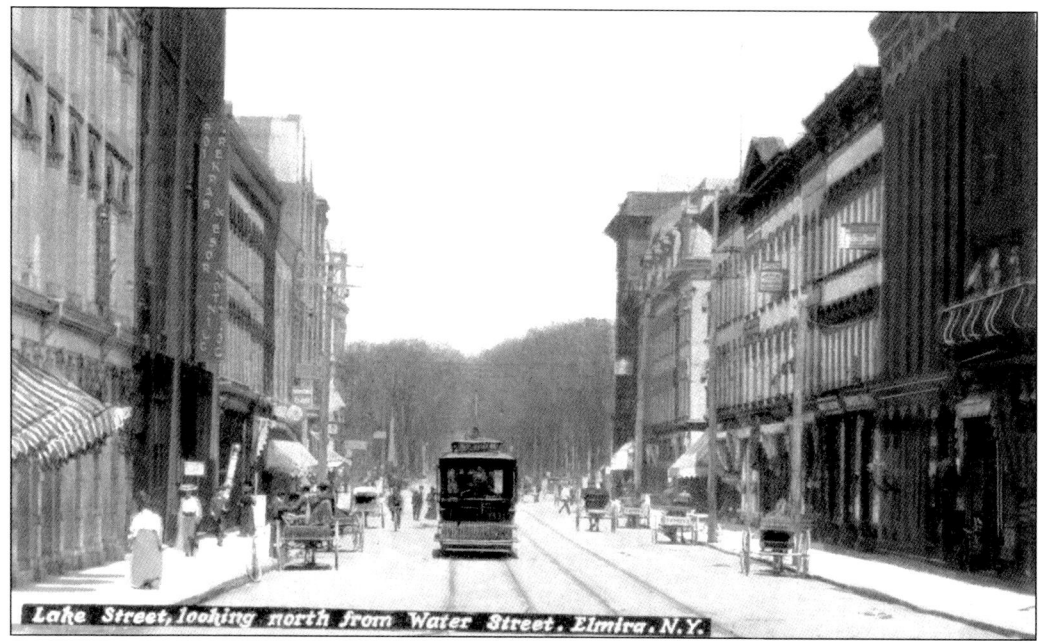

The electric streetcar lines (1890–1939) did not wend just through Elmira, they also connected that city with Corning, Watkins Glen, and other points. Except for a couple of bicycles, all the other vehicles are horse-drawn. Notice that the letters in the vertical sign on the left read disconcertingly from bottom to top.

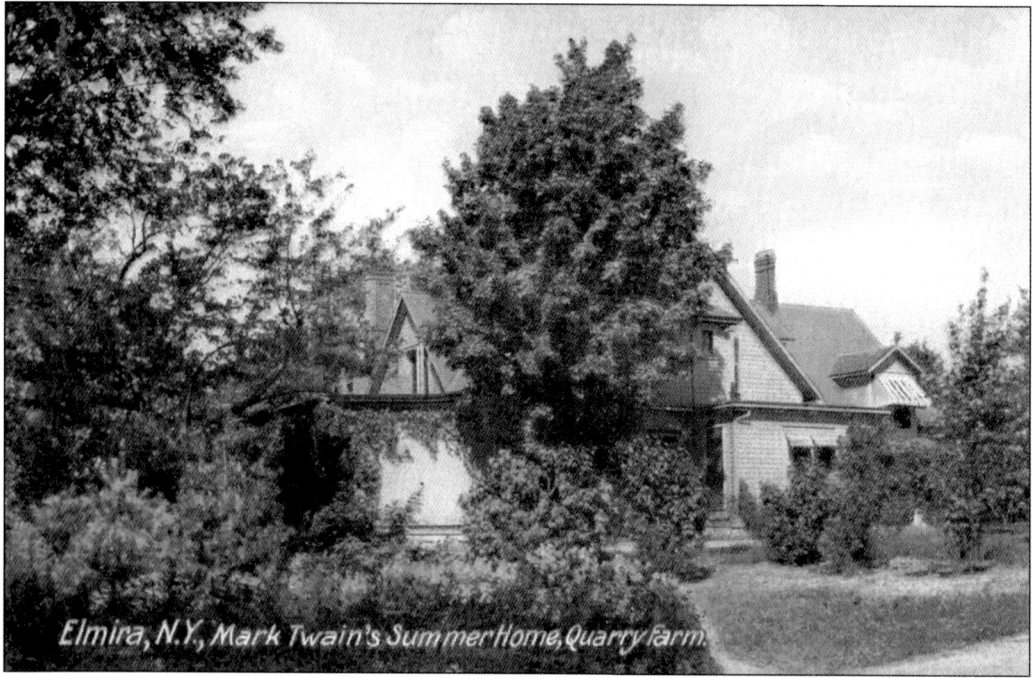

Mark Twain wrote *Huckleberry Finn*, *The Prince and the Pauper*, *Life on the Mississippi*, and other books while summering with his in-laws in Elmira. They built him an octagonal study, now on the grounds of Elmira College. Quarry Farm is also college property.

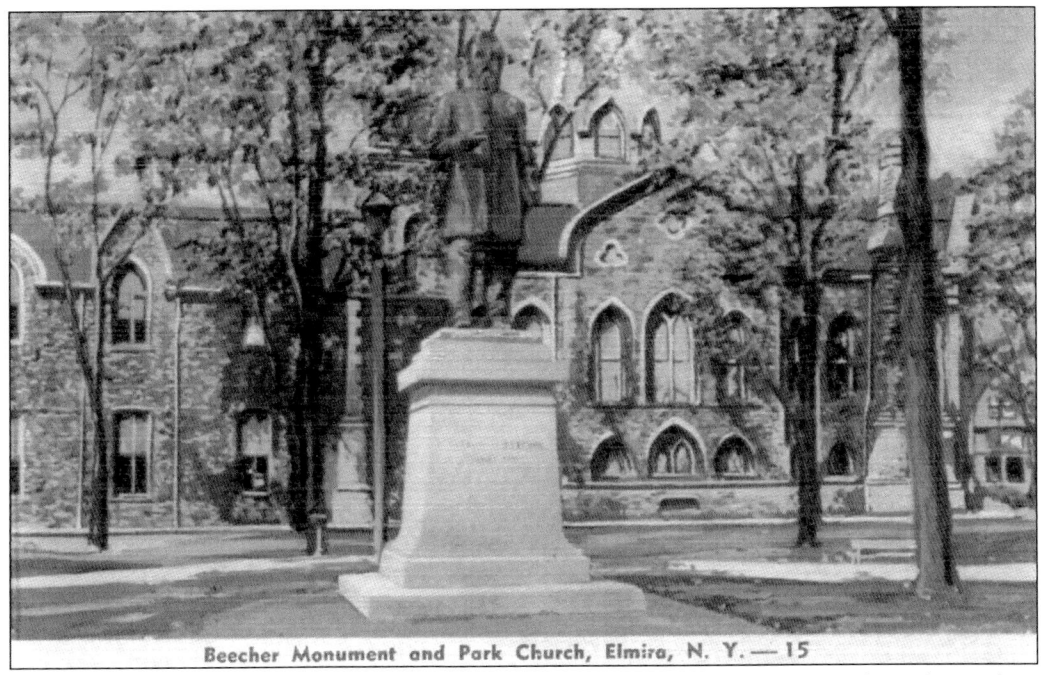
Beecher Monument and Park Church, Elmira, N. Y. — 15

Elmira was a major hub on the Underground Railroad, making congenial settings for such preachers as the brother of Harriet Beecher Stowe. Thomas K. Beecher was an outspoken abolitionist.

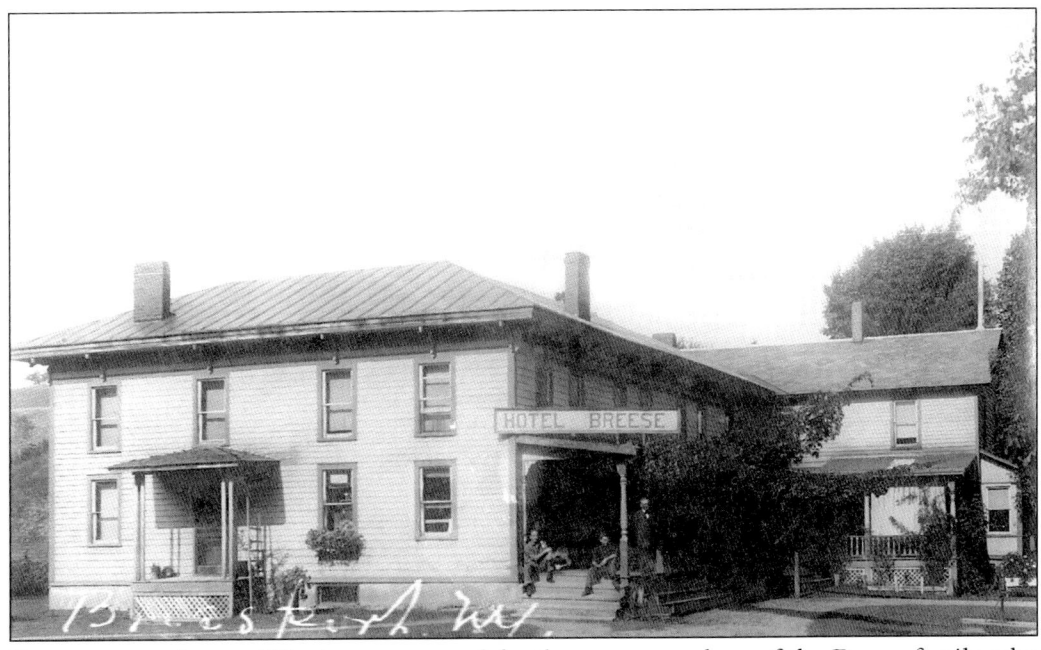
Breesport, northeast of Elmira, was named for the many members of the Breese family who settled there. John Breese was the first white settler in the Chemung River valley.

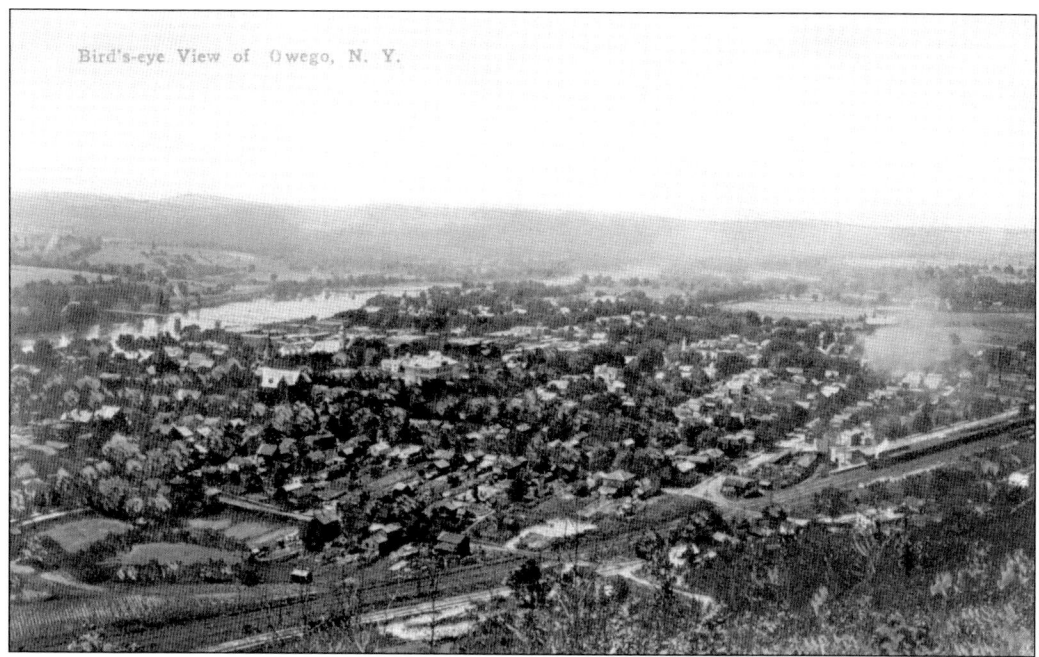

John D. Rockefeller was a boy near Owego, a significant rail town and Tioga County seat. Another native son is Gen. Henry Roberts, who wrote the famous *Rules of Order*. Owego is now home to a major Lockheed-Martin facility. The Susquehanna River is in the background.

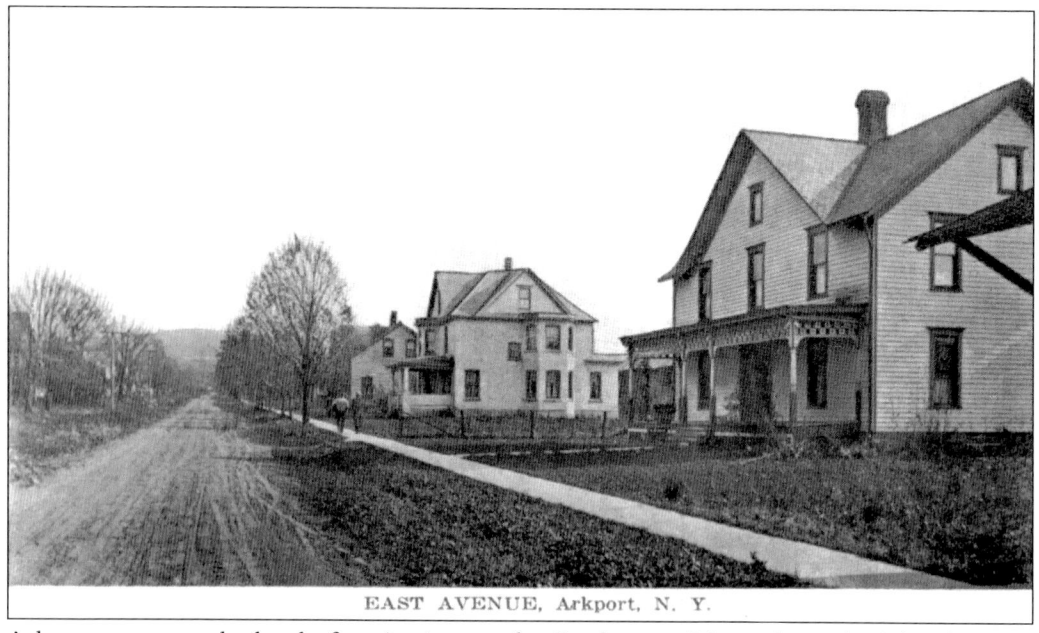

Arkport was once the head of navigation on the Conhocton River; the end of the chain lay on Chesapeake Bay, at the mouth of the Susquehanna. Farmers built wooden arks, filled them with produce, and poled them to Baltimore. There they sold both their goods and their arks (for lumber) and walked back home.

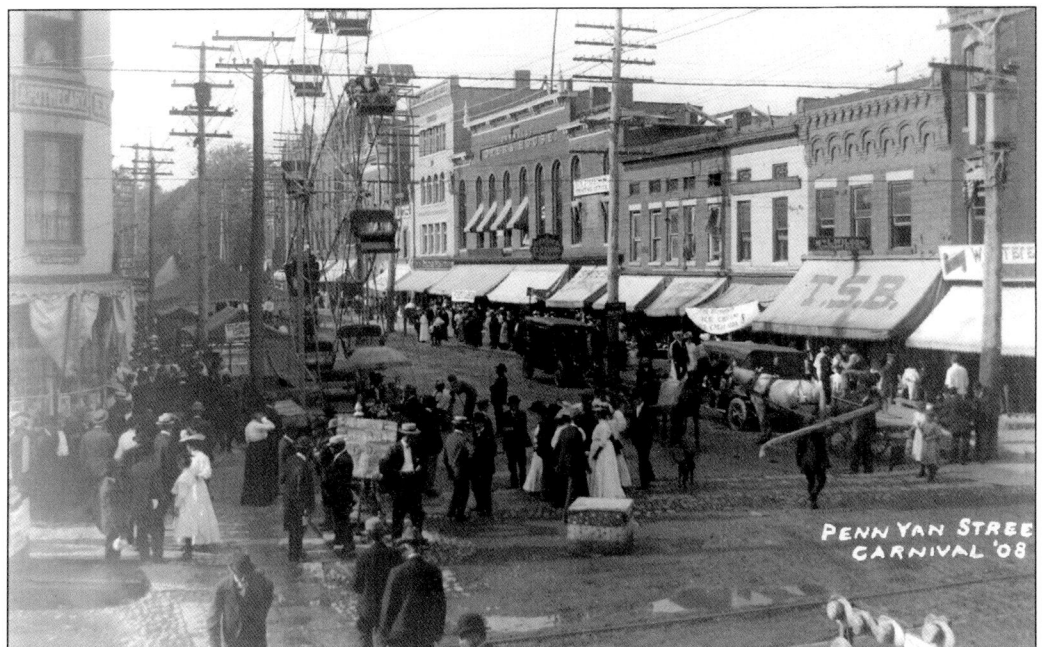

Penn Yan, at the foot of Keuka Lake's East Branch, is the seat of Yates County. Its name came from its early Pennsylvanian and Yankee white settlers, although a small community of escaped slaves existed by the mid-19th century. "T. S. B." on the awning stands for T. S. Burns, early merchant and entrepreneur.

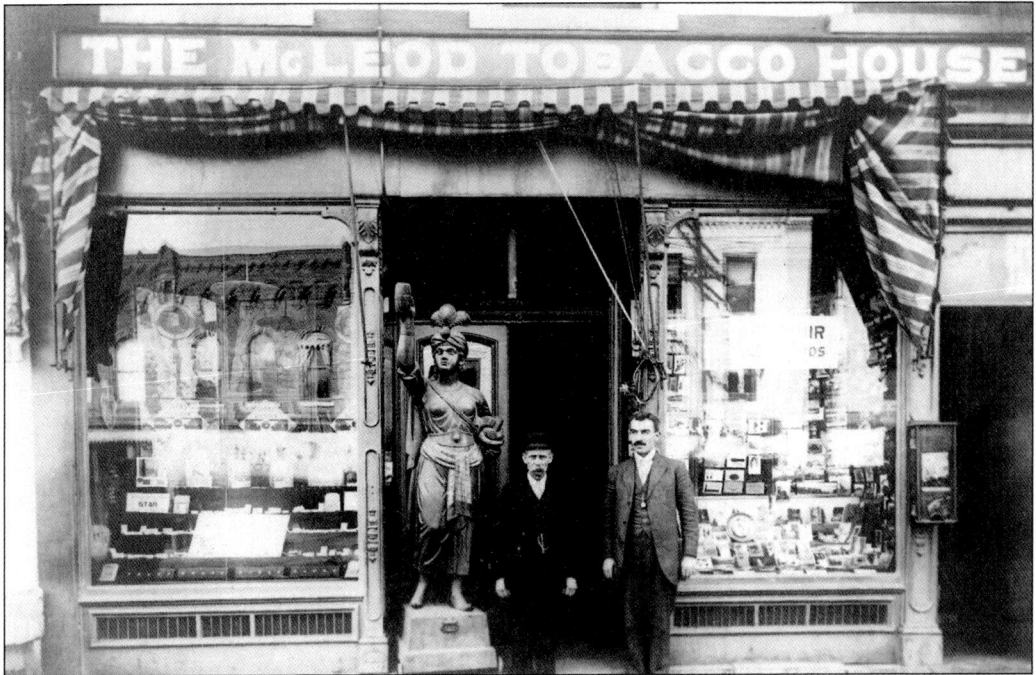

This Penn Yan tobacconist boasts the then-typical wooden Indian. Her garb suggests the Far East more than the New World. Tobacco was commercially grown in the southern Finger Lakes into the 20th century.

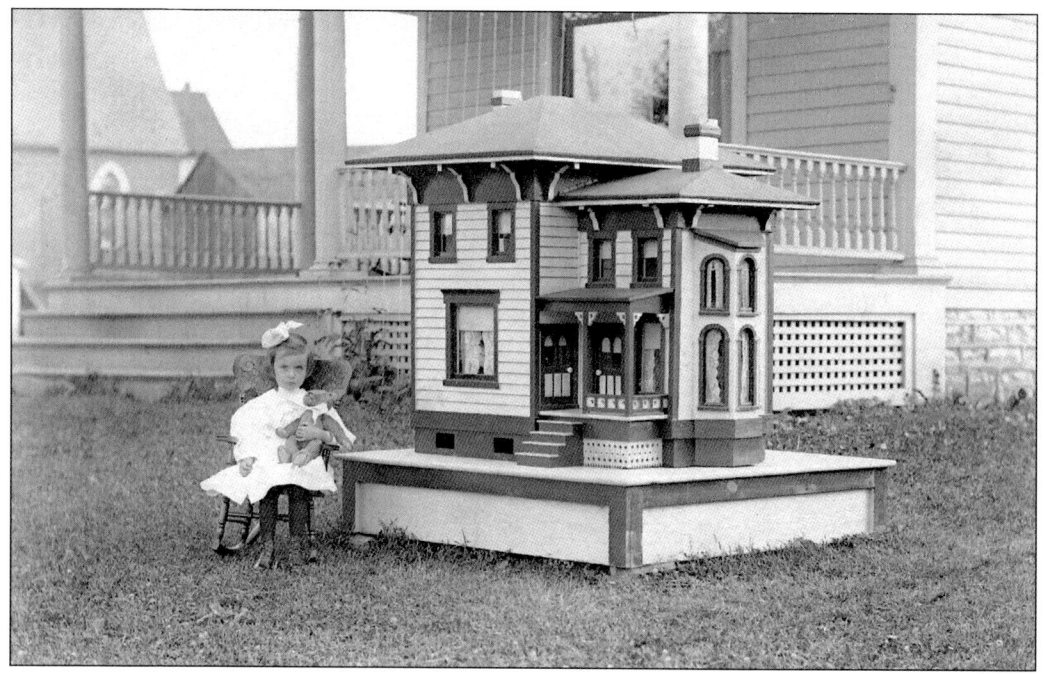
What a fortunate little girl to have a dollhouse like this. Sad to relate, Evelyn Richardson of Penn Yan later drowned in Keuka Lake.

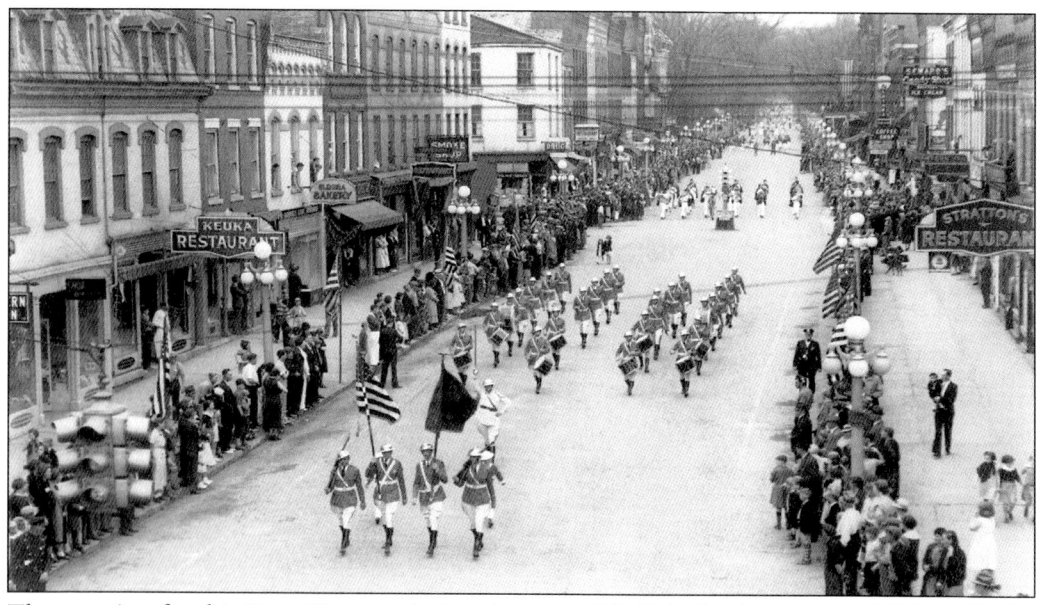
The occasion for this Penn Yan parade is unknown. Of all the business signs visible, only the Keuka Restaurant is still in existence today.

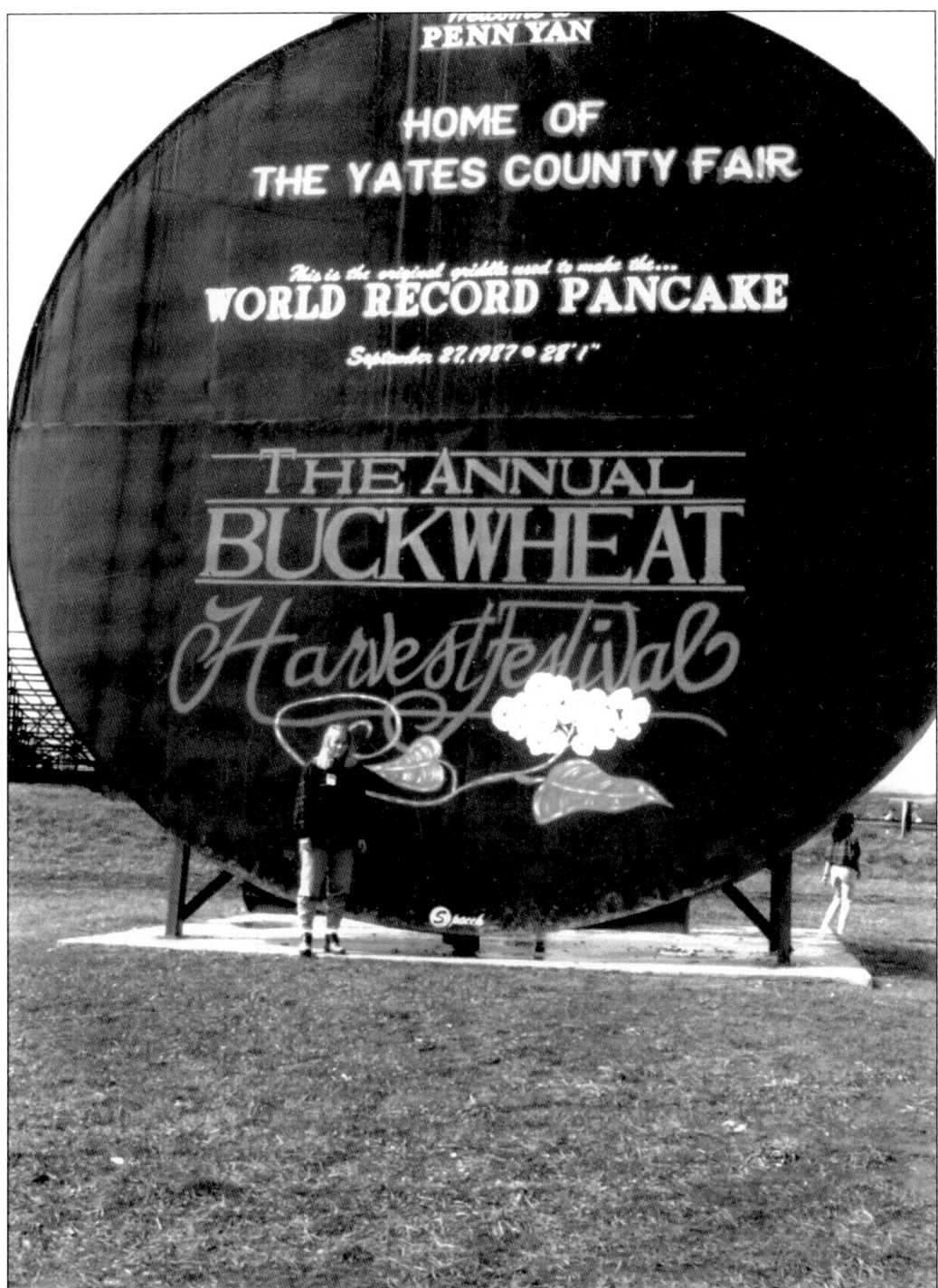

Birkett Mills of Penn Yan, which was founded in 1790, is one of the state's oldest businesses and reportedly the world's largest producer of buckwheat. It clearly has no competition for the world's largest pancake! This griddle at over 28 feet stands as a monument to the 13 annual Buckwheat Harvest Festivals that made Penn Yan come alive.

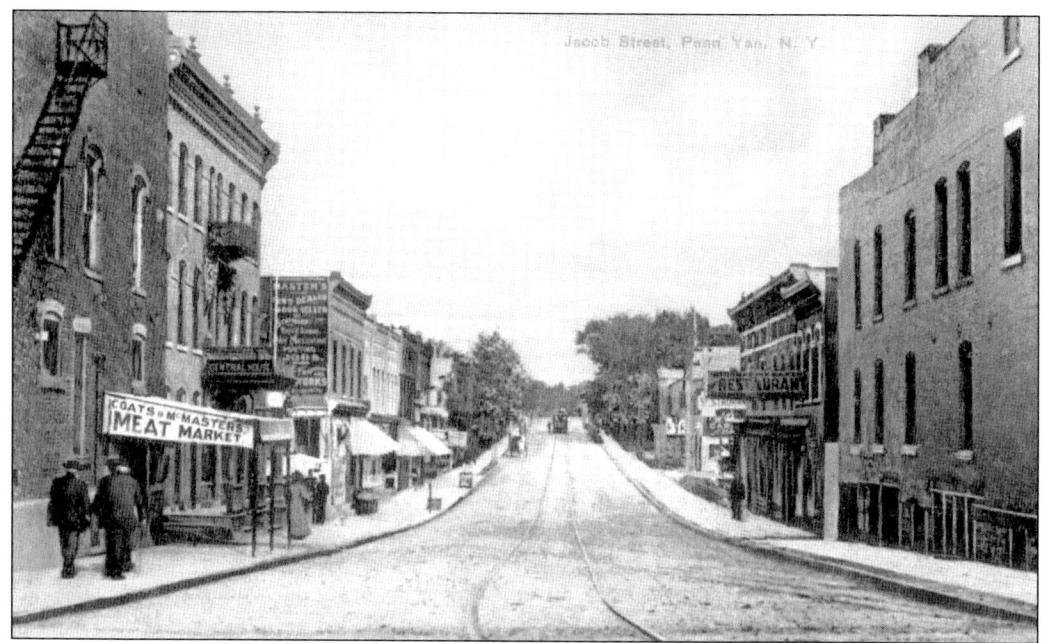

Notice the distant trolley in this view of Penn Yan. The trolley traveled from the Northern Central Railroad, at the top of the image, to Branchport. An artist has removed all the wires from this image, which was not done in the next.

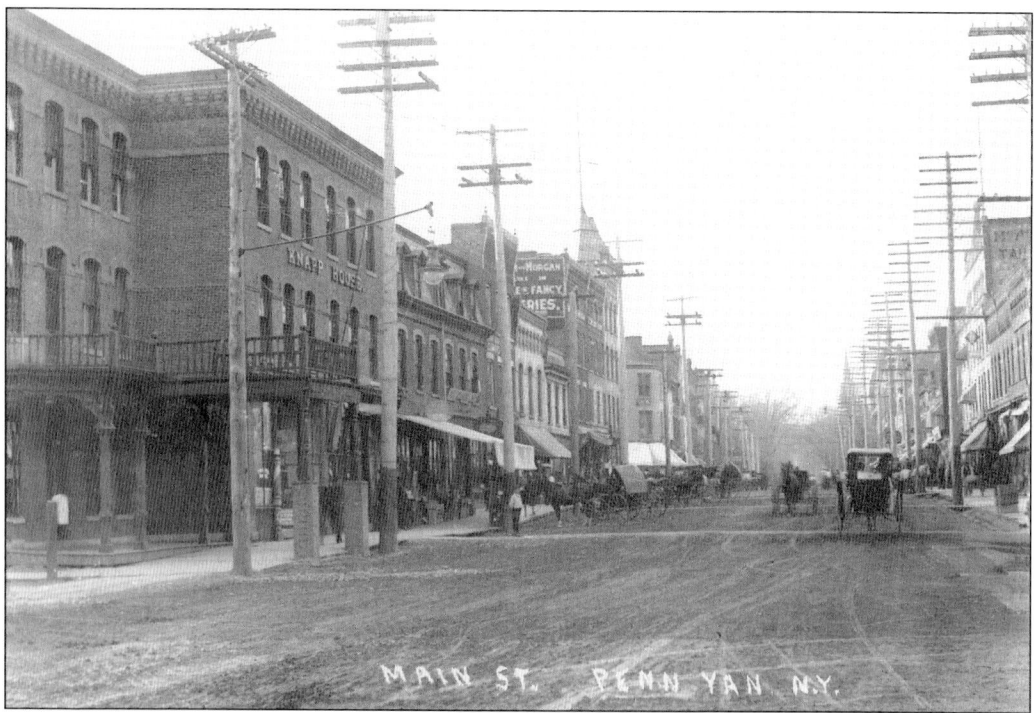

Here one sees the 19th century's dependence on the horse. Consider that each horse daily contributed 36 pounds of waste to the unpaved streets, along with a gallon of liquid. Something that has disappeared and will not be missed is the poles and wires, put underground.

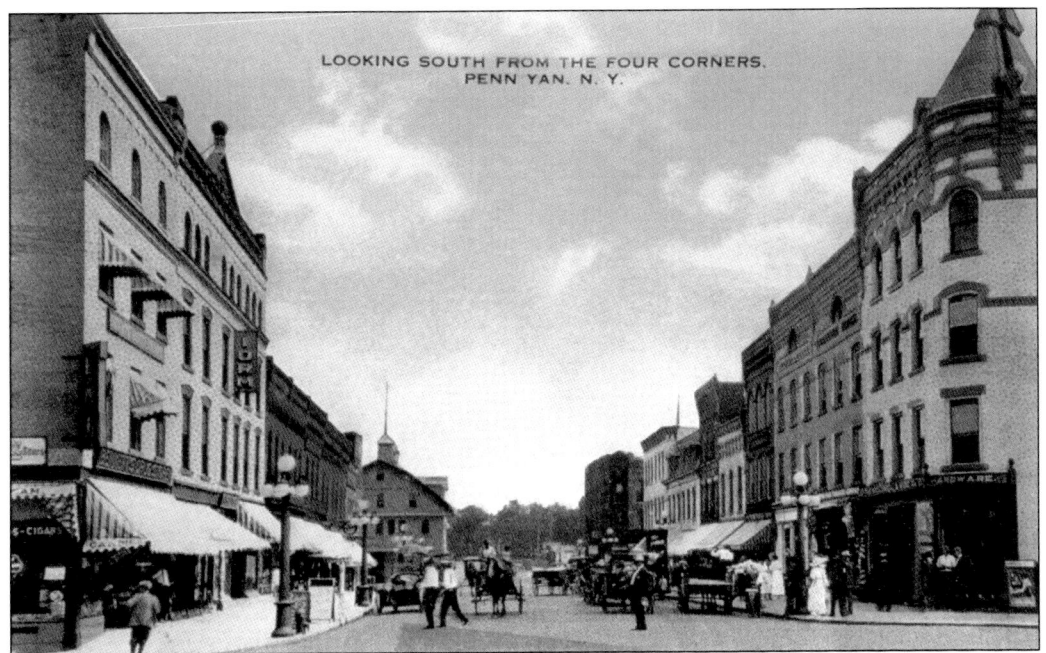

This is the same street as at the bottom of the previous page, just looking the opposite direction. The wires are gone, and some of the horses have been replaced by automobiles. Today there is still that mixture of horses and cars. Conservative Groffdale Mennonites now drive their rigs to town. There are well over 300 Groffdale families in Yates County, with more conservative Anabaptists in Steuben, Schuyler, and other Finger Lakes counties.

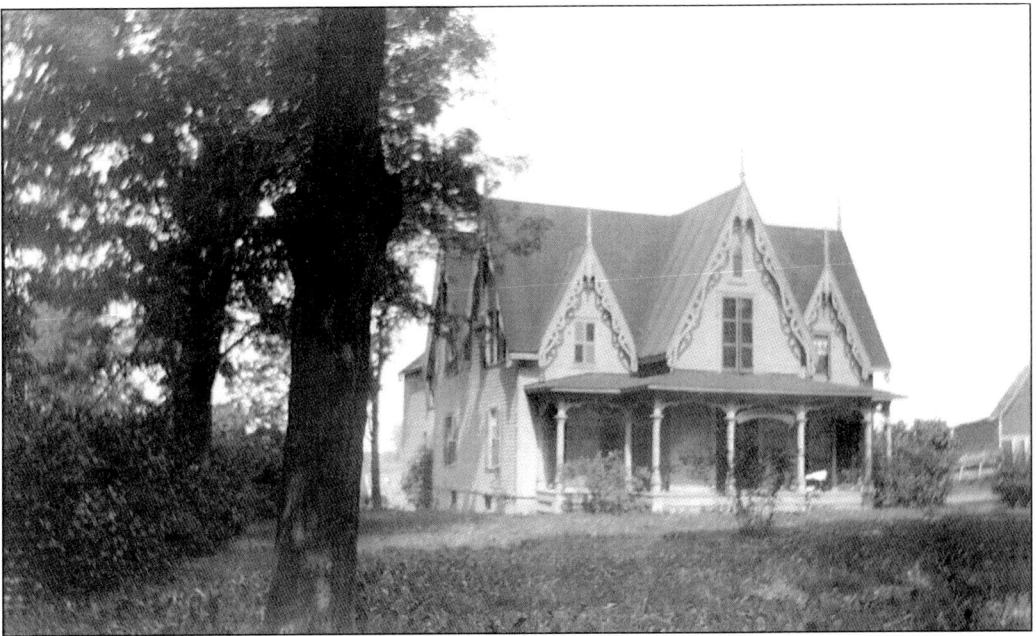

This was the Hatmaker Hospital; the building exists today as an apartment house. If one must go to the hospital, one might as well enjoy those lovely gables. Presumably other professions, and not just hatters, were also allowed.

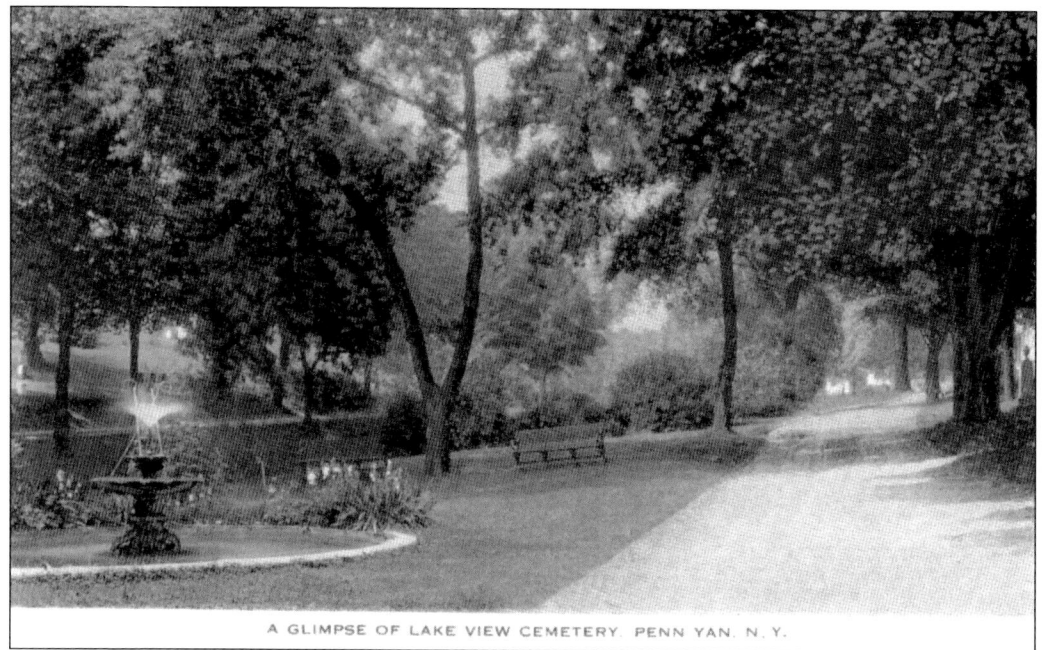

This cemetery makes one almost wish to settle down there, especially with the lake view. Postcards showing cemeteries were often a reflection of community pride and tended to show fountains and pools instead of graves.

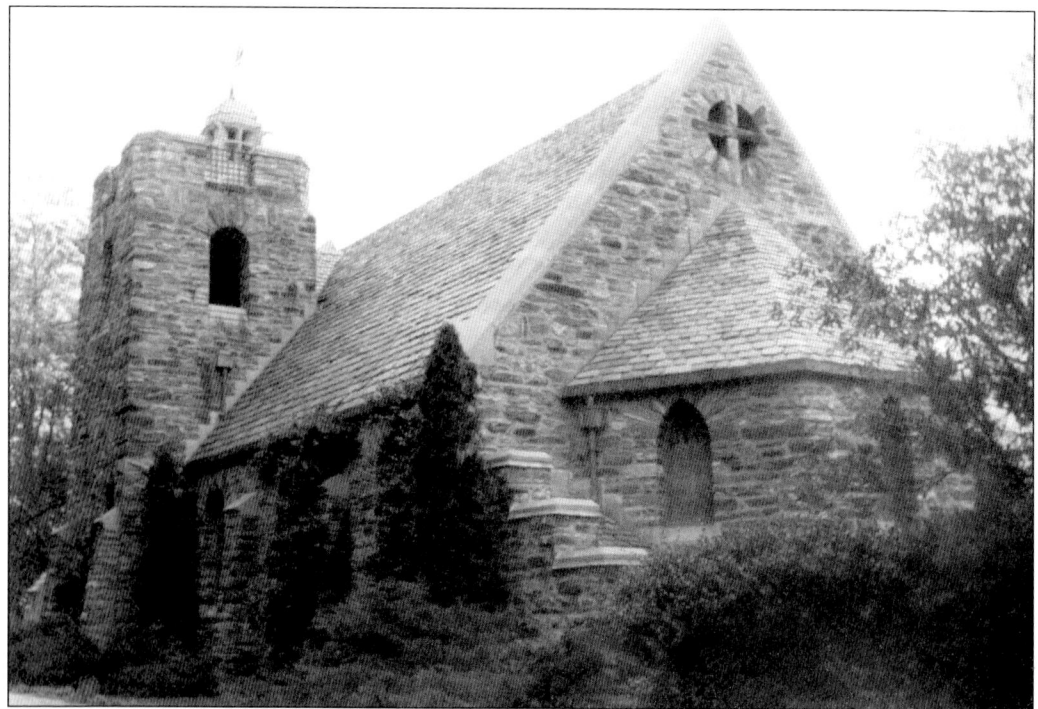

The Garrett Chapel on the Bluff commemorates Charles Garrett, who died too young of tuberculosis. His parents created the memorial, where the Episcopal Diocese of Rochester conducts Sunday morning summer services.

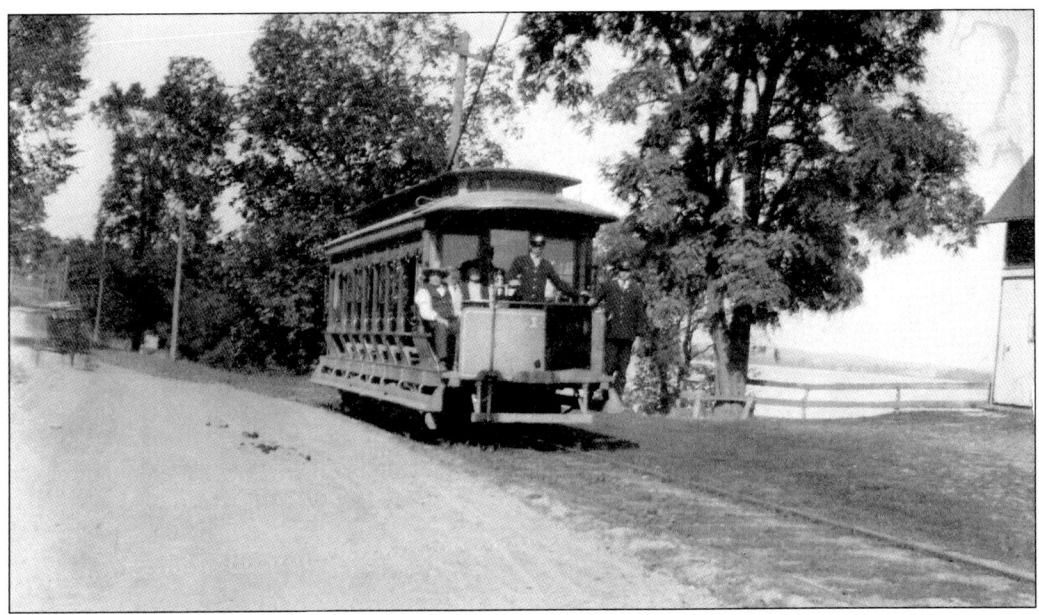

Branchport lies at the head of Keuka Lake's West Branch. Besides being a steamboat port of call, Branchport was also the western terminus of the Penn Yan, Keuka Park, and Branchport (electric) Railroad—the "pie, cake, and biscuit" line. It was once a popular excursion to ride the steamer around the bluff from Penn Yan to Branchport and then return by trolley.

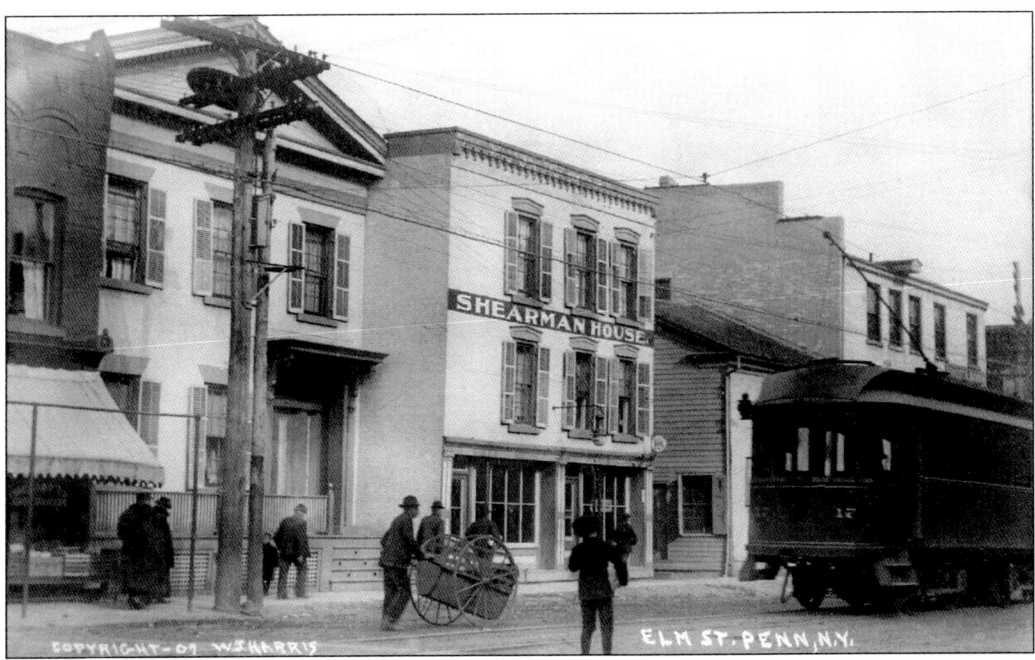

The Shearman House was later the Elmwood Theater and is now the site of the Penn Yan village hall. At the time of this photograph, villagers could make use of the trolley waiting room and the public telephone.

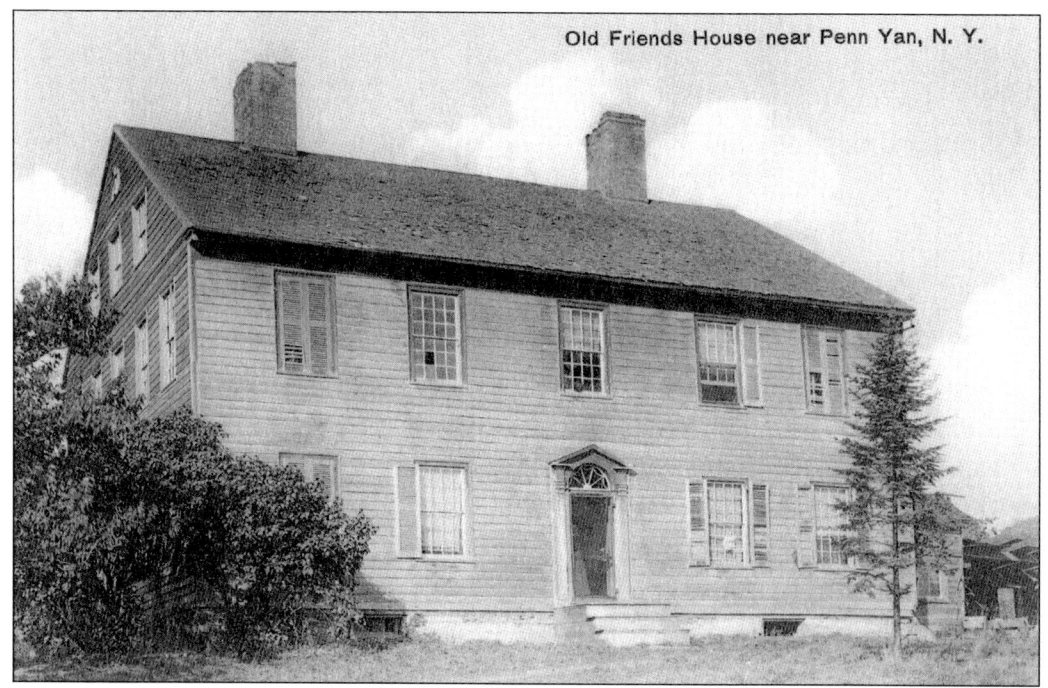

Jemima Wilkinson, who claimed to have died and then been reanimated as the "Publick Universal Friend," centered her religious community first near Dresden (1788) and then in Jerusalem (1794). After she "left time" 25 years later, her following dwindled away, but her 1814 home is preserved today, though not open to the public. The Oliver House Museum in Penn Yan has a number of her personal possessions, including her carriage.

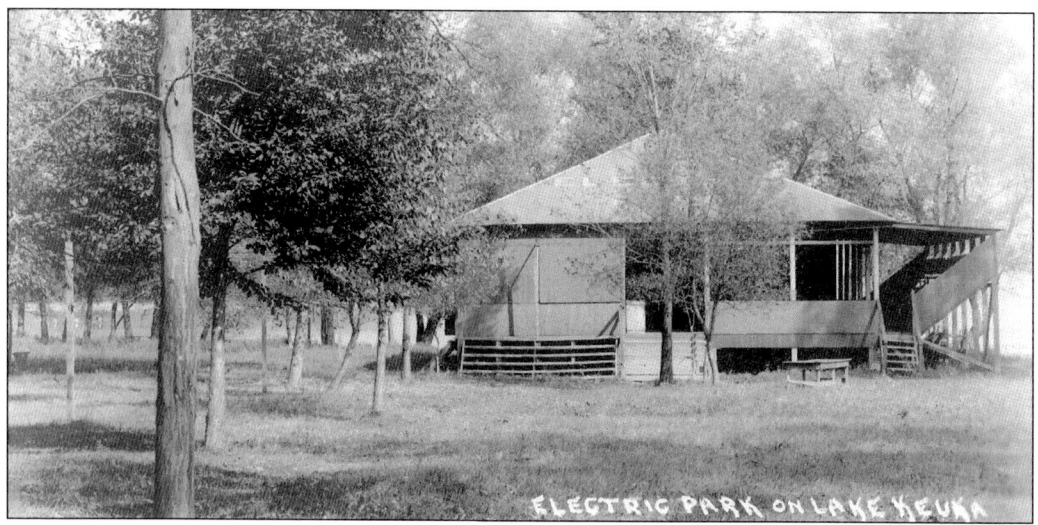

Electric Park on Brandy Bay was typical of arrangements often made by trolley lines. Having the electricity, the tracks, and the rolling stock, they set up amusement parks to stimulate ridership (also profiting from park revenue, of course). Penn Yan residents and Keuka College students were glad they did. The park banned liquor, lest the students be corrupted.

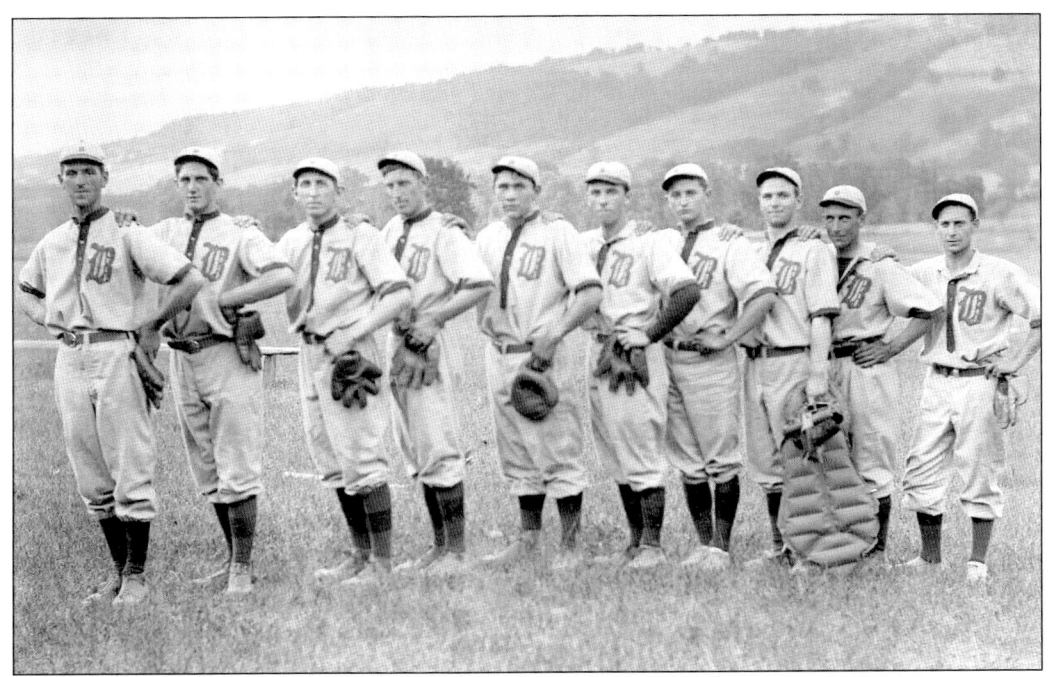

Notice the full-fingered gloves that most of the Branchport town team players have. Branchport took great pride in the baseball team, and in a time of fewer sports venues than today, the games were well attended.

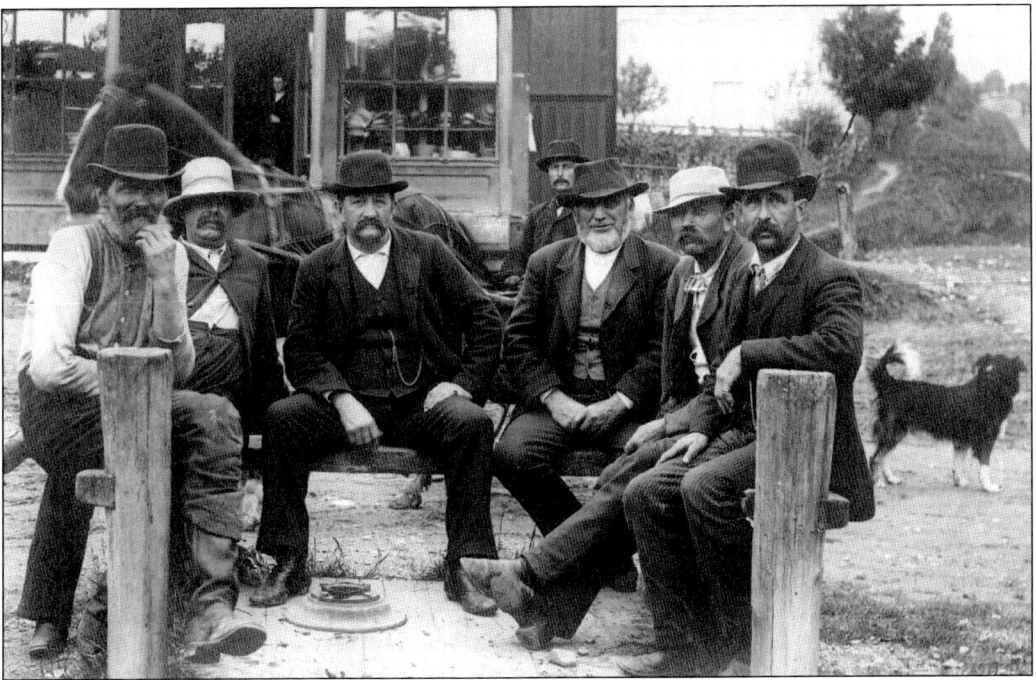

These Branchport gents no doubt remembered being young like the ballplayers, but the youngsters probably never envisioned taking a seat on this bench.

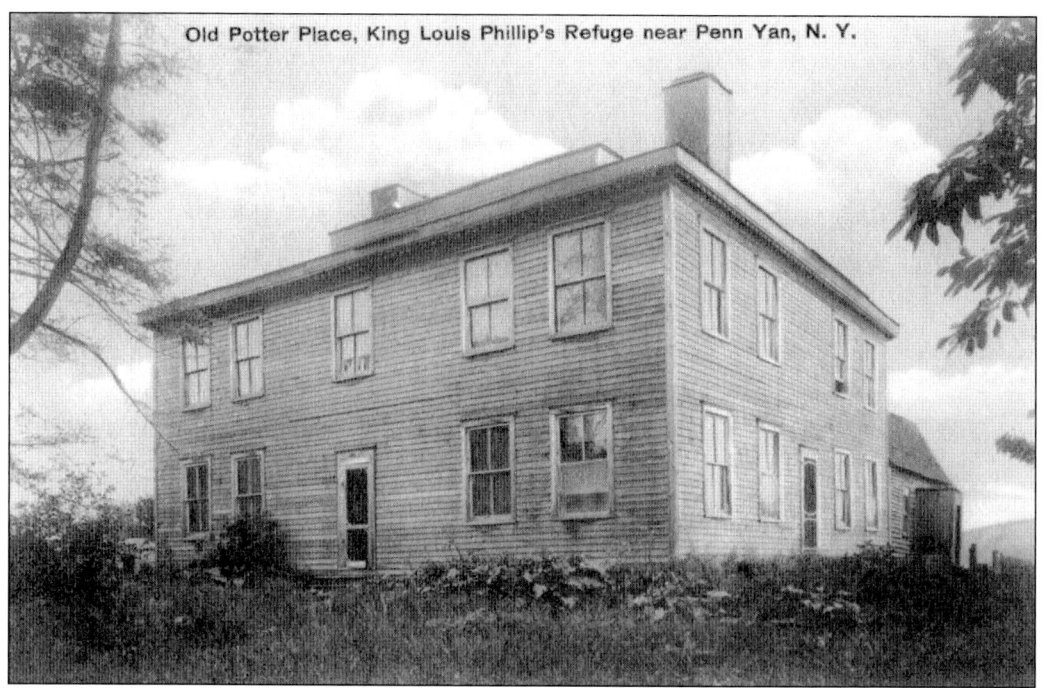

The future King Louis Philippe of France spent time at the Potter Mansion. This house is one of the oldest in Yates County, built by early setter Arnold Potter.

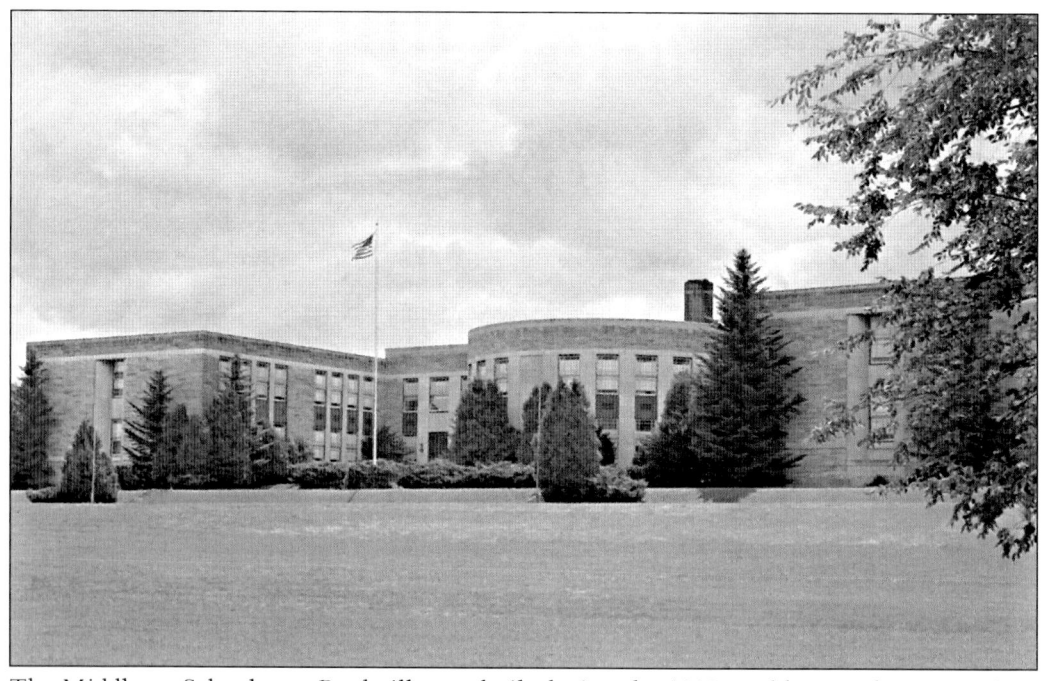

The Middlesex School near Rushville was built during the 1930s and has an elegant art deco facade. During World War II, Rushville had a camp for Italian POWs.

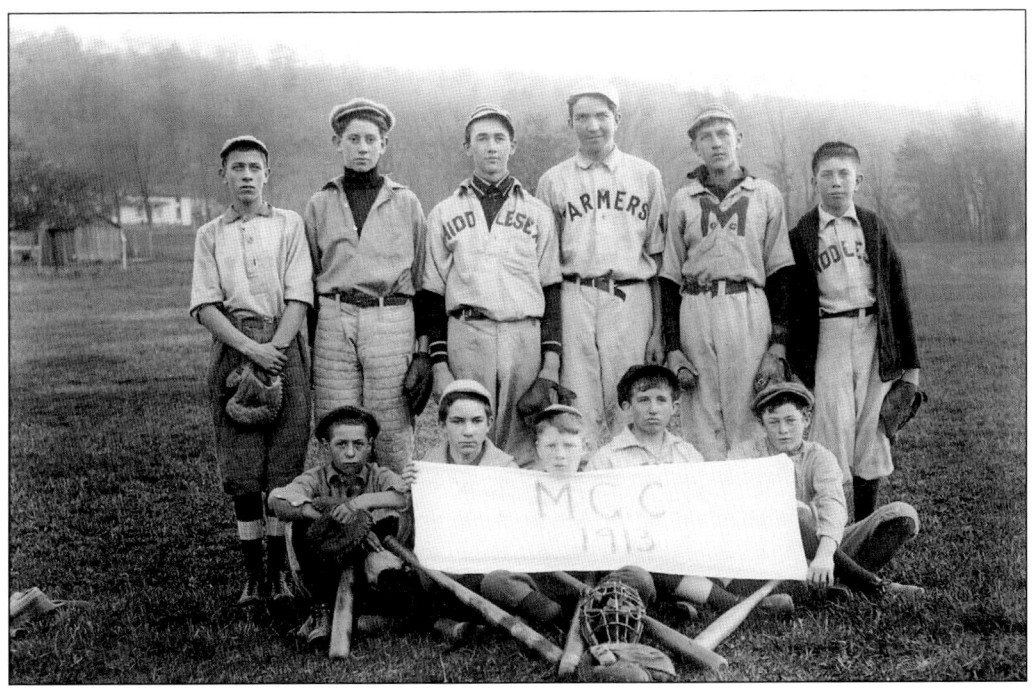

Most of these Middlesex ballplayers wear flannel, but the two standing at left have heavy quilted pants. Some do not appear to have uniforms at all.

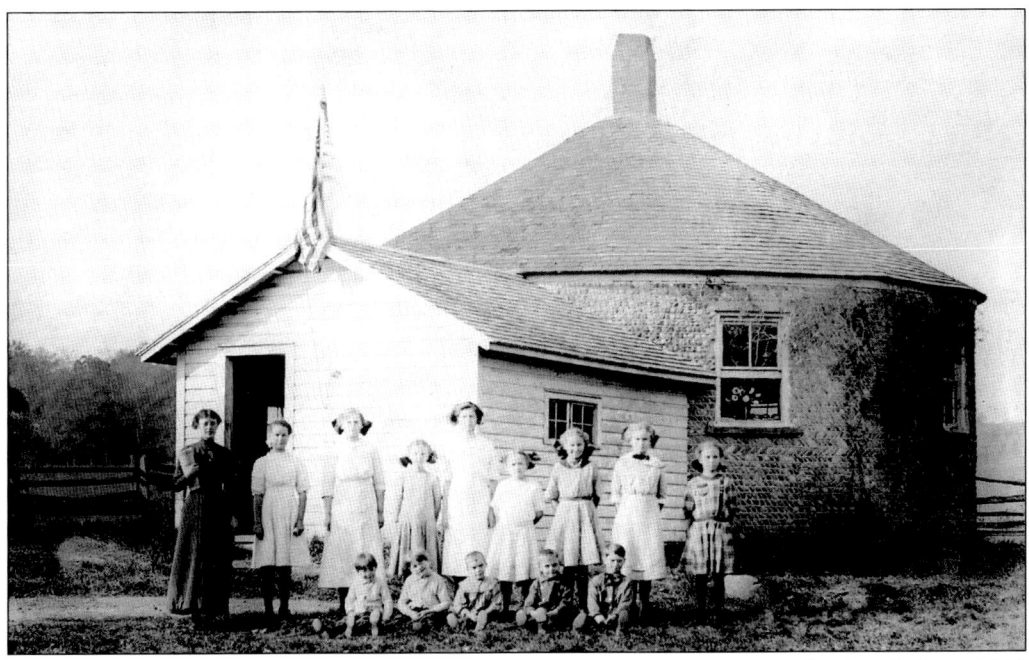

The circular cobblestone school in the town of Potter was a Yates County landmark from 1838 until 1920. It burned and was replaced by a wood school structure in 1921.

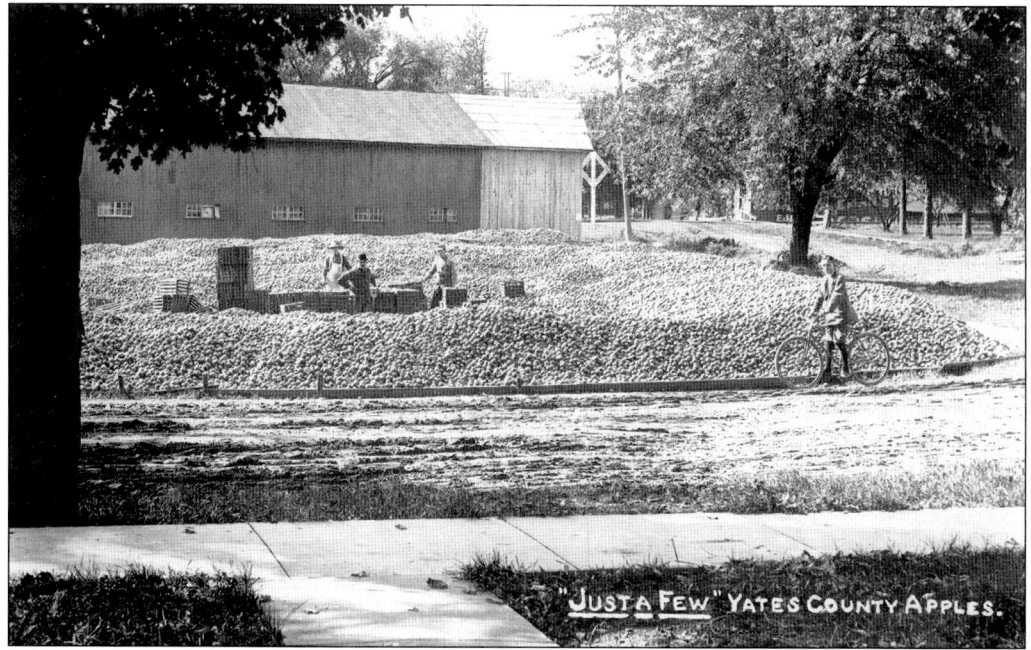

It is a big day in Himrod! Notice the delicious details this postcard inadvertently preserves: the concrete walkways beside the rutted dirt street; the schoolboy on his safety bike, with suit and knickers; and the diamond-shaped crossing sign.

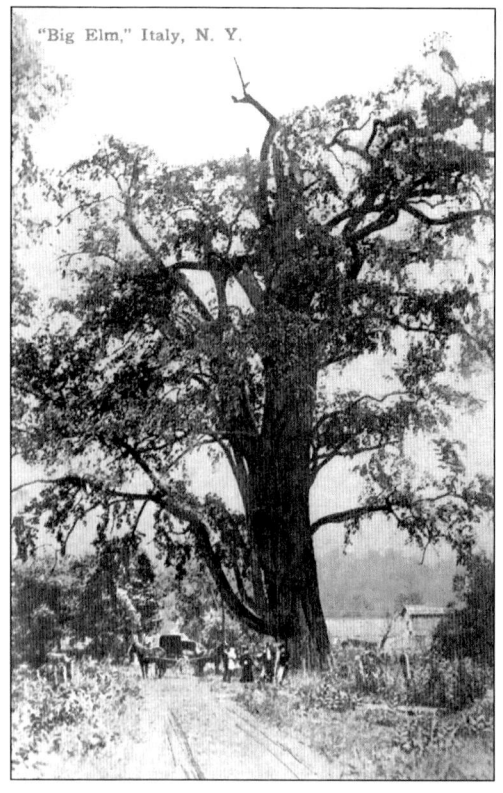

Sad to say, elms are rarely seen nowadays, thanks to a killing blight in the 20th century. They are slowly being restored now, with plantings of European elms. This particular tree, which lasted until 1933, had a circumference of 29 feet.

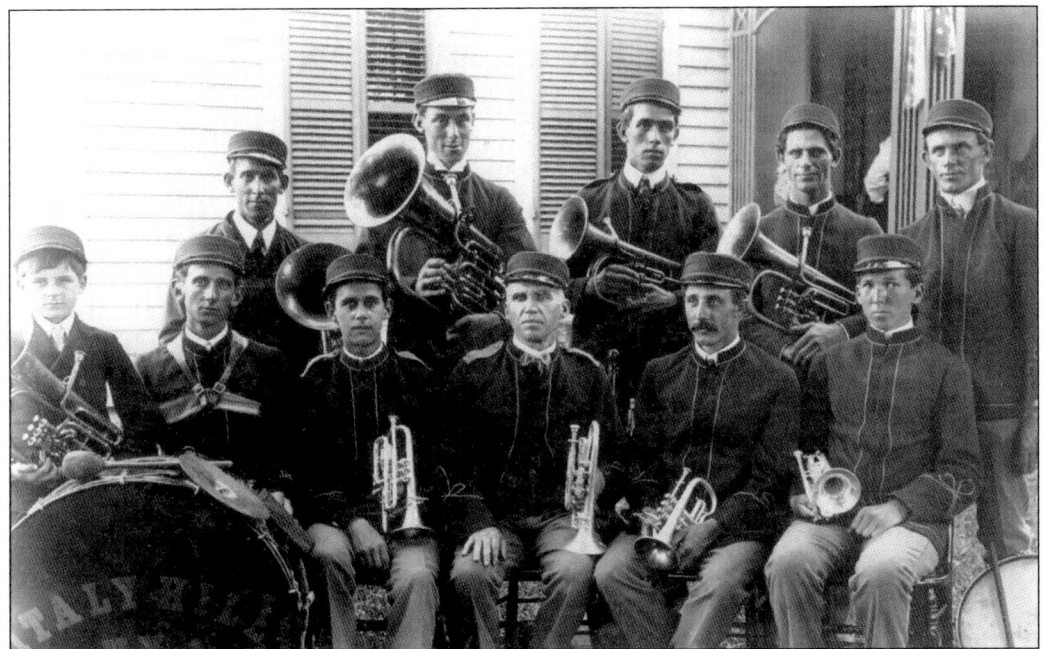

Up into the early 20th century, even small communities had their own bands. Italy Hill, between Branchport and Naples, was no exception.

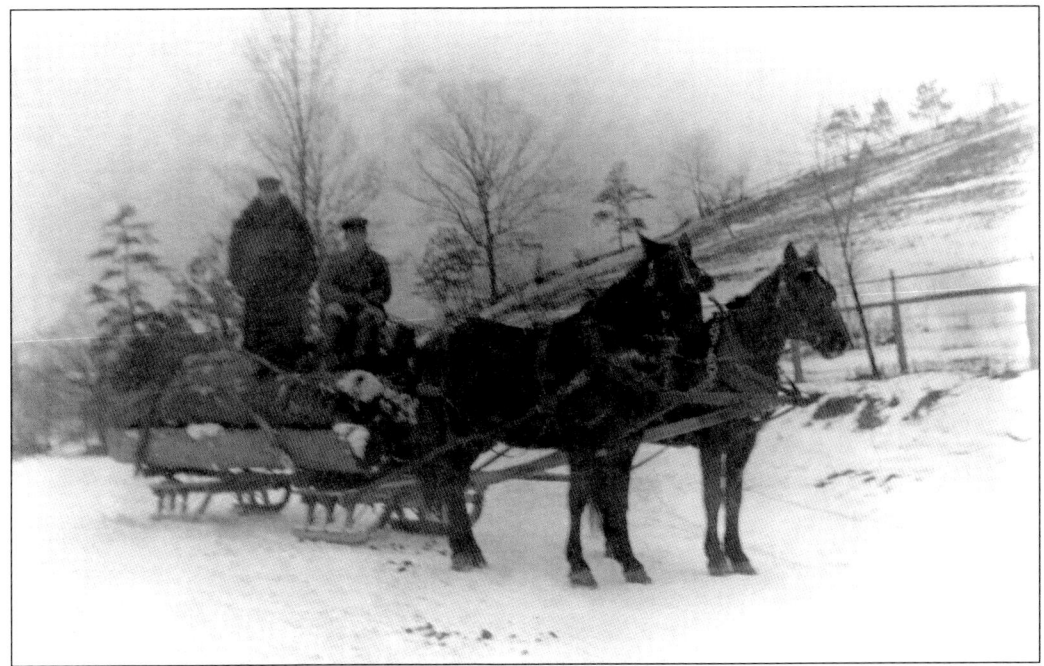

"This load scales 1,612 feet," according to the inscription. Lumbering was an important regional industry, so important that the land was largely cleared by 1900. As less land is farmed, the forest returns, and so do forest species such as black bears and turkeys.

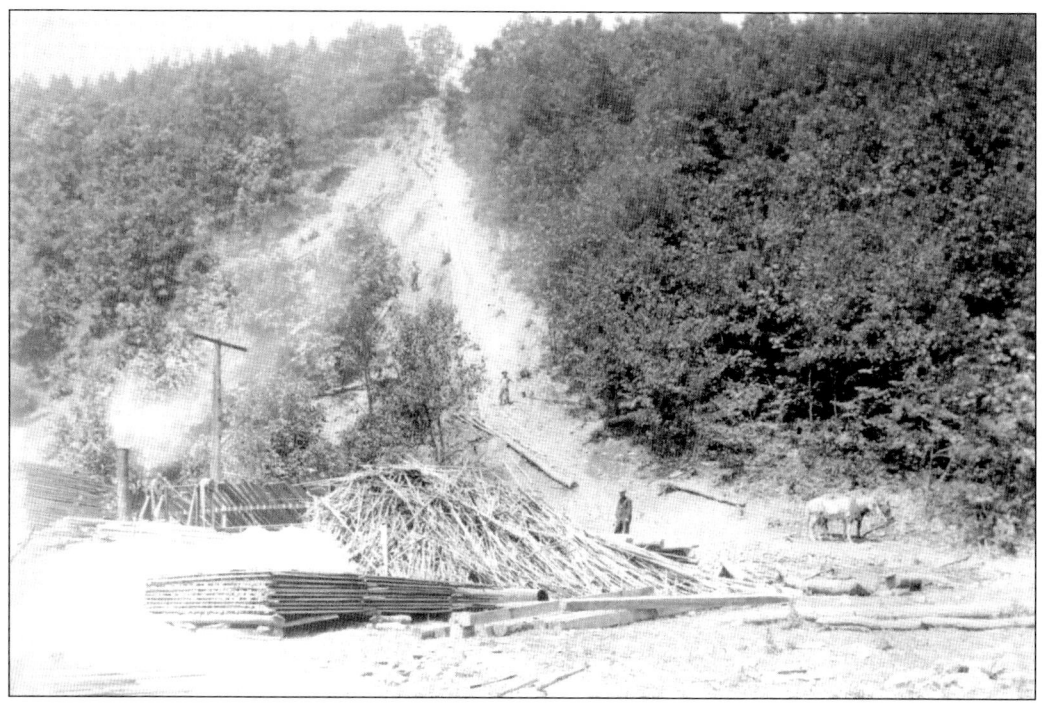

Lumbering remained a major occupation in the Finger Lakes for many years and still continues on a smaller scale. At right is a horse team that hauls logs down the slip from the hill. At left, the smokestack for the sawmill's steam engine puffs away.

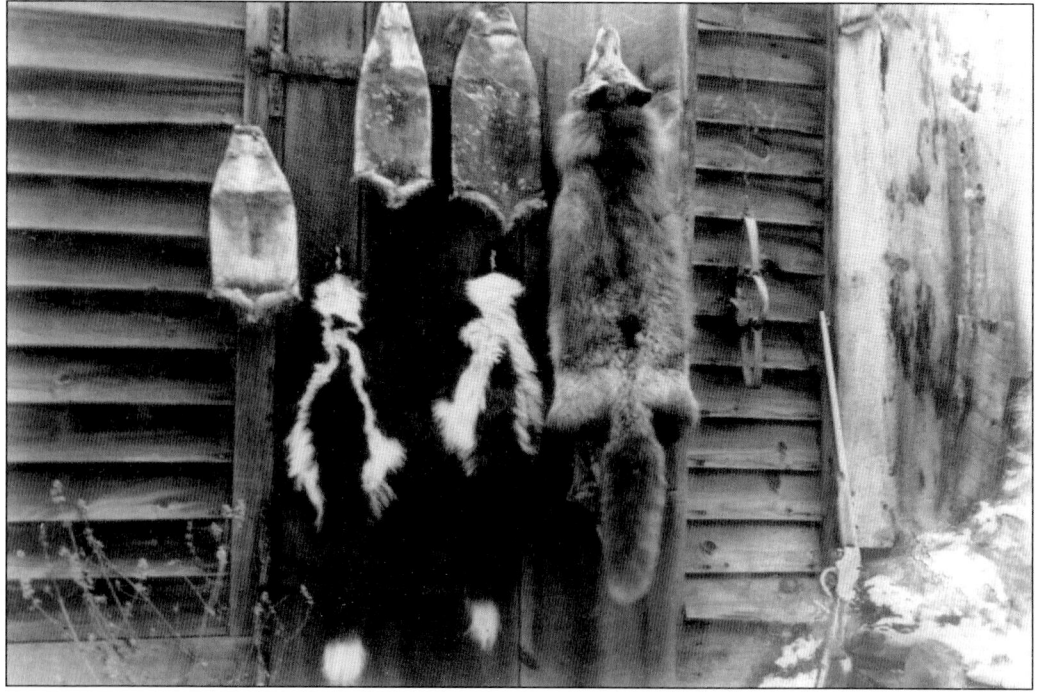

Trapping also is no longer the occupation it once was. The pelts on this shed include fox and skunk. Notice the trap hanging to right and the long gun propped to the right.

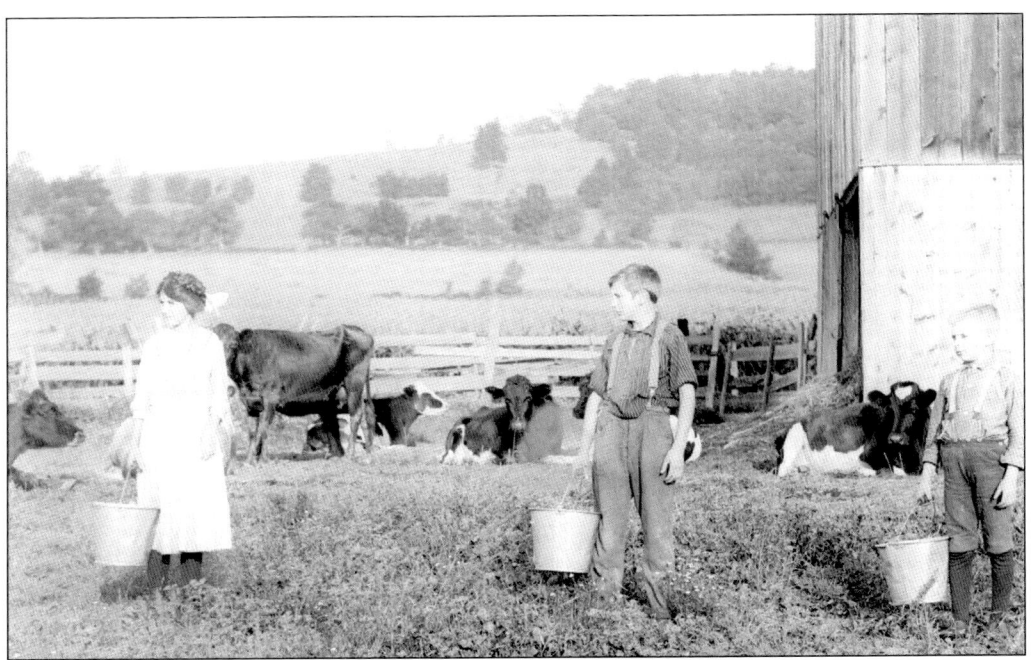

Whatever one's age, there is always plenty of work on a farm, although one may wonder whether the girl at left is really dressed for outdoor chores.

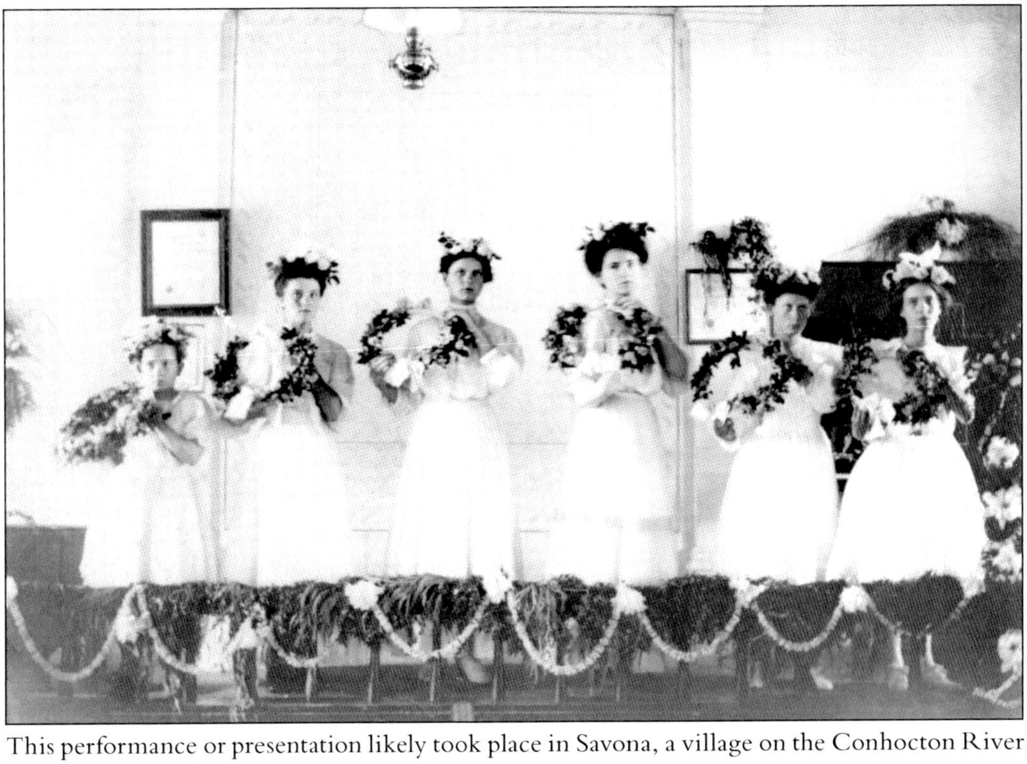

This performance or presentation likely took place in Savona, a village on the Conhocton River between Bath and Corning.

Open fields and long ridges still abound in the Finger Lakes, and sheep still safely graze. The land- and labor-eating split rail fences in the background, while picturesque, have mostly been replaced by the barbed-wire fences in the fore.

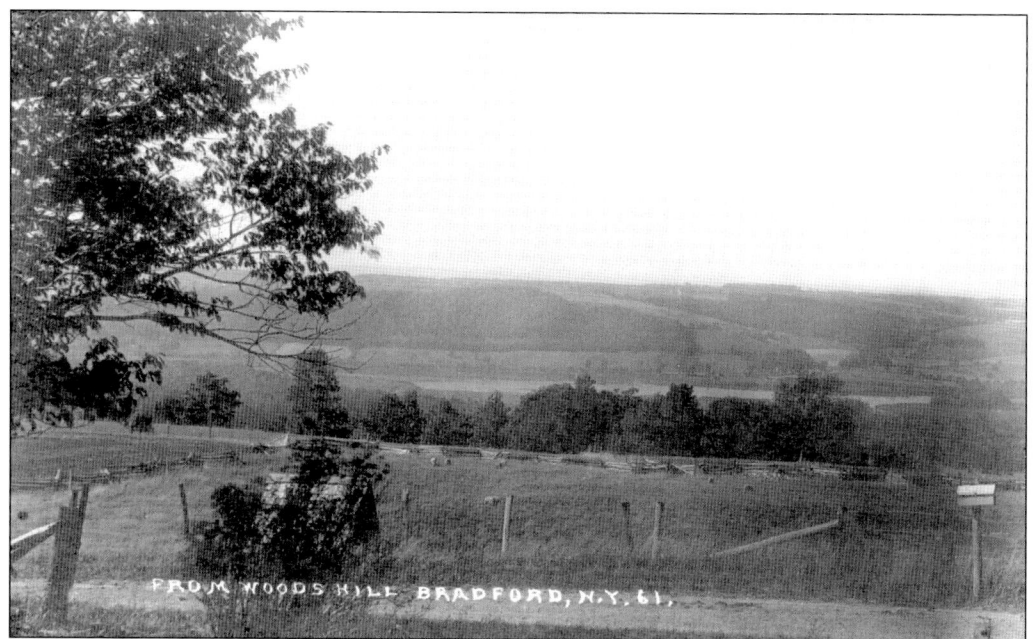

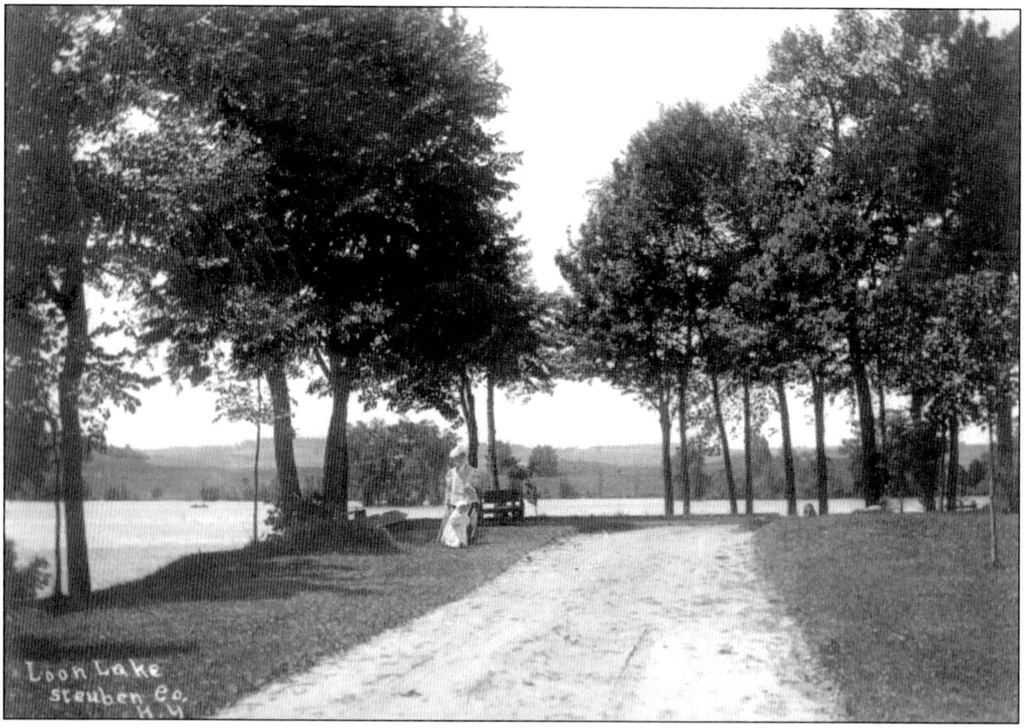

Loon Lake in Steuben County, although small, was the site of a resort hotel built in 1870. It is now a residential area. F. A. Owen of Dansville published this postcard.

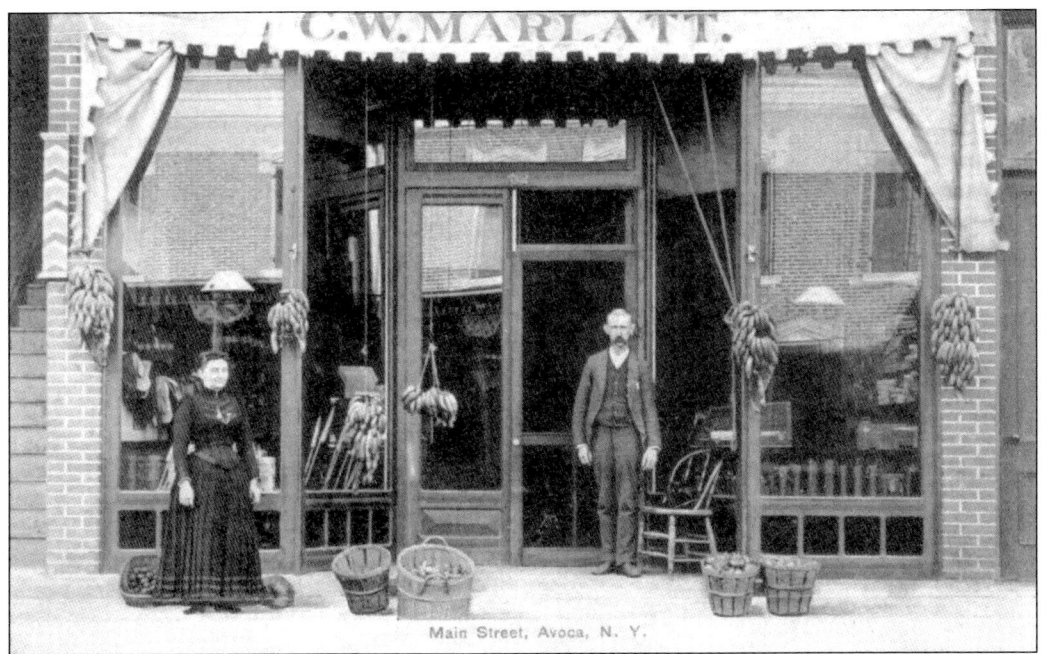

The Marlatt store in Avoca is meticulously ready for business. Perhaps there is a barber on the second floor—notice the striped panel, suggesting a barber's pole, to the right of the stairs. "Hello old sox," reads the message on the back. "Does this postal look natural[?]" Before World War II Avoca became a regional starting point for potato production, thanks to farmers brought in from Maine.

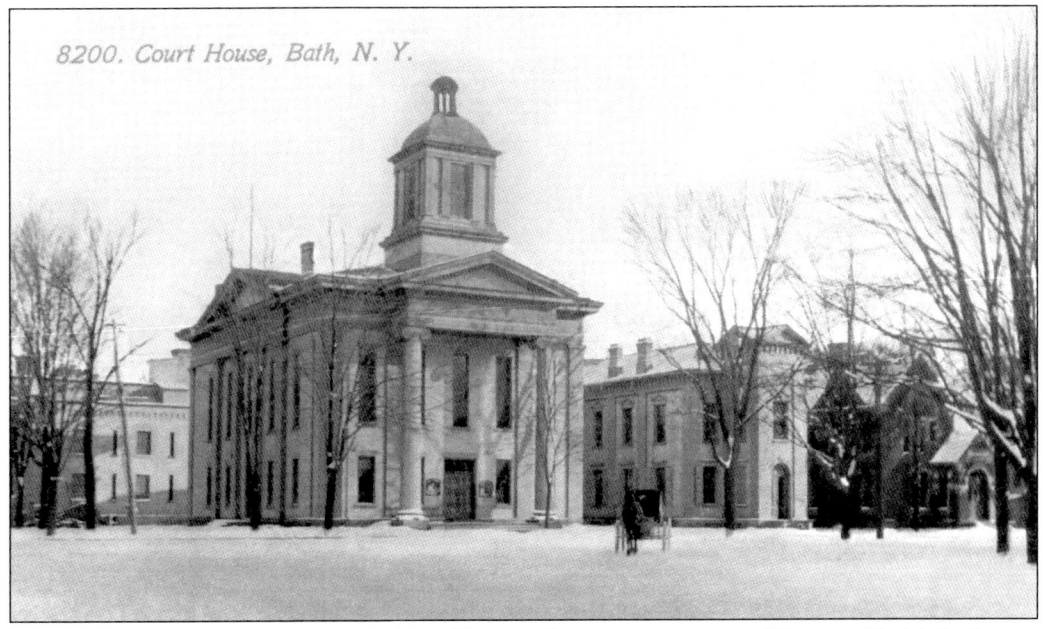

The 1860 courthouse, county clerk's office, and surrogate court still grace Bath's Pulteney Square, but the buildings in back have given way to parking lots. Conservative Anabaptists sometimes drive buggies to town, but they rarely have the whole street to themselves as the driver on this card does.

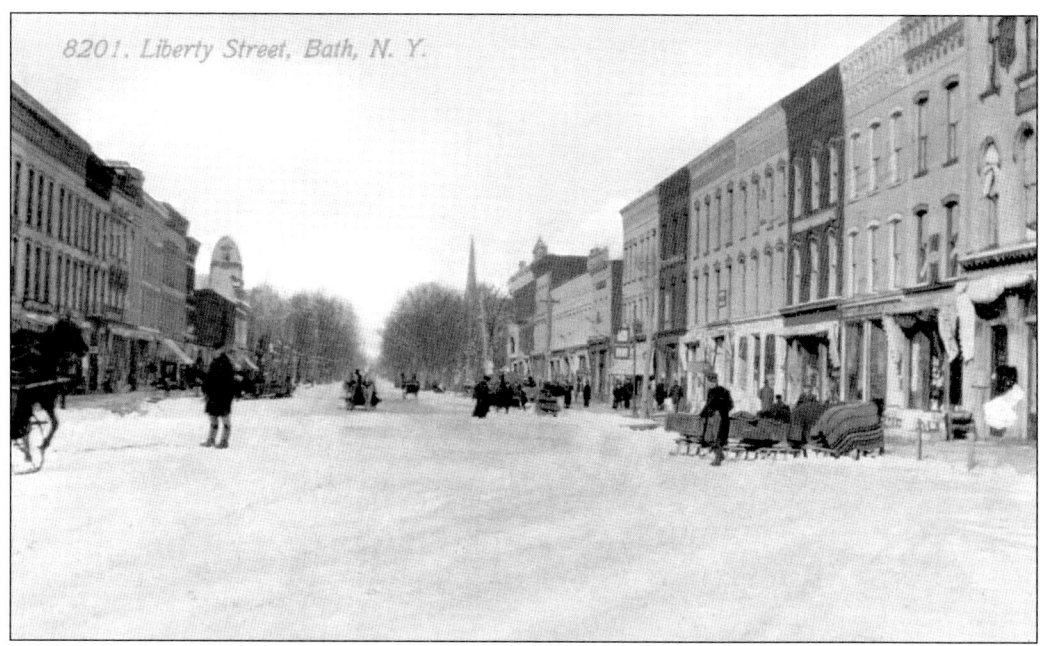

Sleighs, sledges, and heavy blankets mark this wintry street scene on Liberty Street in Bath. Remarkably, the street is little changed today, except for the sleighs.

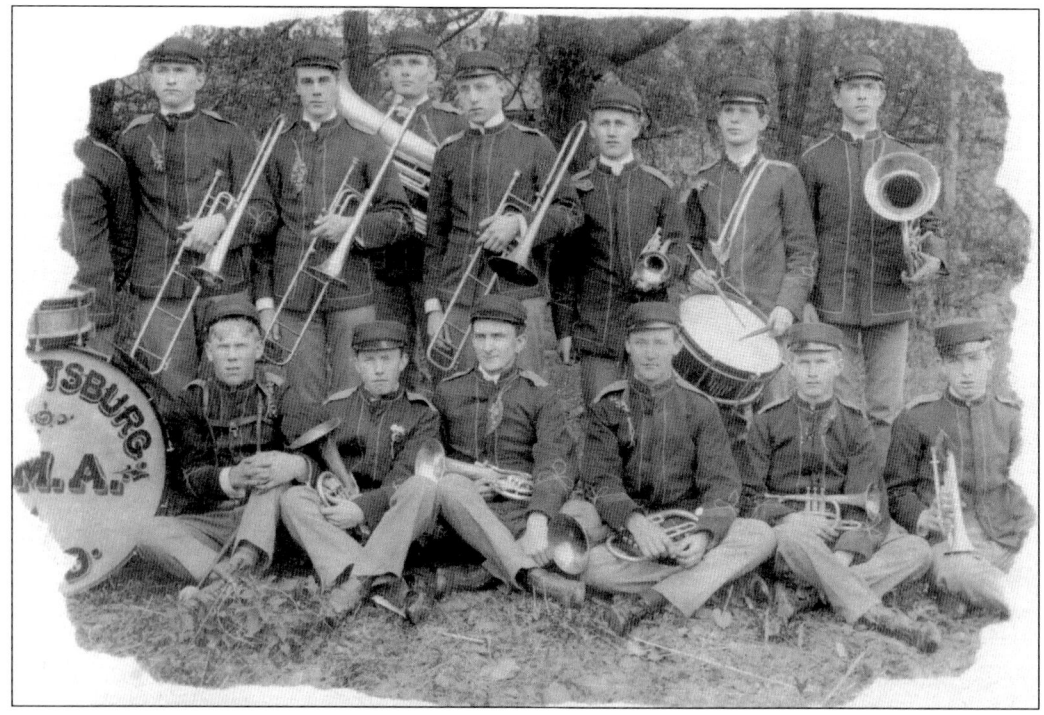

Prattsburgh (then spelled without its terminal *h*) likewise had its band. At concerts young women would stroll around the bandstand, while young men circled it a little farther out in the opposite direction. After enough perambulations, a fellow sometimes worked up sufficient courage to reverse direction, spiral down to the inner circle, and ask a young lady to walk with him.

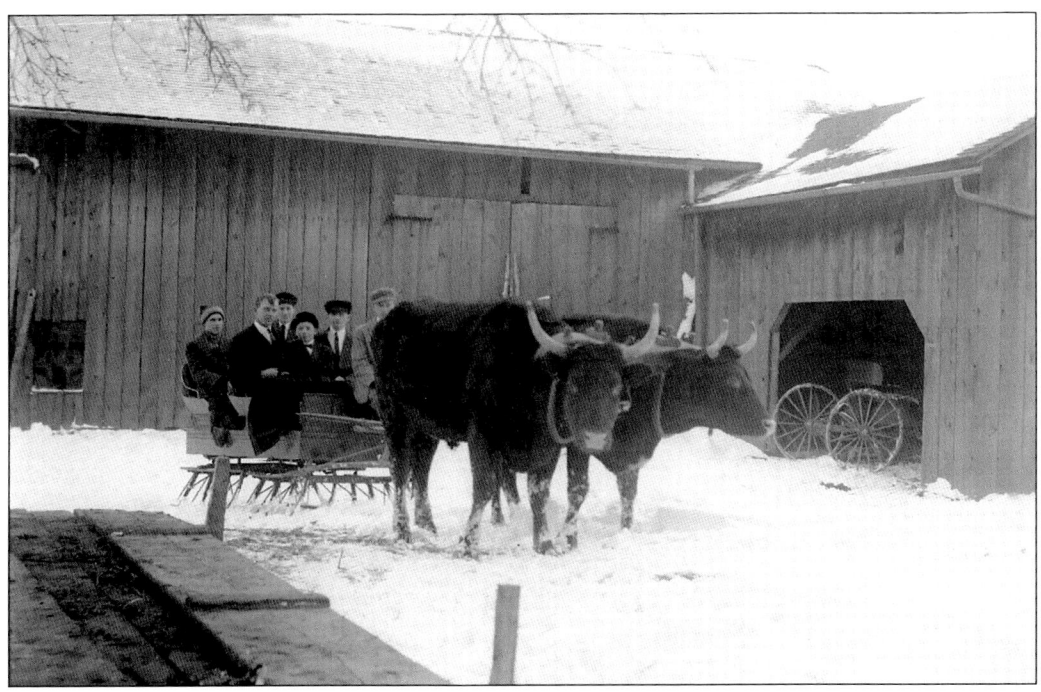

The location of this wintry scene is uncertain, but the riders presumably went plodding through the snow in their two-ox open sleigh. Two horses would certainly have been faster.

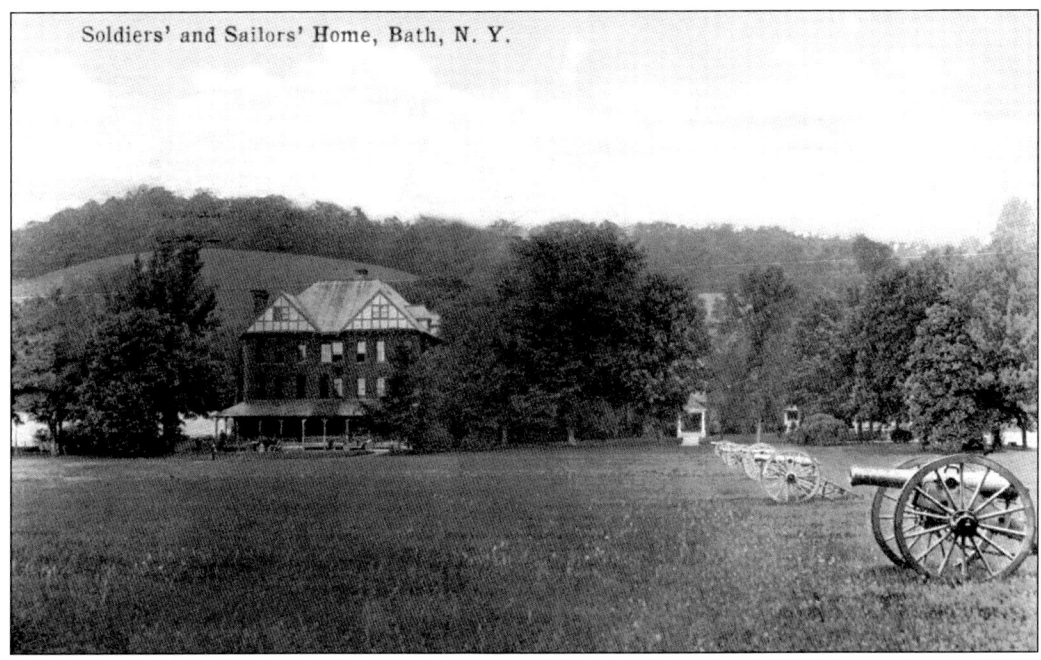

Bath campaigned mightily against Watkins, Penn Yan, and Elmira to host the New York State Soldiers' and Sailors' Home after the Civil War. The home is now a VA Medical Center.

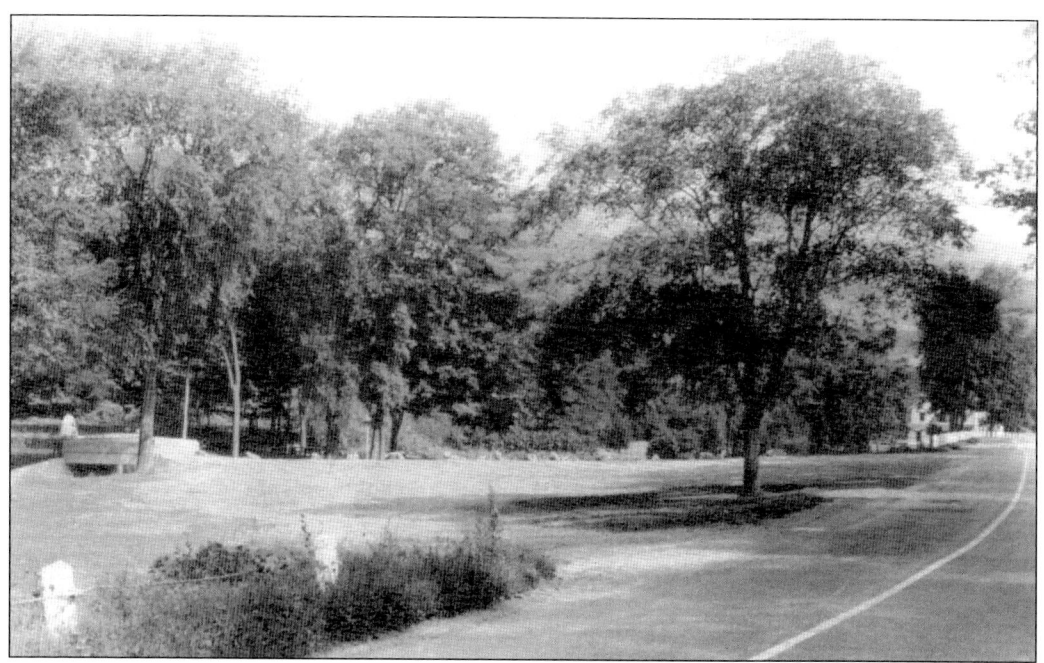

This pleasing hand-colored picture of Bath Fish Hatchery graced the 1941 calendar of the Farmers and Merchants Trust Company. Frank Campbell, who had been president of Farmers and Merchants and was state comptroller from 1890 to 1892, was instrumental in founding the hatchery.

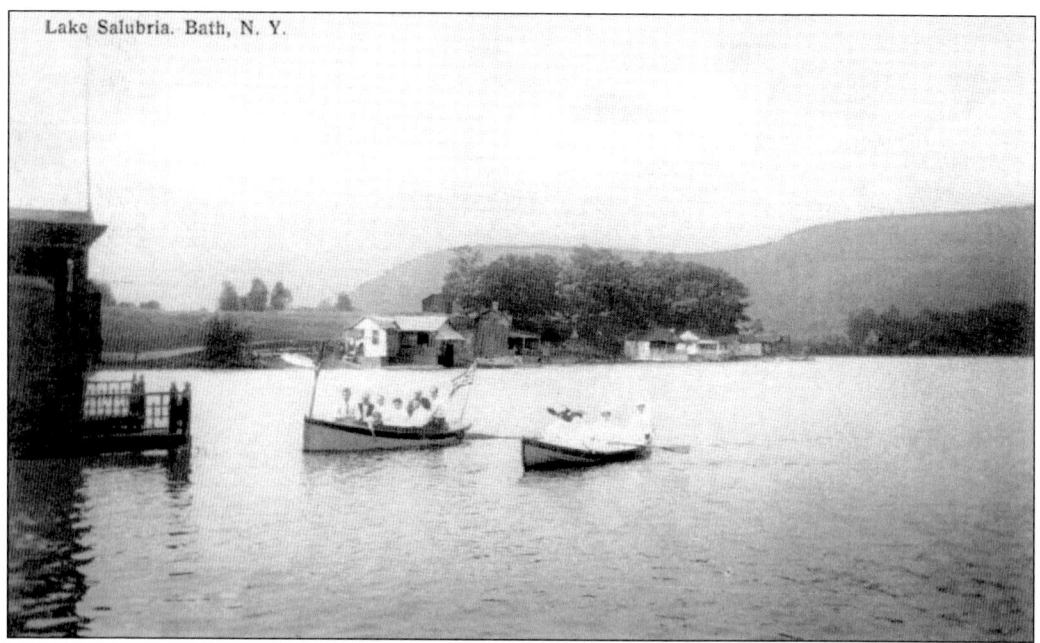

Bath residents improbably described Lake Salubria as a mile wide and a mile across. The dock and the boats are both very elegant in this German-made card published by G. H. Ferris 5 and 10 Cent Store. The message on the back reads, "oh you kid-o."

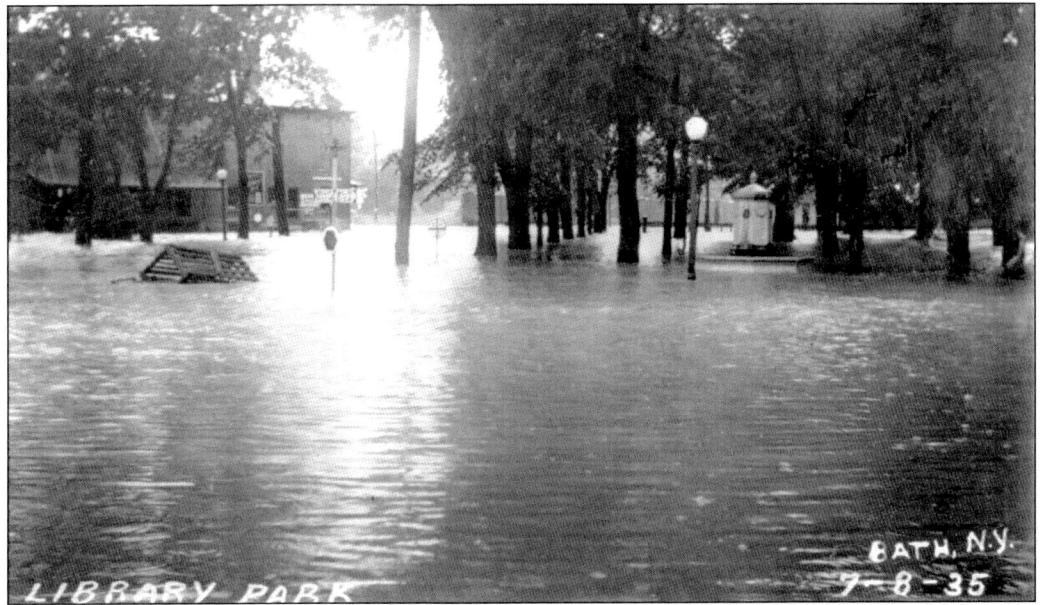

The 1935 flood was a disaster throughout the southern Finger Lakes. It looks as though the fountain in front of the Magee House in Bath has overflowed.

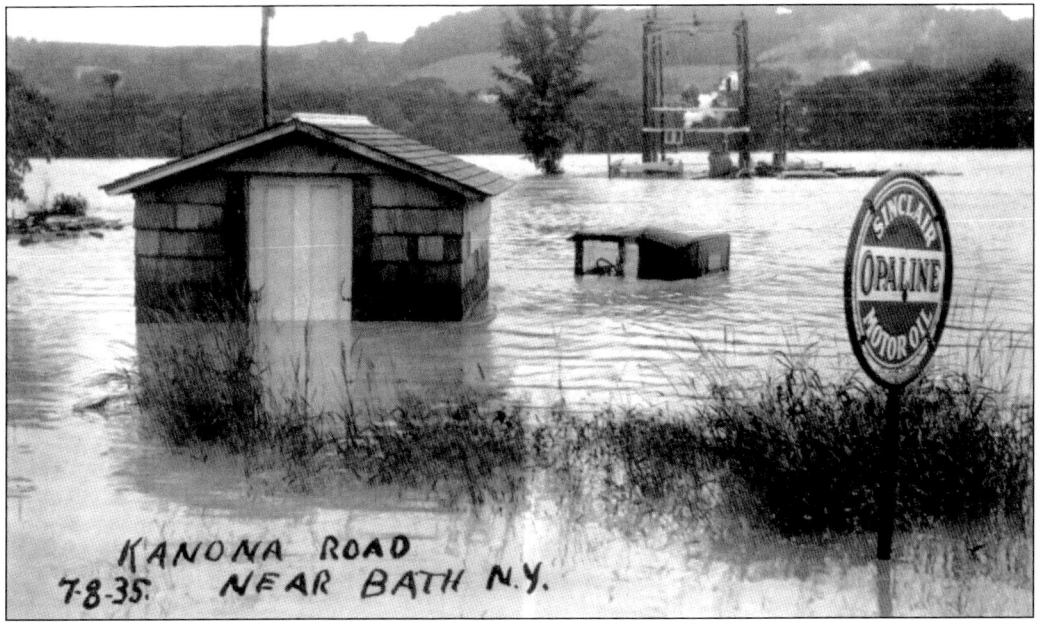

The main road and even the bridge were drowned near Kanona. The car is going to need more than Sinclair Opaline Motor Oil.

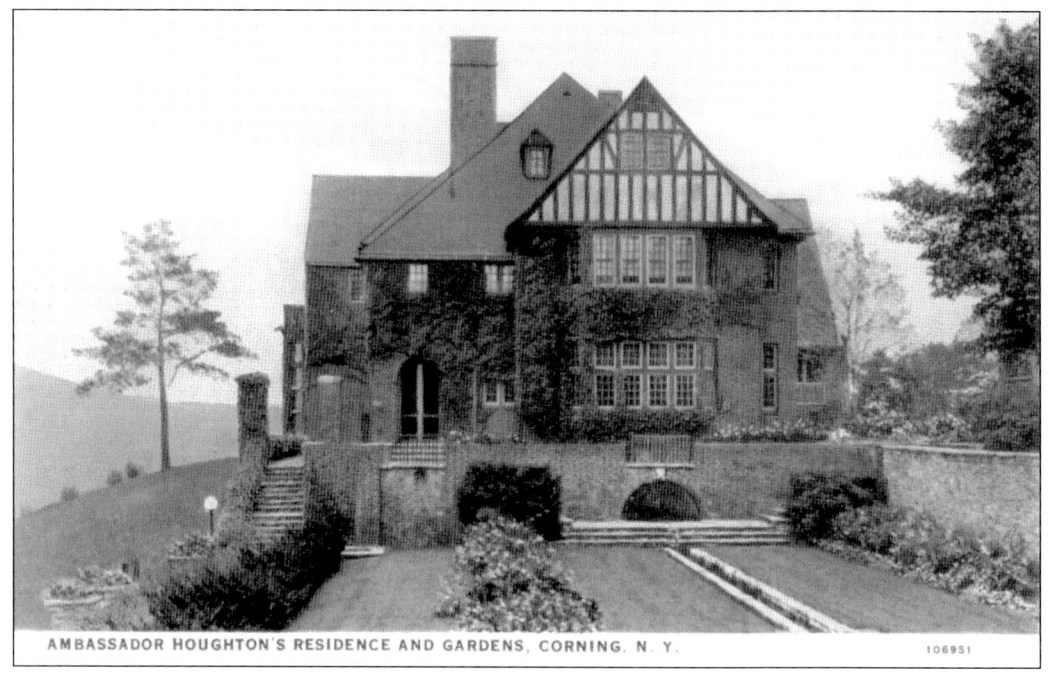

AMBASSADOR HOUGHTON'S RESIDENCE AND GARDENS, CORNING, N. Y.

The Houghton family has traditionally been well represented in the leadership of Corning Glass Works (now Corning Incorporated), but they do not stop there. Ambassador (to France during Eisenhower's administration) Houghton's father and son each represented the district in Congress.

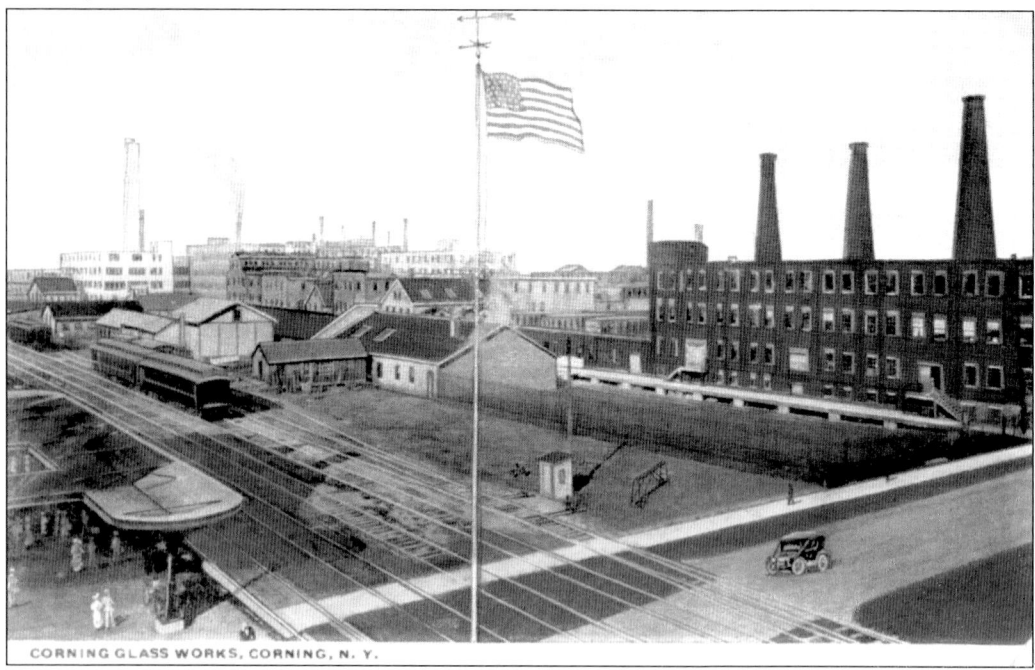

CORNING GLASS WORKS, CORNING, N. Y.

Most of these structures are now gone, along with the extensive downtown rails, but the shot tower at left still dominates the Crystal City's skyline. The tower was used in fabricating thermometer tubing.

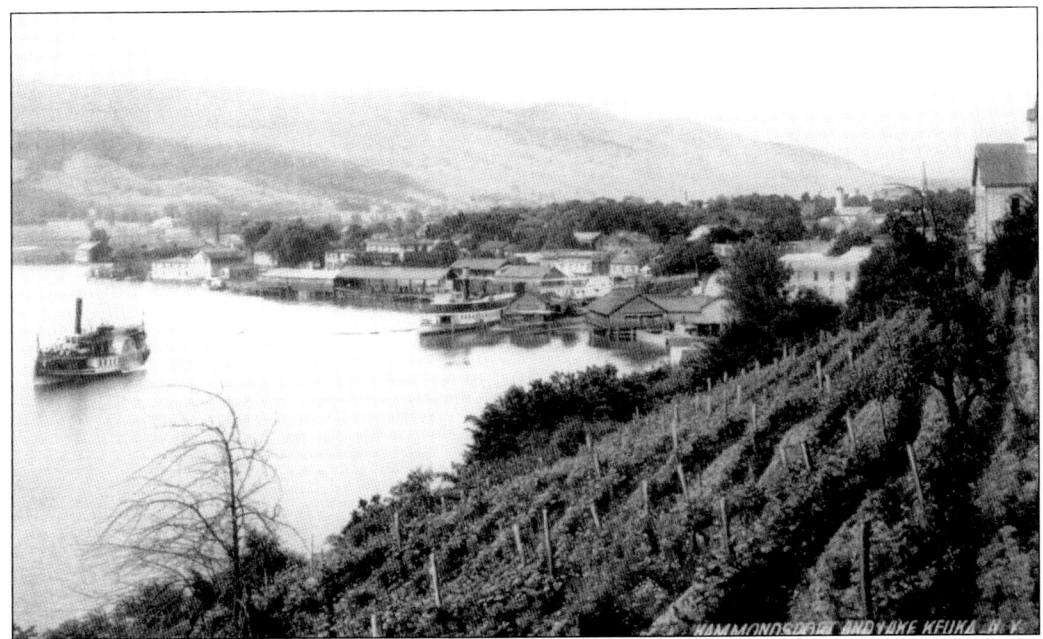

The hillside vineyards, the village in the vale, the two steamboats, and the mirror-smooth lake—what an incredible picture of Hammondsport. The building with the spire at right is Orchestrion Hall. Visitors came from miles around, by water, road, and rail, to listen to a huge mechanical music apparatus.

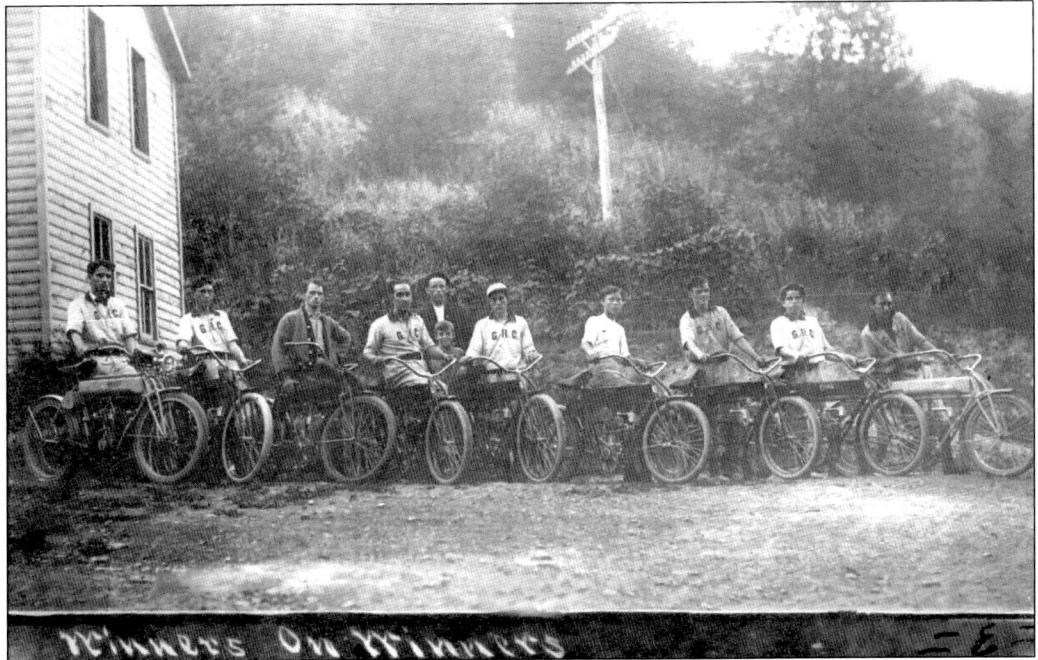

For the first 15 years of the 20th century, Hammondsport was a significant producer of motorcycles. Judging from the uniforms these "winners" are wearing, they belong to the Curtiss plant baseball team. Their steeds, of course, are Curtiss motorcycles.

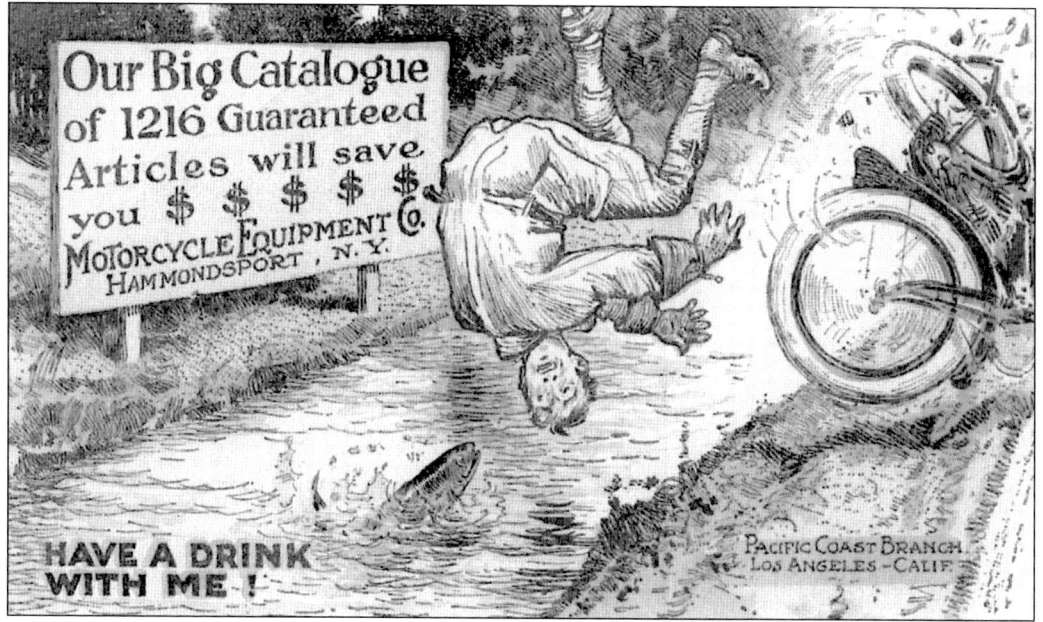

Another Hammondsport business specialized in parts and like Curtiss branched out to the West Coast.

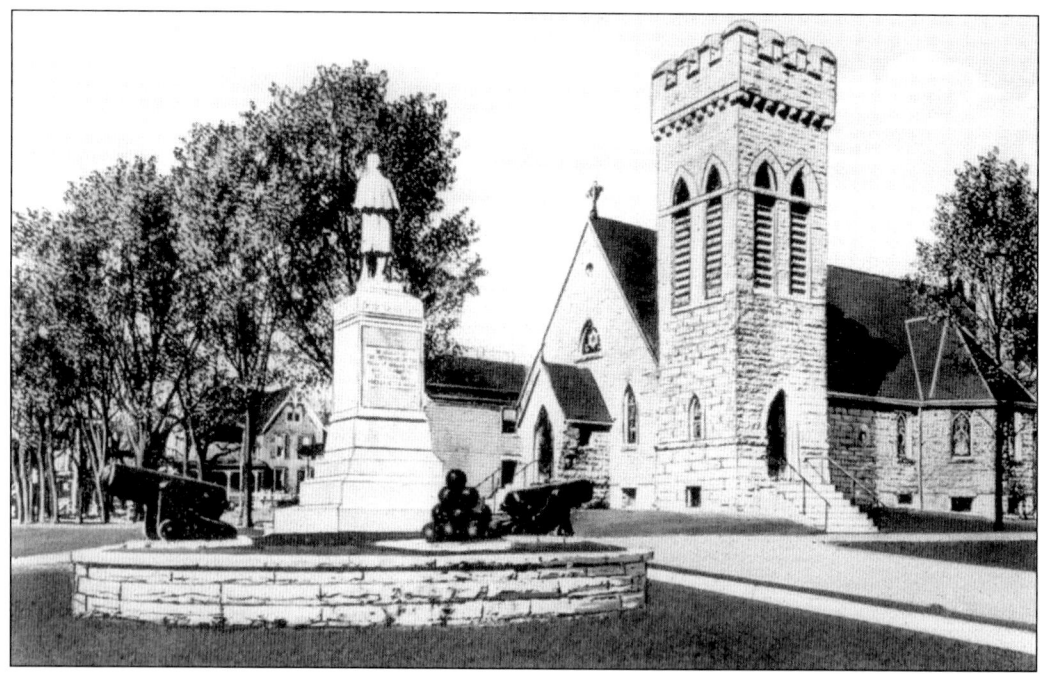

The Episcopal Church in Hammondsport is mostly unchanged, but the 1901 Civil War statue has moved from the intersection to the nearby lawn of what was lately the municipal building. The cannon and cannonballs have vanished, perhaps to some world war scrap drive.

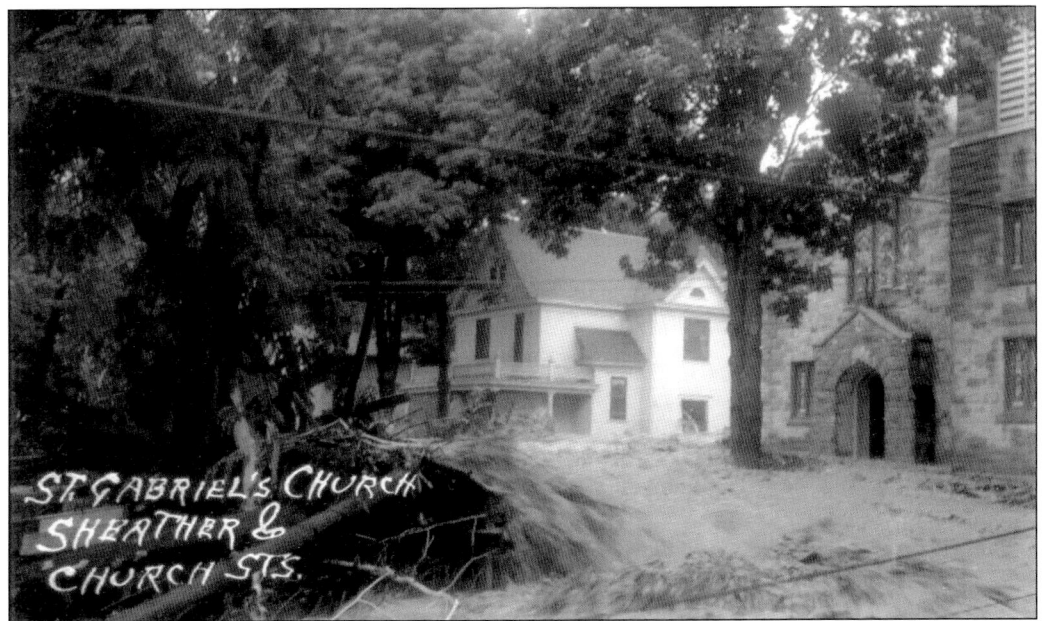

In July 1935, much of the southern Finger Lakes were hammered by sudden and disastrous floods following nonstop cloudbursts.

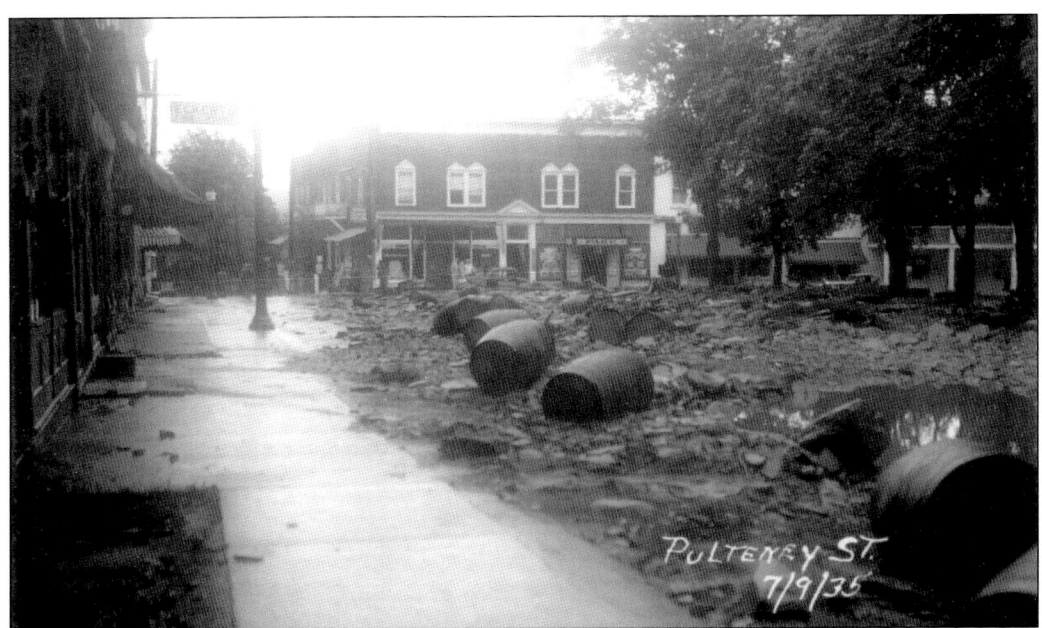

Brandy barrels from a warehouse in the Hammondsport Glen washed down as far as the lake. How many casks there were, who got them, and what happened to them are still topics of avid conversation.

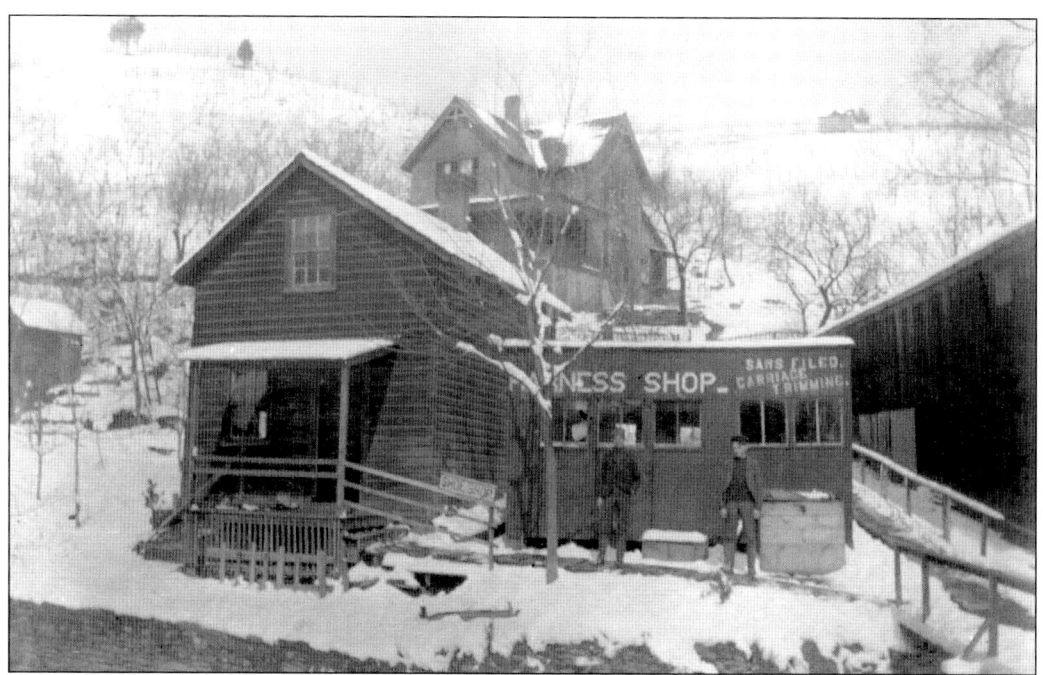

This Hammondsport harness shop sets off hillside vineyards covered with snow. Vineyards and wineries remain a significant aspect of life around Hammondsport. Rev. William Bostwick made the first Finger Lakes wine here in 1829. Pleasant Valley Wine Company (established 1860) is the region's oldest.

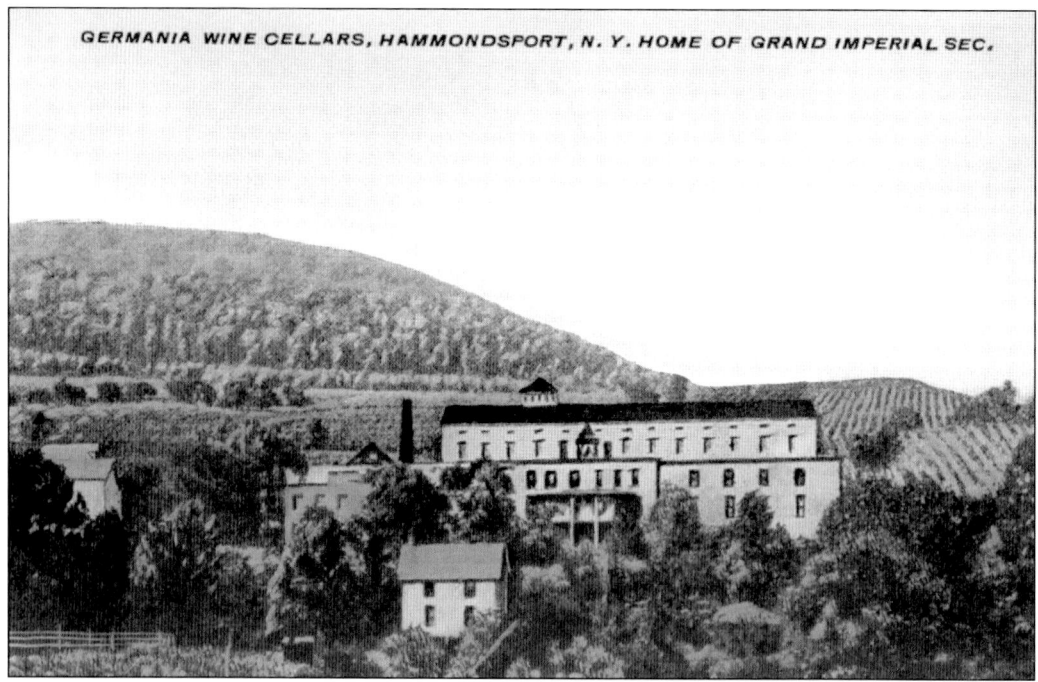

Germania's facilities are now part of the next-door Pleasant Valley Wine Company. Faced with anti-Teutonic sentiment after the World War I, Germania for a spell became Jermania.

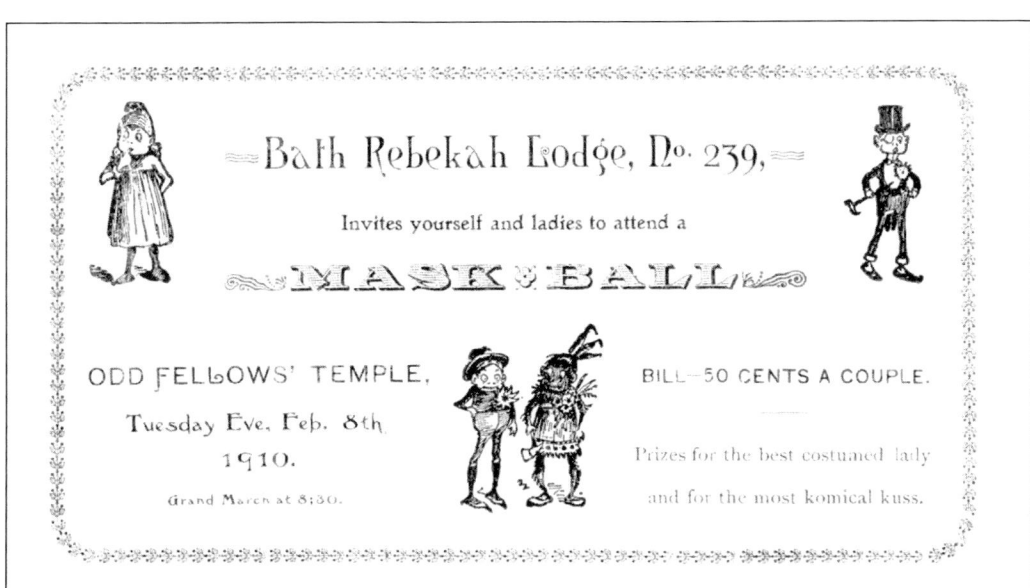

Bath (settled by whites in 1793) is the Steuben County seat. The International Order of Odd Fellows (with their affiliated Daughters of Rebekah) are a fraternal lodge. The curious figures on this card are Brownies, Palmer Cox's beloved creations that even lent their name to the Eastman Company's new camera line in Rochester.

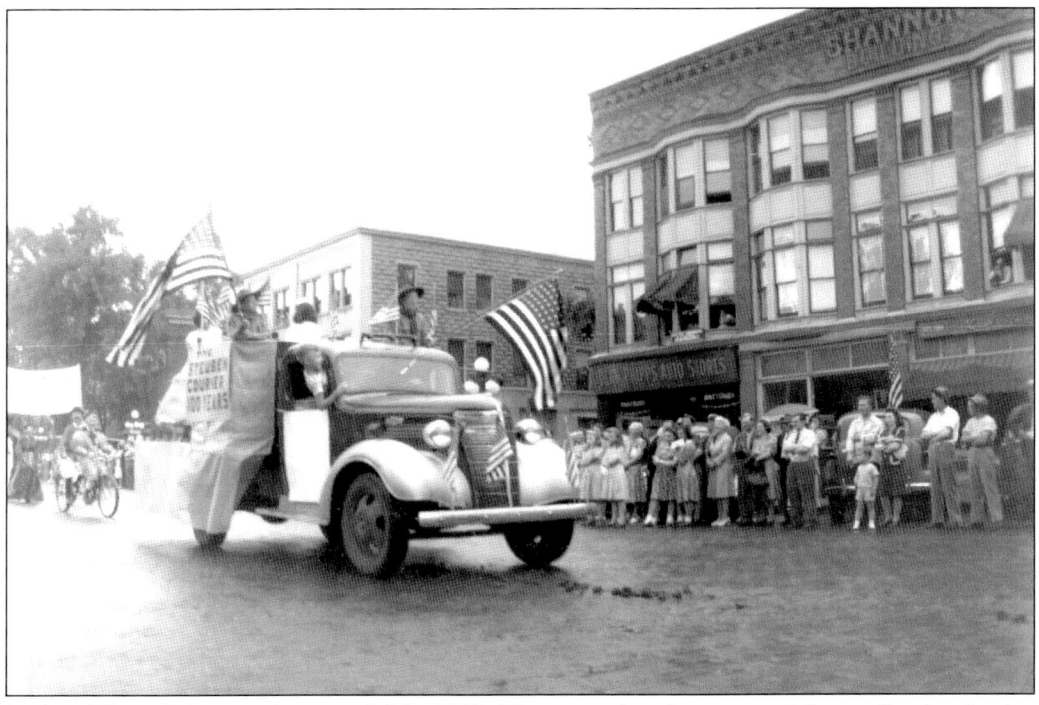

Bath celebrated its sesquicentennial in 1943. That was also the centennial year for the *Steuben Courier*, a weekly paper that is still impatiently awaited on Sunday mornings. Notice the Boy Scouts on the truck.

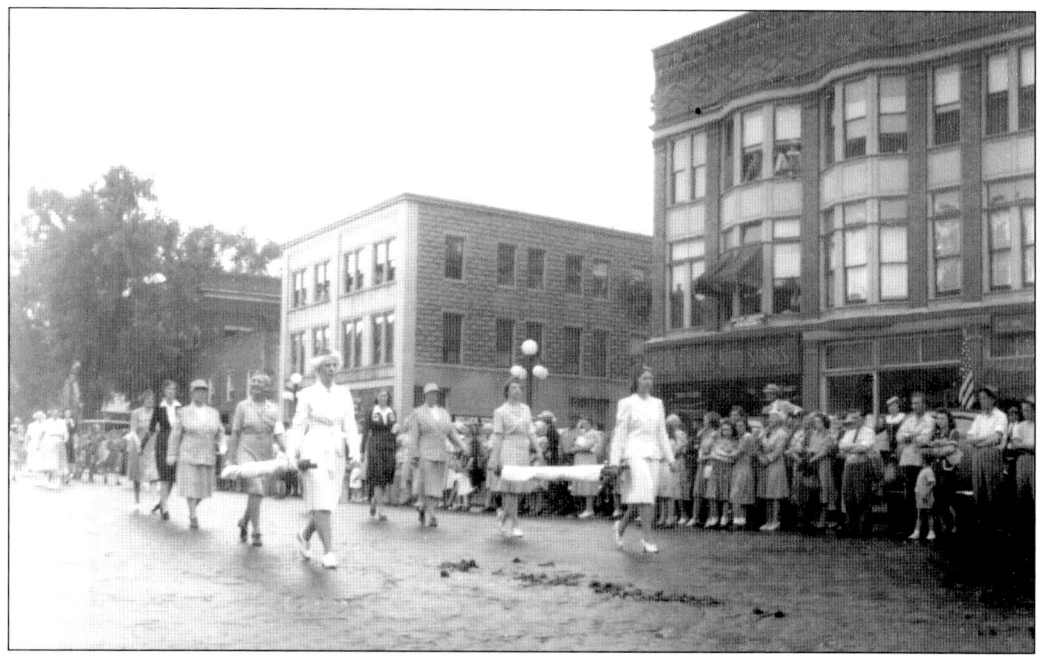

Since 1943 was a war year, it is not surprising that Red Cross volunteers played an important part in the parade, conveniently spaced to avoid the horse droppings. All the buildings shown here are still in use, although the street is no longer paved with brick.

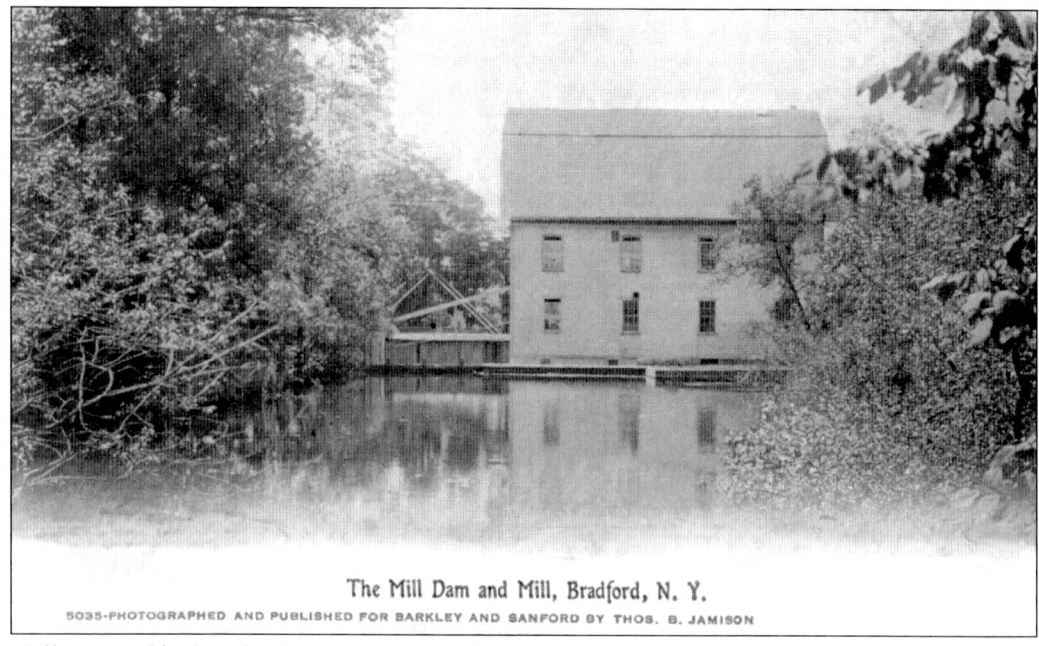

Mills in Bradford took advantage of Mud Creek water from the "Little Lakes"—Lamoka and Waneta—that lie in Schuyler County between Keuka and Seneca Lakes.

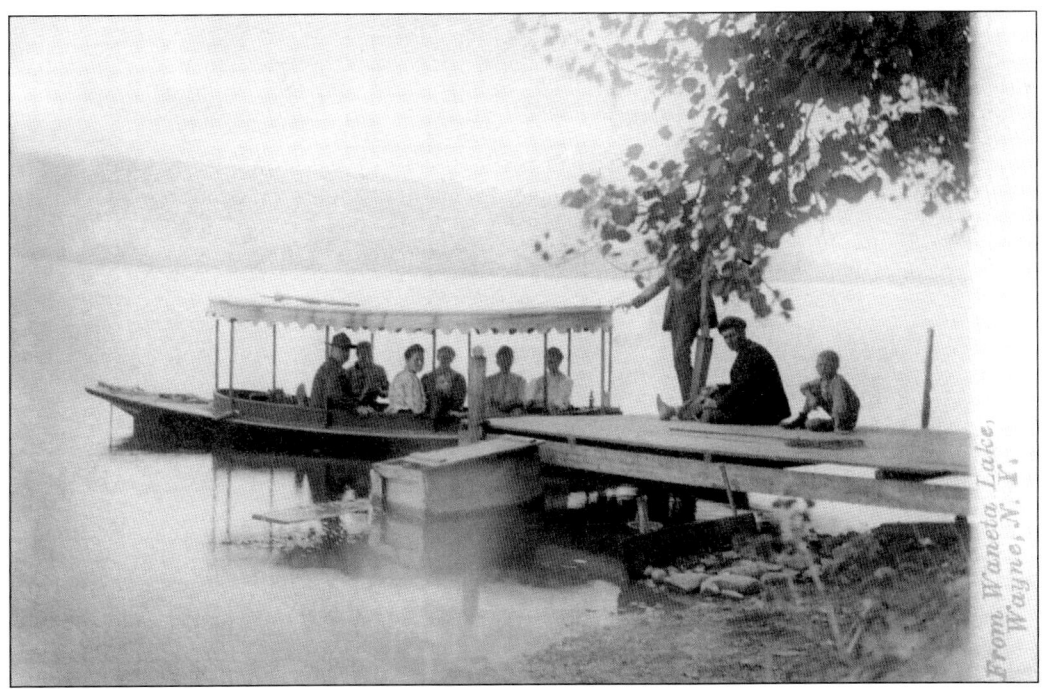

This interesting-looking boat is probably powered by a naptha engine, converted from a steam engine. Fishing is the major attraction on Waneta Lake today.

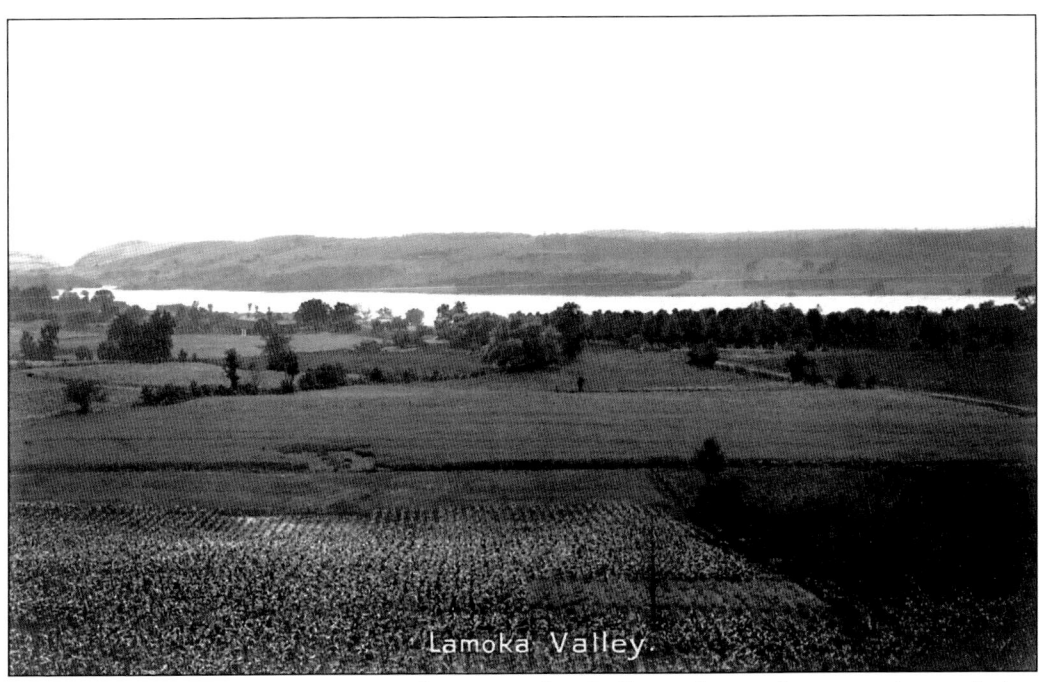

Lamoka Lake gives its name to a prehistoric Paleo-Indian culture whose remains are being excavated near the inlet. Camp Lamoka (Baptist) is on the west shore.

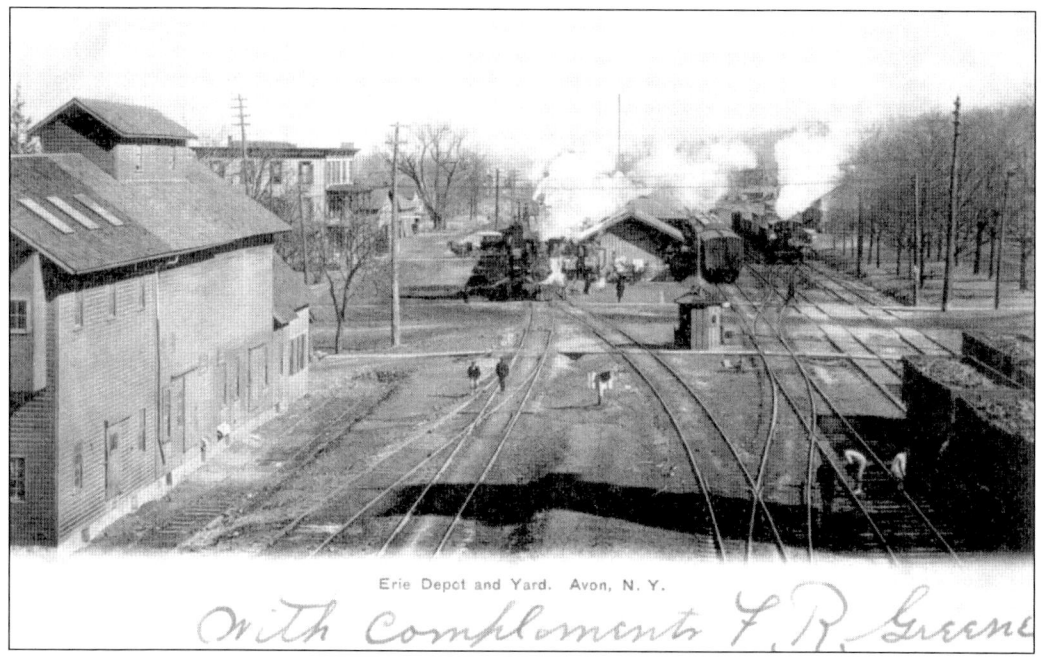

The freight train still stops in Avon, which remains an important transportation point. An even earlier canal is gone, but Interstate 390 crosses New York State Routes 5 and 20 nearby, while the Lakeville, Avon, and Livonia Railroad is a significant regional operator. Senecas once lived here in their town of Canawaugus. Avon was once famed for sulfur springs, harness tracks, and horse breeding.

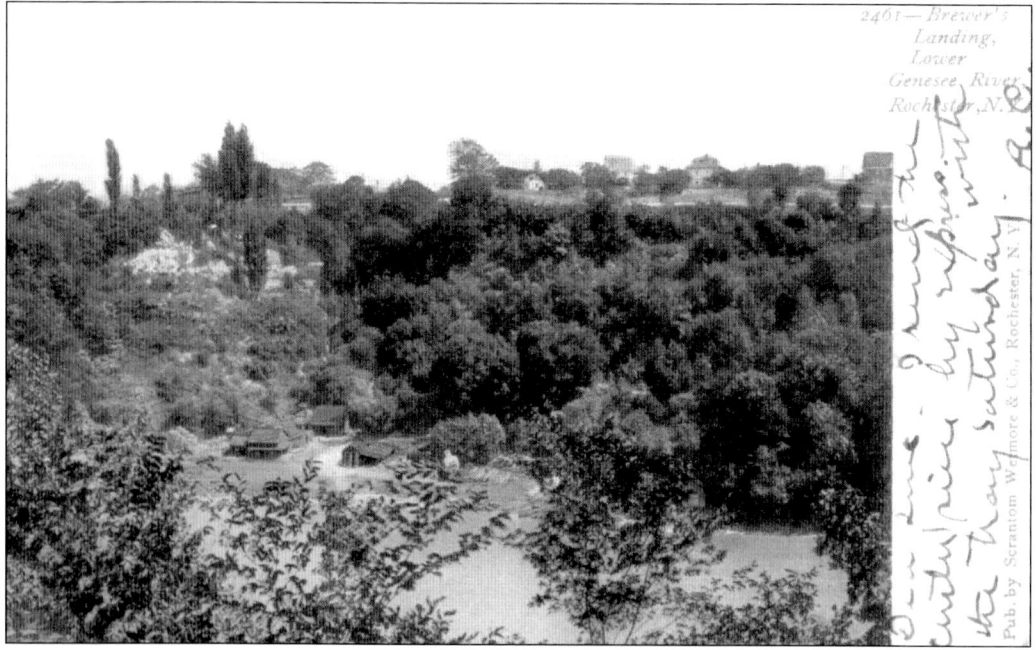

The Genesee River forms the traditional western edge of the Finger Lakes region, as it did the western limit of the 1788 Phelps and Gorham Purchase. The Erie Canal crossed the Genesee in Rochester, while the upriver Genesee Valley Canal connected that river with the Allegheny.

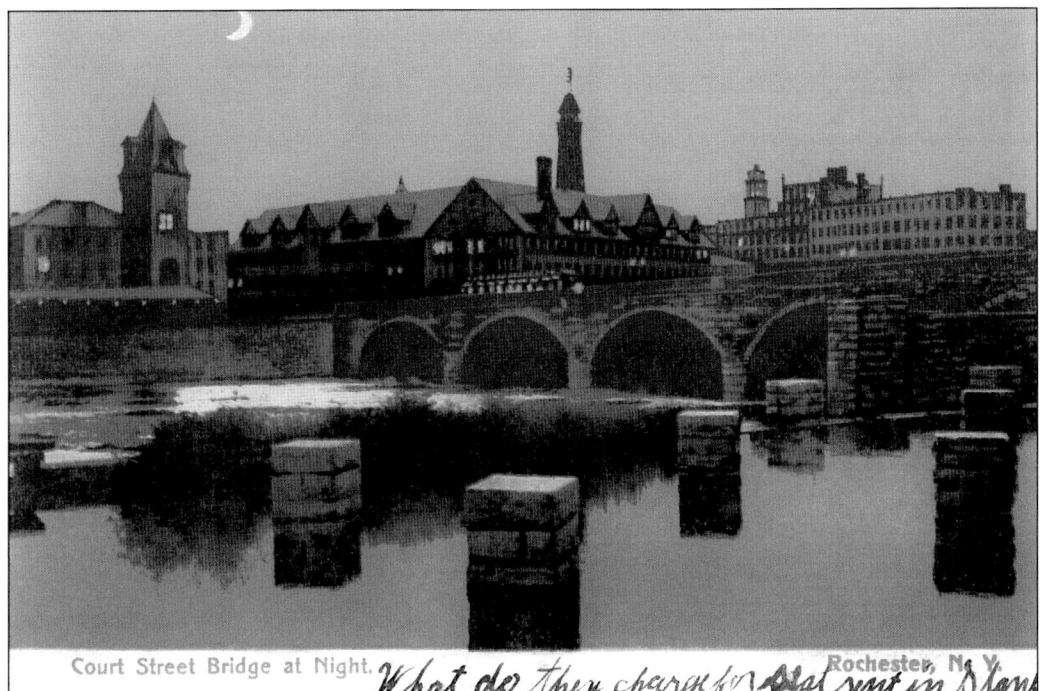

The towered building at left is the Lehigh Valley Railroad terminal. The Erie Canal no longer goes through the center of Rochester. It has been suggested that parts of it be restored to help revitalize downtown.

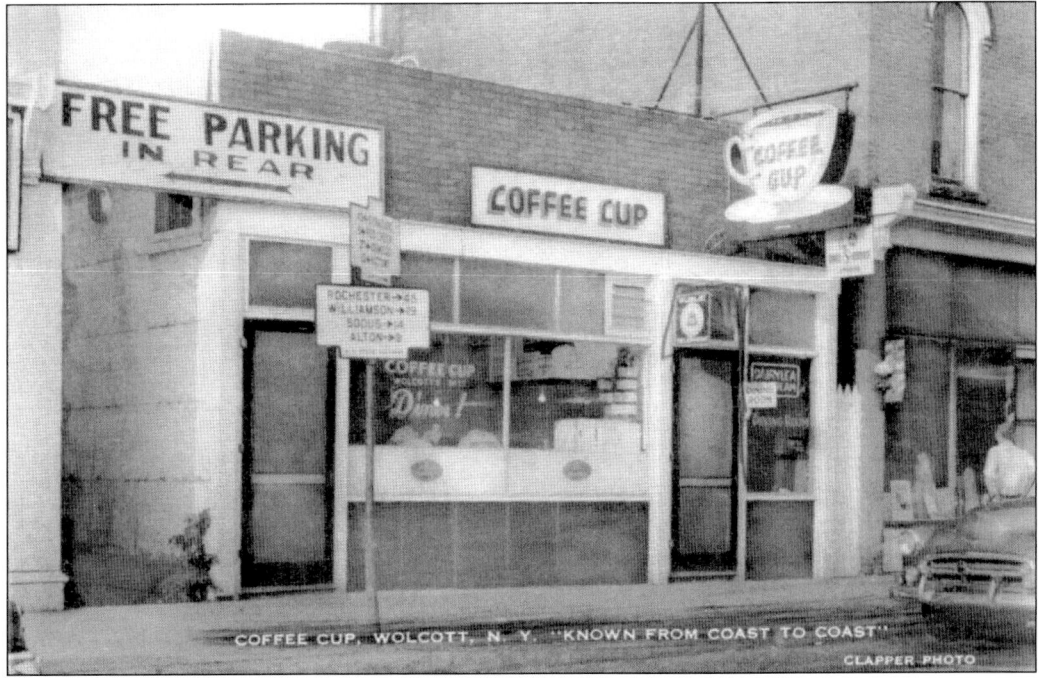

It may not have been "known from coast to coast," but it was well known on Route 104, about halfway between Syracuse and Rochester.

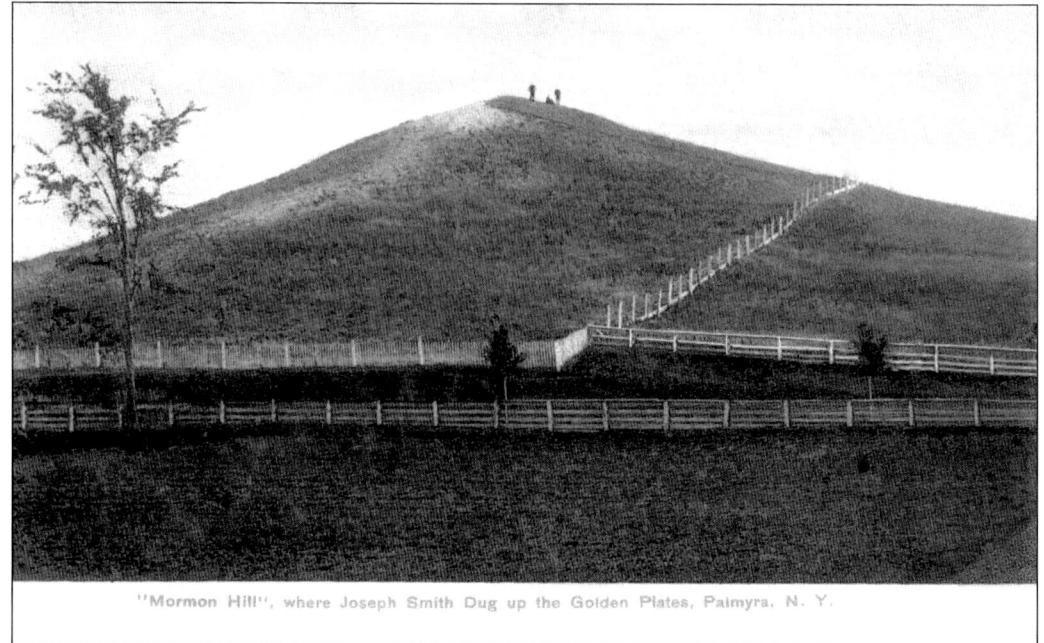

The Hill Cumorah Festival—a sound-and-light spectacular dramatizing the Book of Mormon—now takes place here on summer evenings. Science-fiction great Orson Scot Card scripted the current version.

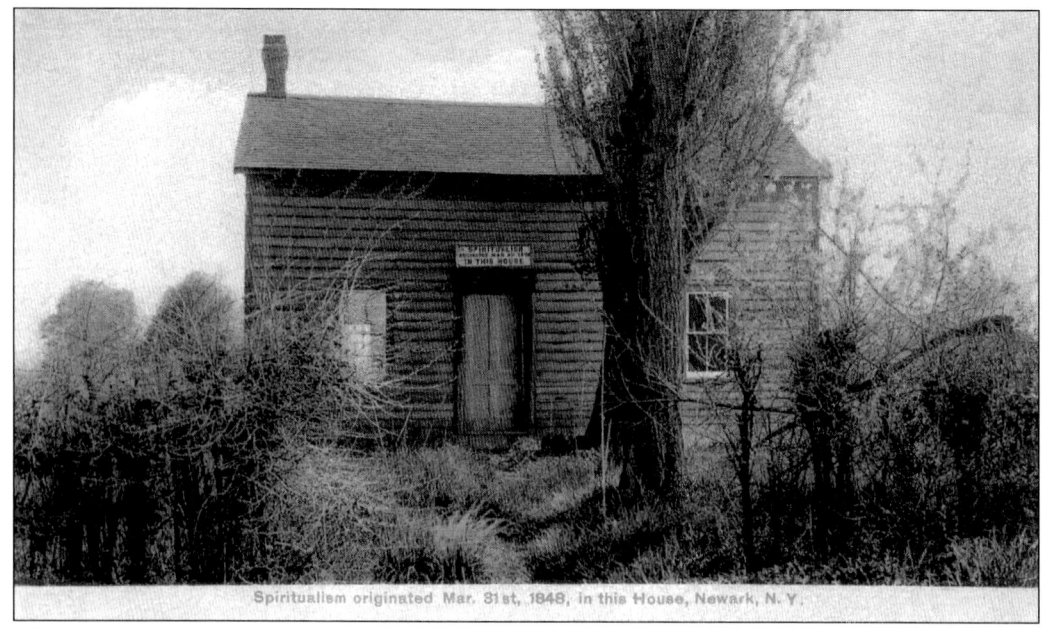

The Finger Lakes and western New York fermented with new ideas in the 19th century. Here at Hydesville in Wayne County the Fox sisters experimented with rappings and other phenomena, an inquiry that grew into Spritualism.

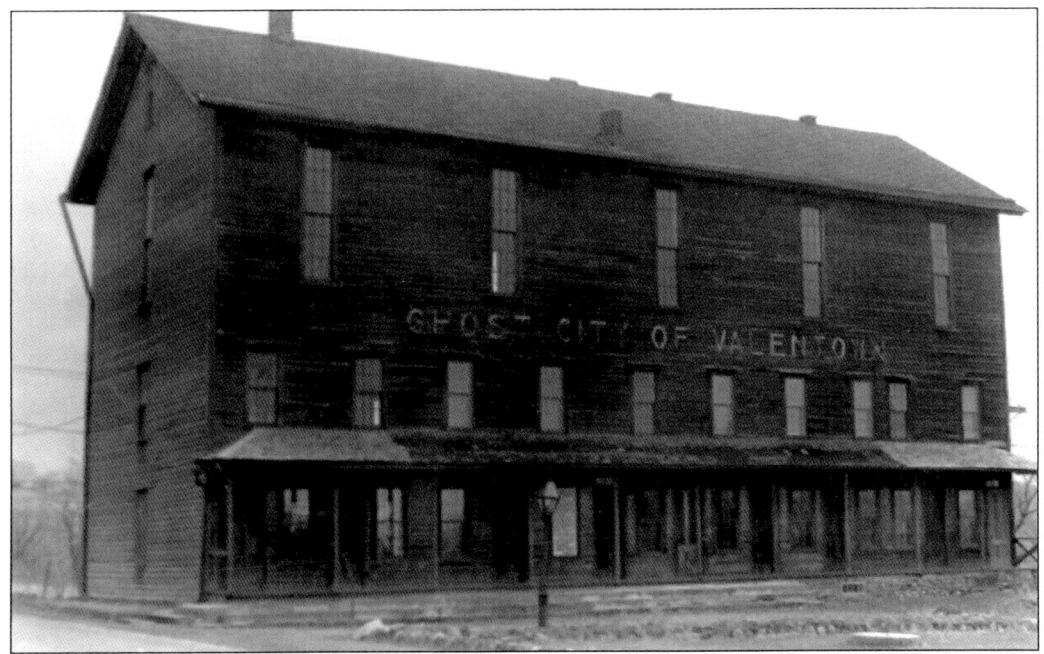

Regional historian J. Sheldon Fisher turned the 1879–1881 Valentown Inn (where his parents met, at a dance) into a museum. "Shel," who still worked on that roof when he was nearly 90, was pushing 100 and still going strong when his sparkling life finally closed. Valentown Museum is now part of the Victor Historical Society.

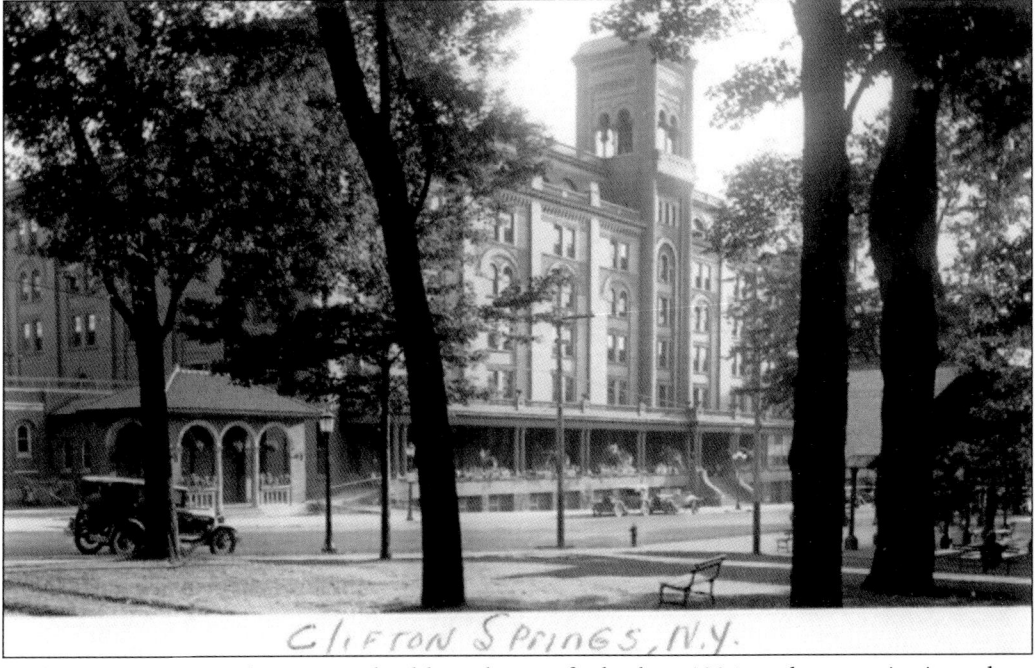

Clifton Springs started attracting health-seekers as far back as 1806, and one sanitarium alone treated 3,000 visitors a year. The small town is a still a major medical center, although they do not depend on the sulfur so much these days.

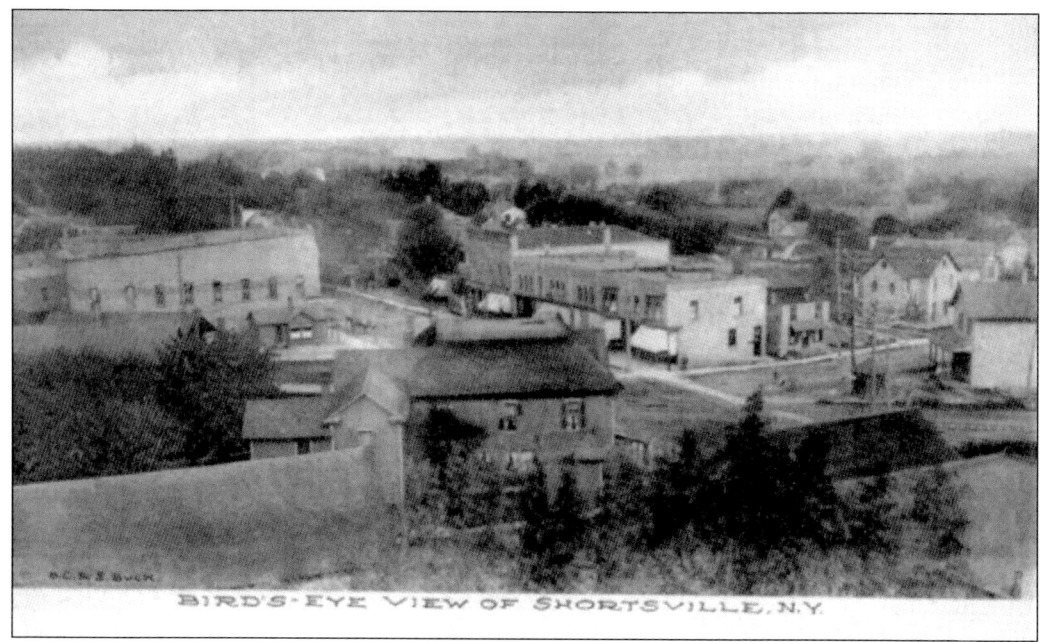

Prior to aerial photography, any image from a high vantage point was referred to as a bird's-eye view.

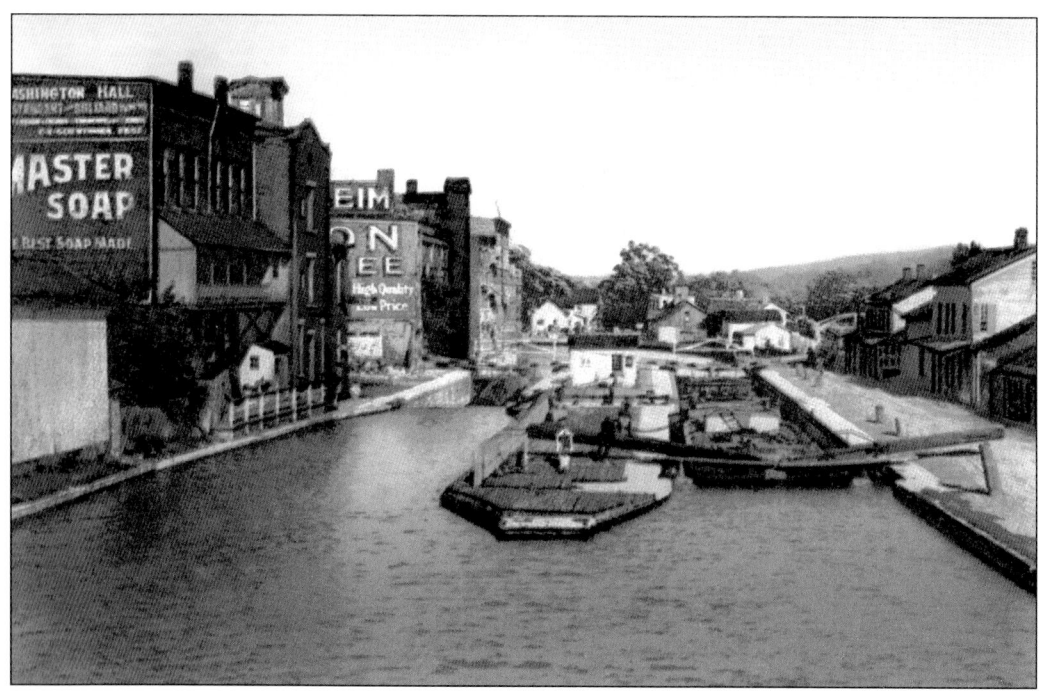

The 1825 Erie Canal (here at Lyons) turned the northern fringe of the Finger Lakes into a boom region. Lyons in the 19th century produced half the nation's peppermint oil.

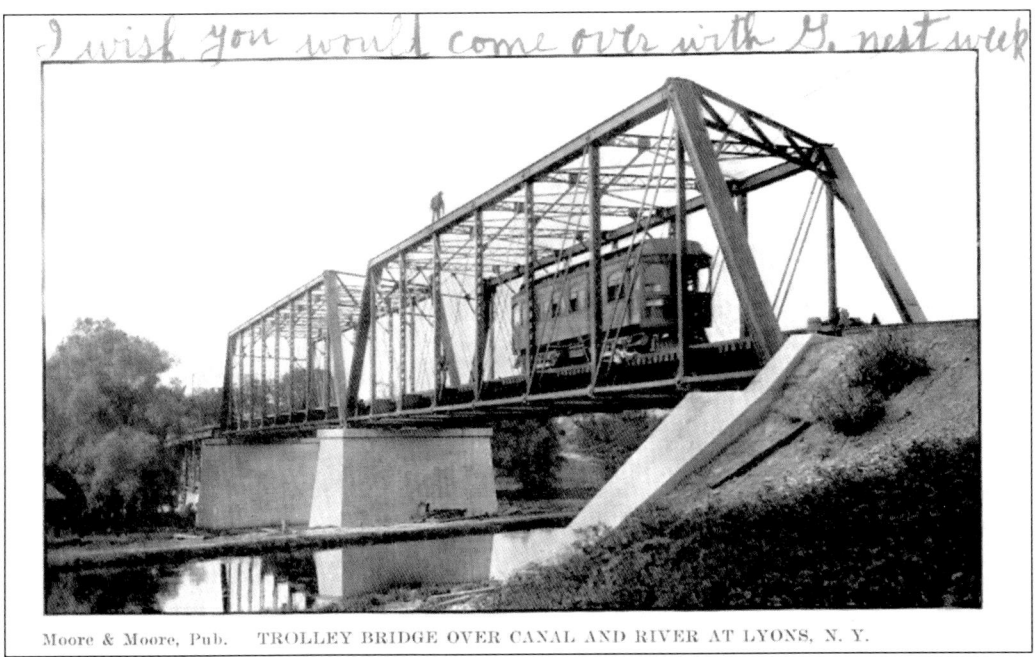

As in most of the Northeast, electric interurban railways crisscrossed the region. This trolley is crossing over the Erie Canal. But what is the man doing on top of the bridge?

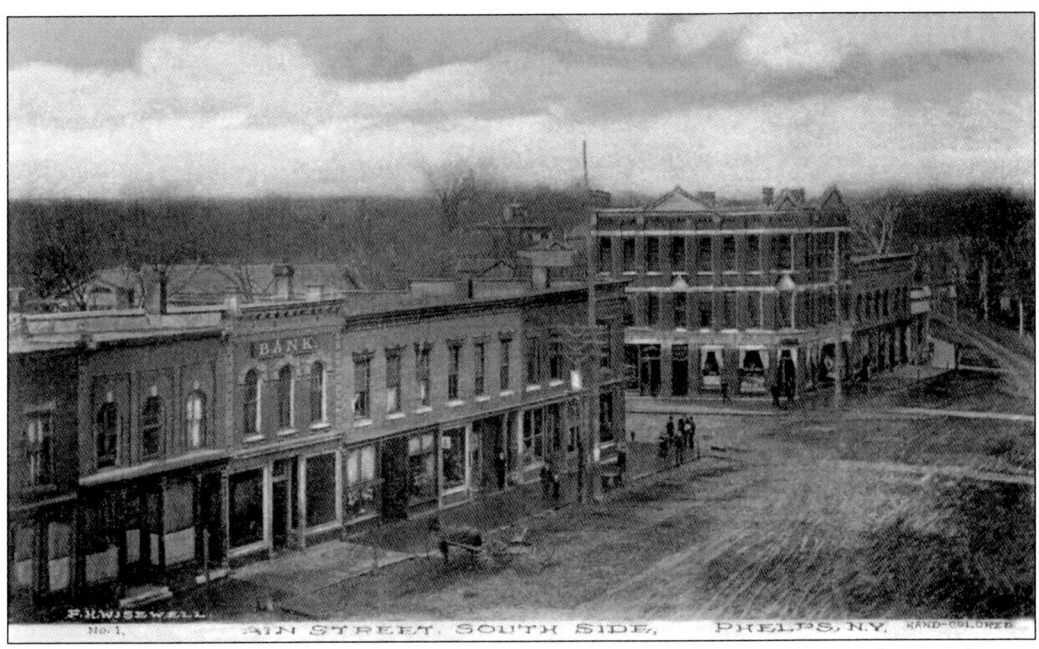

Phelps's downtown business district managed to combine an air of prosperity with a comforting atmosphere of welcome. An annual sauerkraut festival attracts visitors from far and wide.

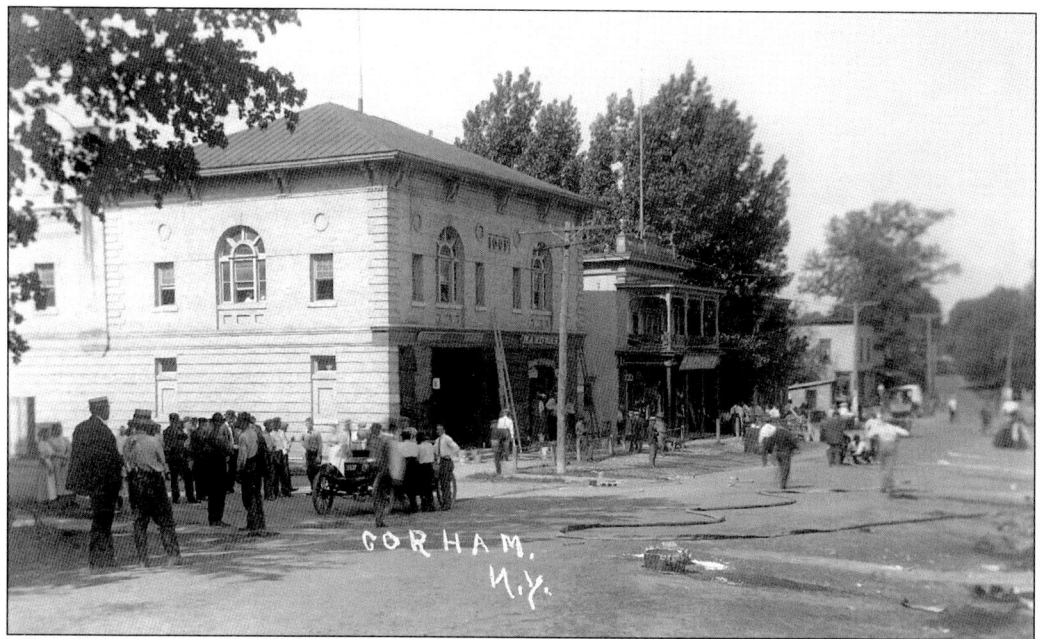

Judging from the hoses in the street, this crowd in Gorham collected to watch a fire. The towns of Phelps and Gorham are named for early proprietors of vast holdings in the Finger Lakes.

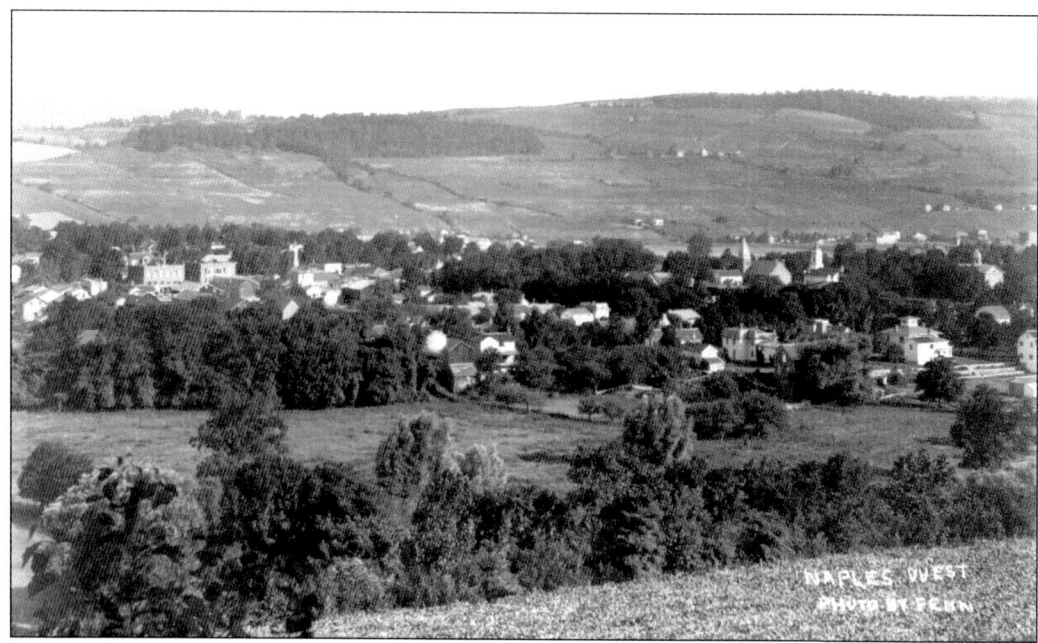

Naples, not far from Canandaigua Lake, is home to Widmer's Winery. Among other products, Widmer's makes Manischewitz. The Naples wine industry started with German workers, served by a Lehigh Valley spur line.

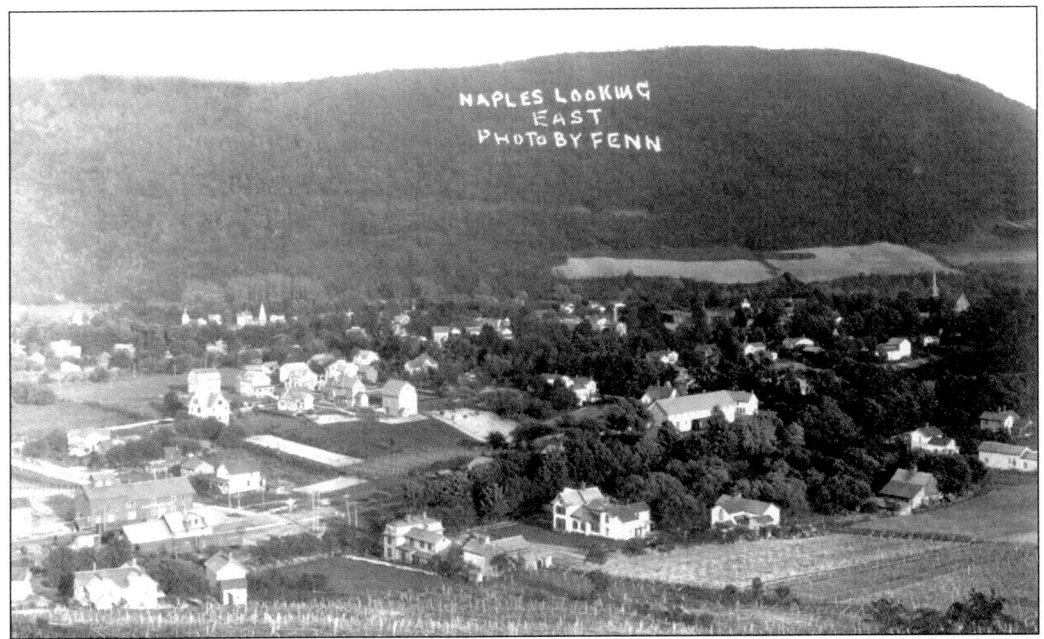

Mark Jennings was on the road with his baseball team in September 1916 when he wrote to his wife in Troy, Pennsylvania, "Dear wife/ -how are you/ am at Naples/ Penn Yan won 6 & 4/ I am staying all/ night. Good bye/ With love Mark."

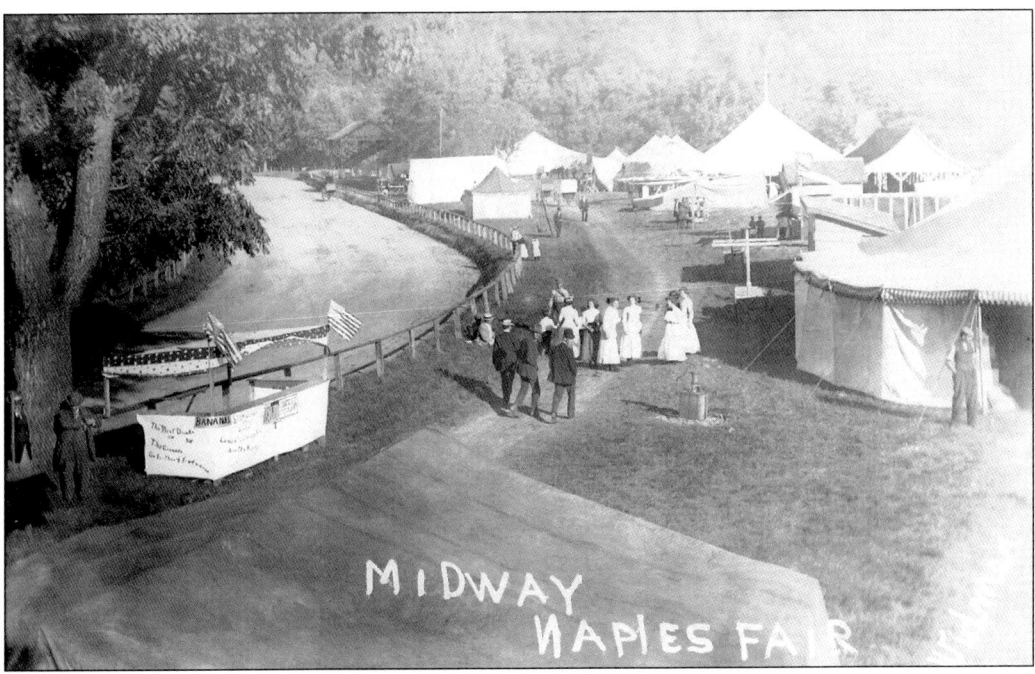

The old-time Naples Fair was almost as big as the modern-day Naples Grape Festival. Notice the handmade sign by the railing of the track.

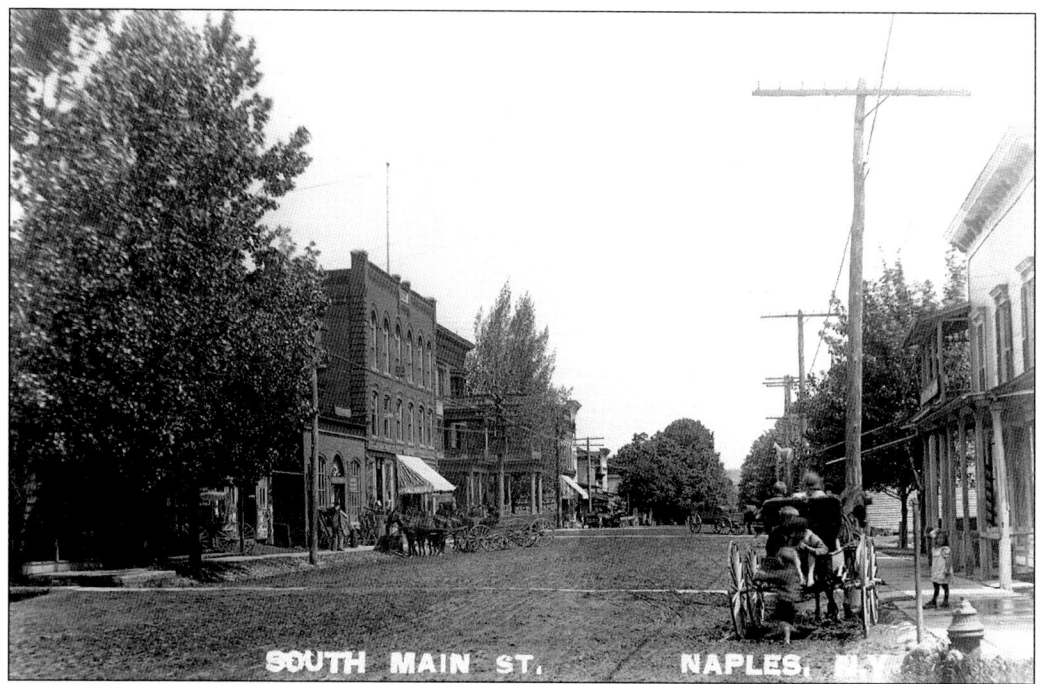

Naples is situated in a valley between large hills, making the village long and narrow. A mile-long Main Street makes for a lovely, if strenuous, walk.

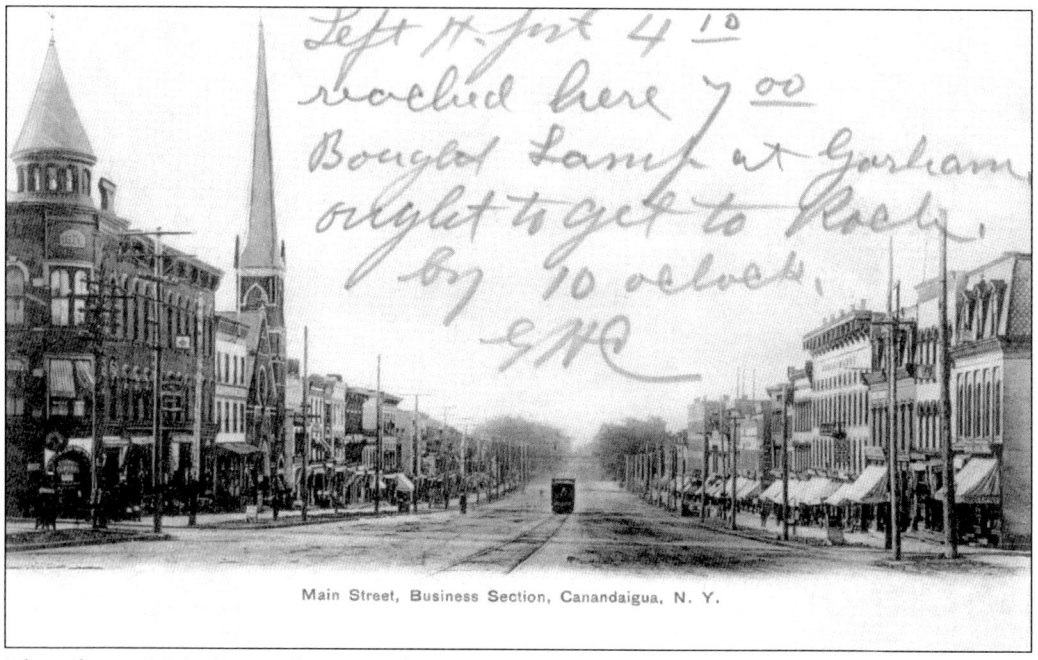

The vibrant Main Street shopping district still slides beautifully down toward Canandaigua Lake. Glenn Curtiss was making excellent motorcycle time on 1907 roads, especially running after dark.

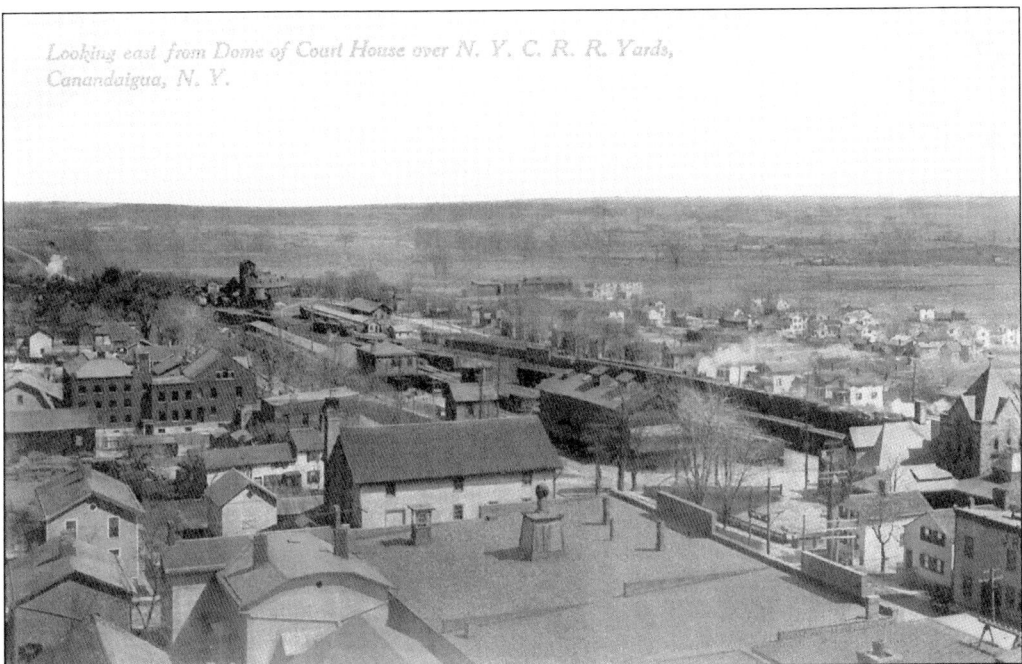

In Canandaigua's Ontario County courthouse, Susan B. Anthony and several other women were convicted of voting in the 1872 election, along with the male officials who admitted them. "I will never pay one cent of your unjust fine," she snapped at the judge —and she never did.

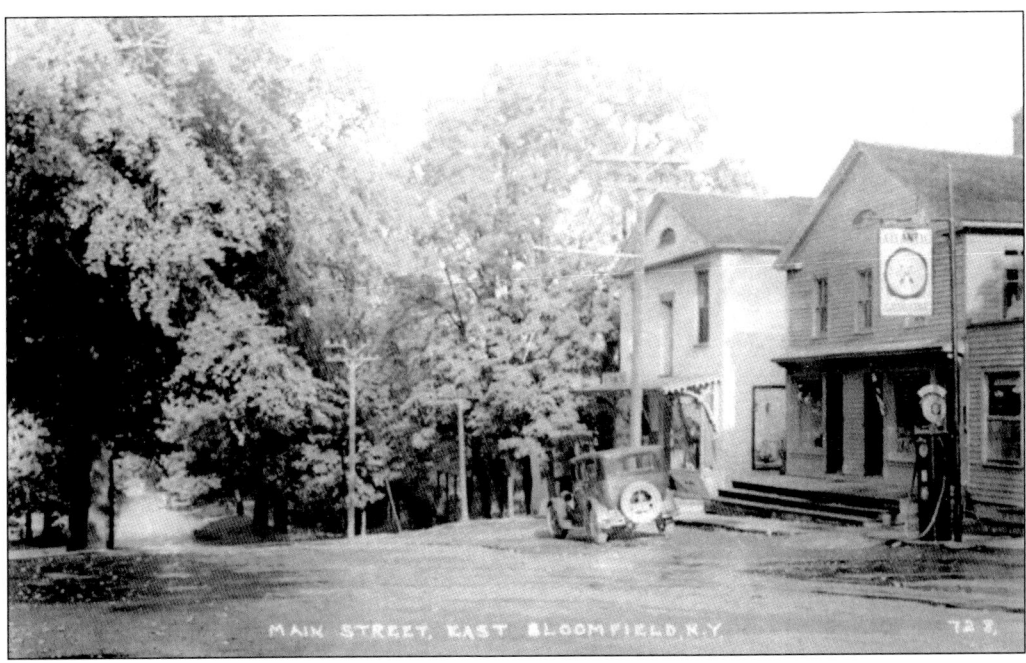

The Sieur de Denonville with French troops destroyed the Iroquois village of Gannongarae at East Bloomfield in 1685. The town now boasts a beautiful green and a wireless museum.

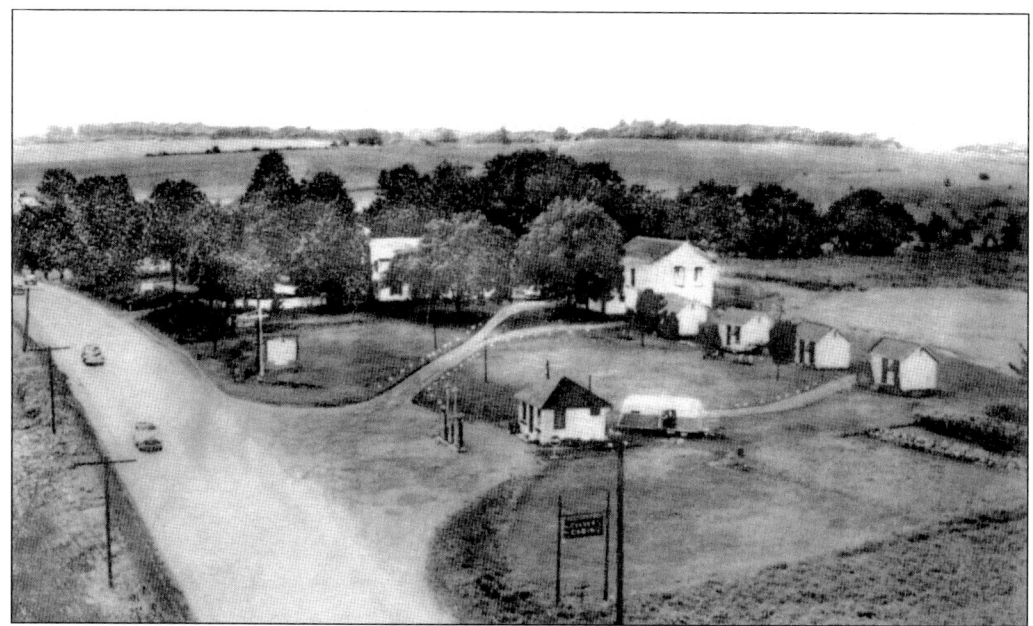

Routes 5 and 20 (on the left) were a major westward highway when the Erie Canal was in its heyday, and remained the primary land route until the New York State Thruway opened. As touring and motoring became wildly popular after World War I, facilities like Culver's Cabins in East Bloomfield succored the weary traveler—in Culver's case, with steam heat and private baths.

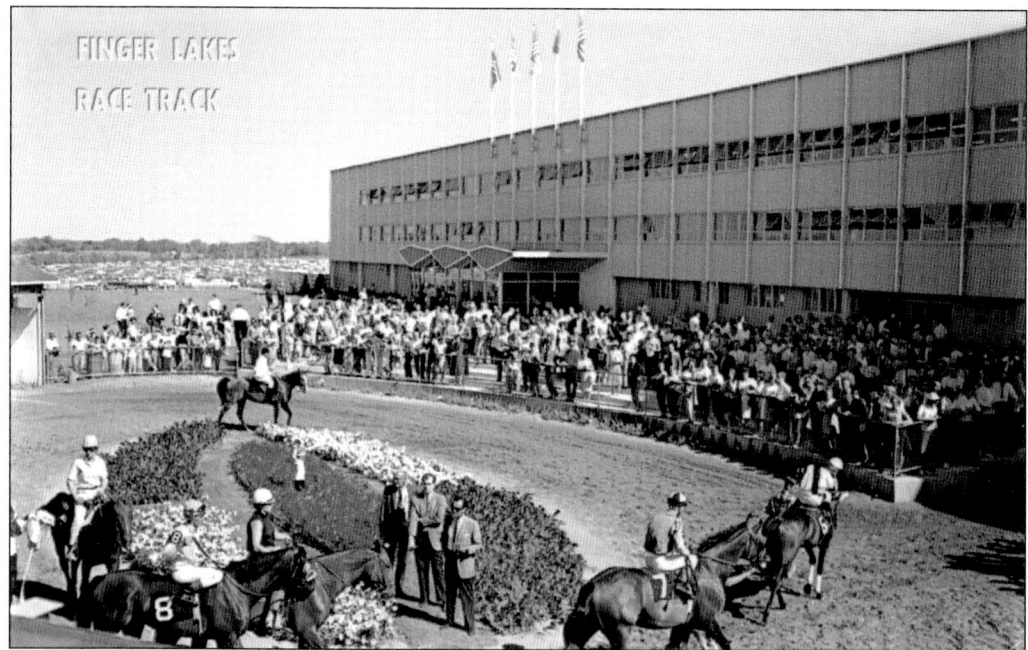

In 1796, Charles Williamson sponsored a horse race near Bath, drawing spectators from Canada, Massachusetts, and Maryland. Thoroughbred racing now takes place at Farmington, near Canandaigua.

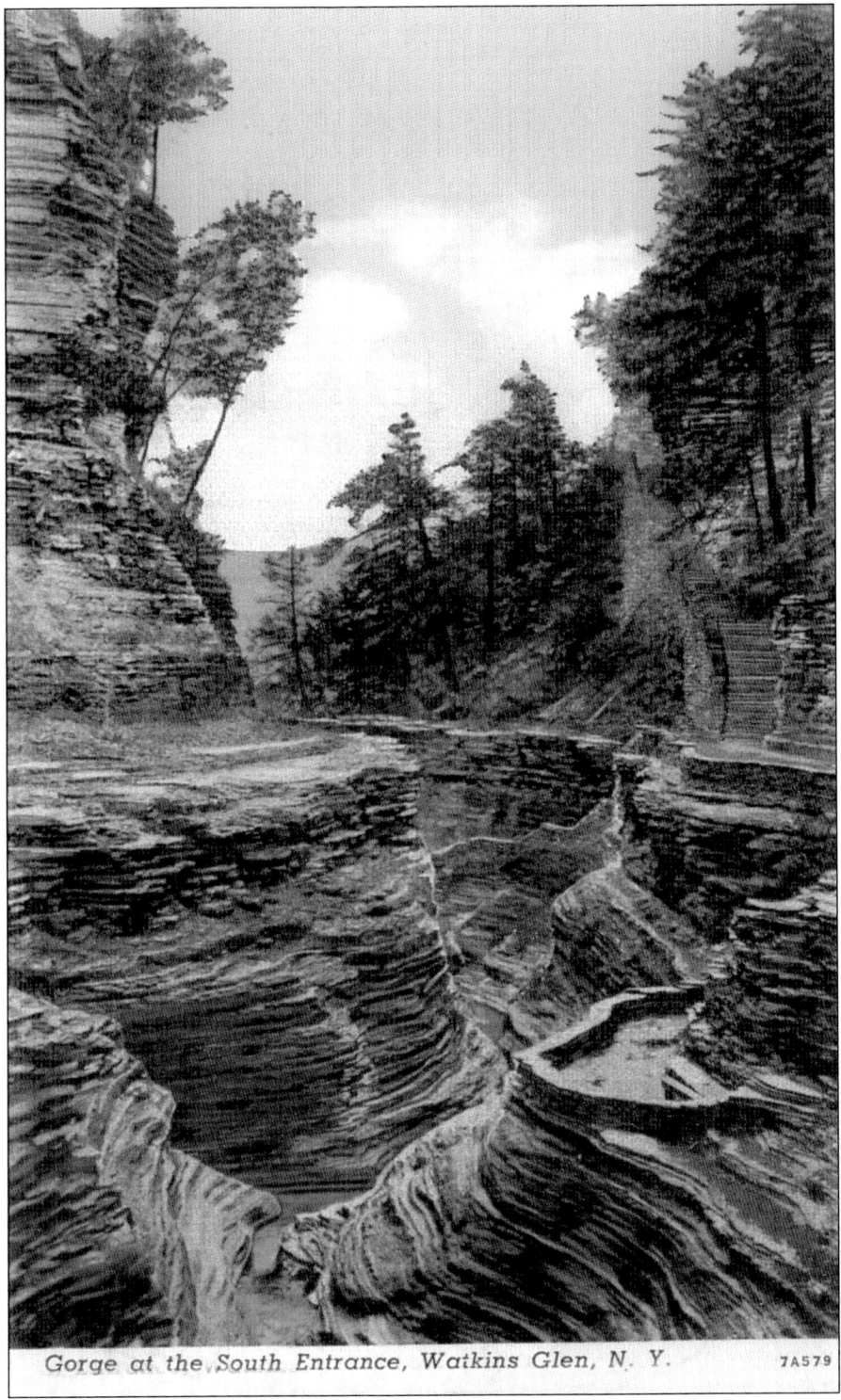
Gorge at the South Entrance, Watkins Glen, N. Y.  7A579

The remarkable gorge of Watkins Glen attracts visitors from across the globe. One can walk up to view the rock formations or, as more experienced visitors do, park at the top and walk down.

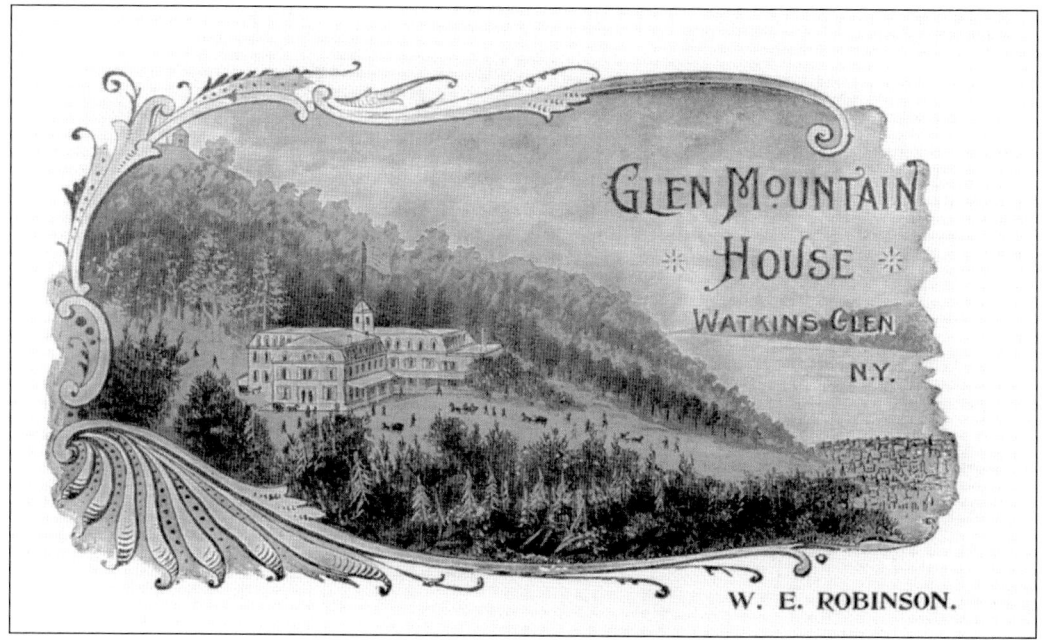

Even foreign-language travel guides in Europe extolled the Glen Mountain House. The hotel offered its guests regular bus service (horse-drawn, in the early days) to and about the village.

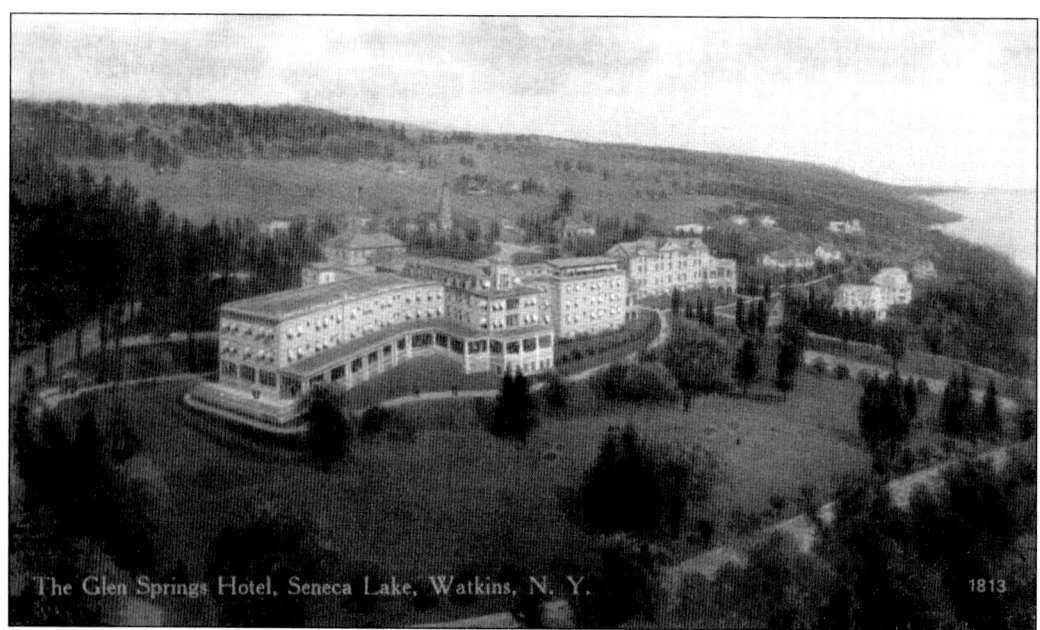

Yet bigger facilities welcomed the 20th-century traveler. The Glen Springs Hotel offered golf, health-giving springwater, and all the amenities.

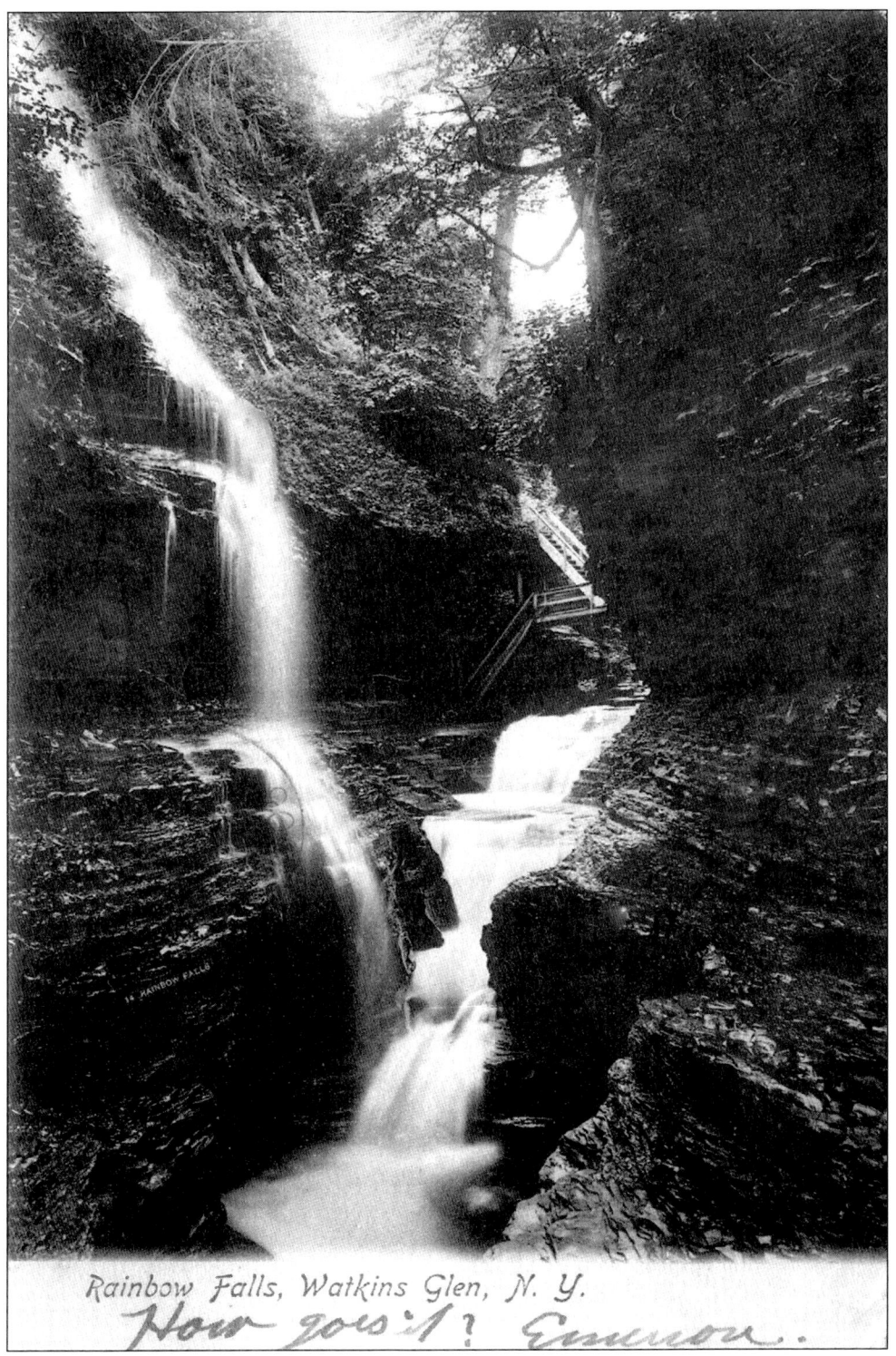

Rock itself gives way to ever-flowing waters. One of the phenomena that makes Watkins Glen interesting is that the water flows from so many different places at the same time.

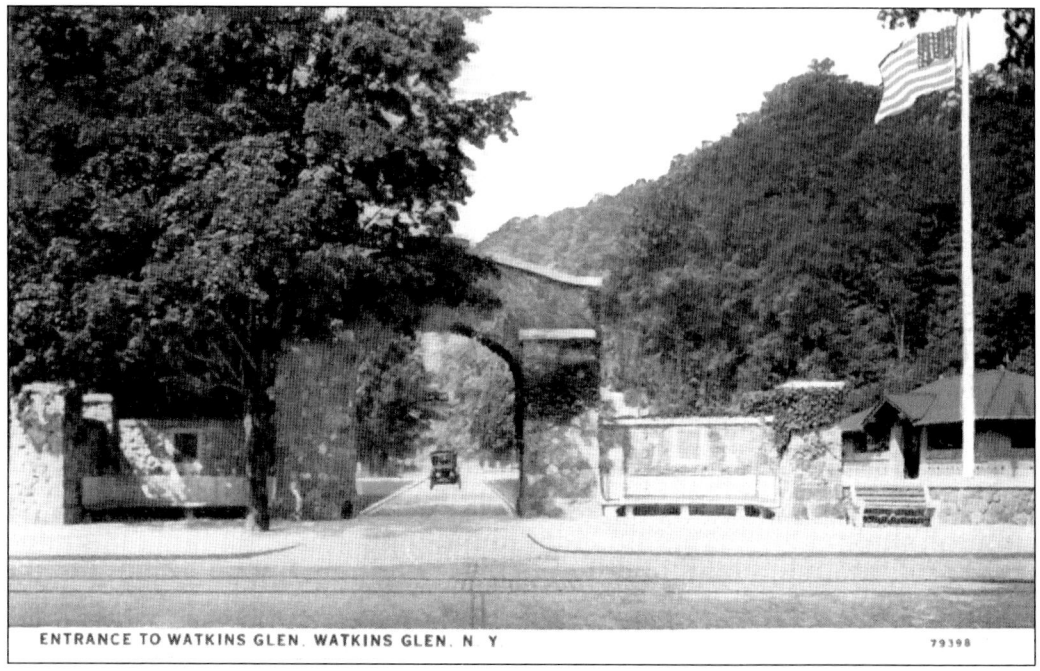

The old entrance to the state park prior to the flood of 1935 introduces an interesting before-and-after pair.

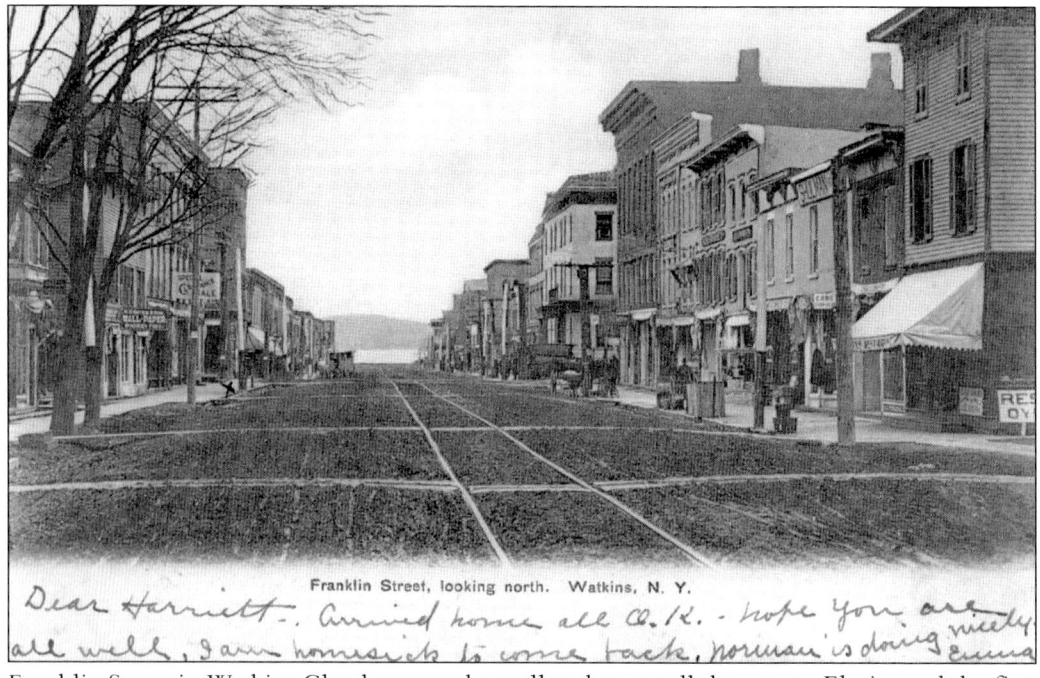

Franklin Street in Watkins Glen has seen the trolley that ran all the way to Elmira and the first grand prix races in the late 1940s. Later a road track was built on the hill outside town. Today this track hosts NASCAR races.

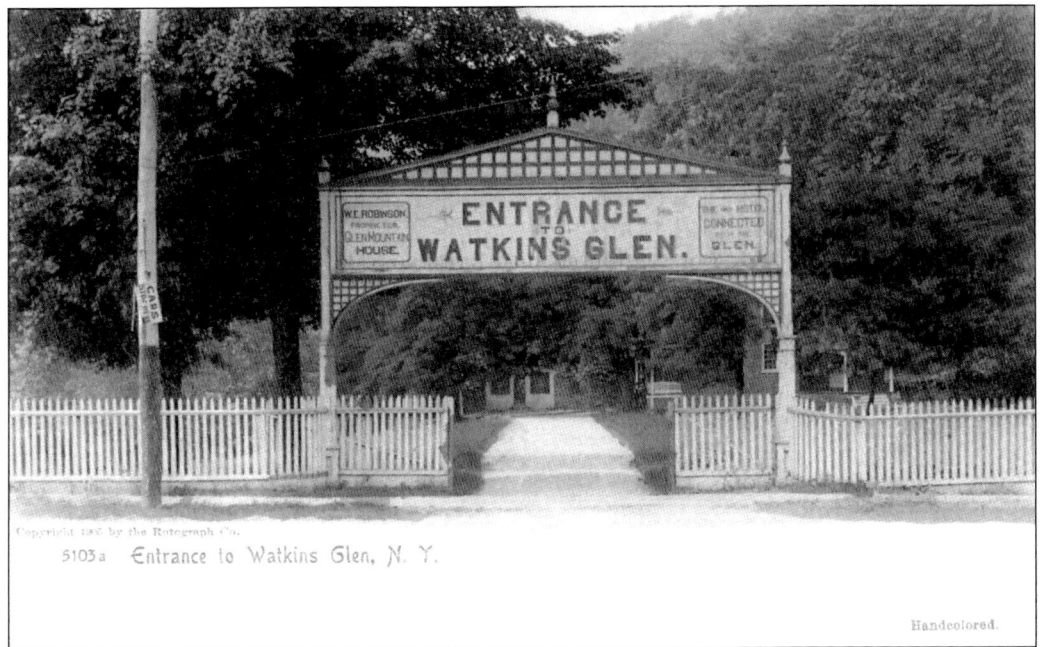

An earlier entrance was less permanent but in some ways even more interesting. At this time the Glen Mountain House was still in business and the glen was in private hands.

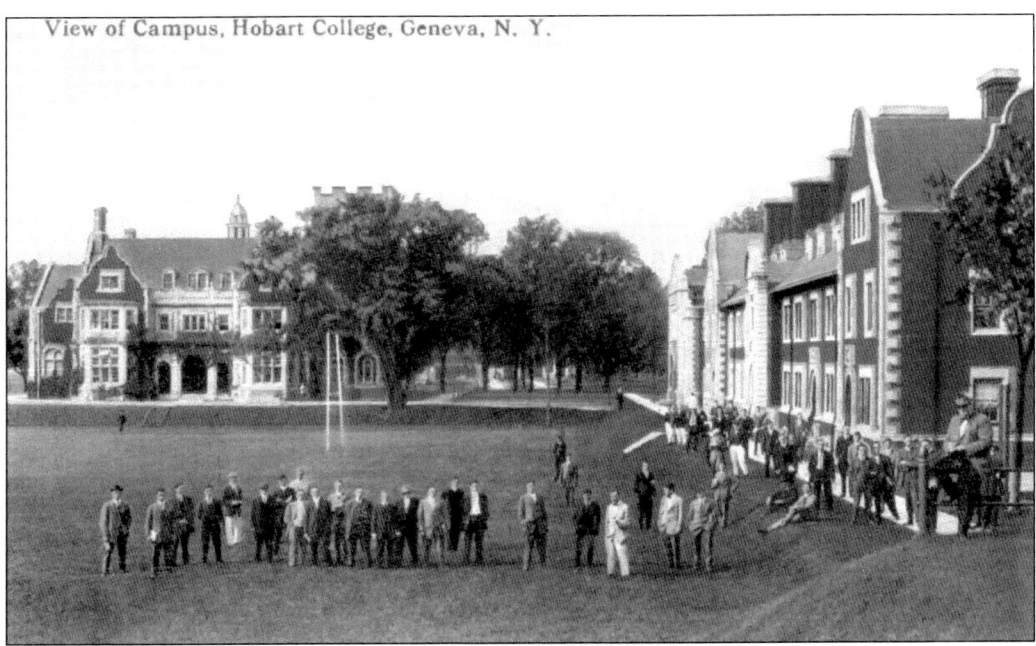

Hobart College goes back to Geneva College (1822) and Geneva Academy (1796). Here Elizabeth Blackwell was the first woman in America to earn a medical degree, in 1849. William Smith College (1908) was a coordinate institution for women. Since 1943 there has been a single corporate entity, Hobart and William Smith Colleges. Drivers approaching the city from the west shore of Seneca Lake enjoy the beautiful old campus buildings.

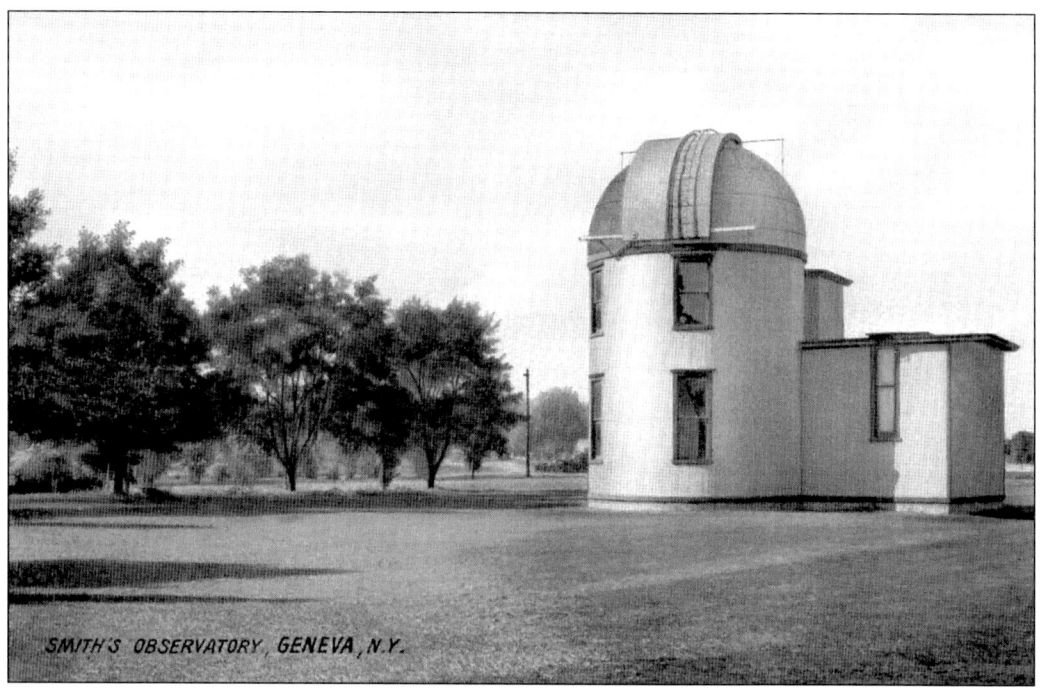

Dr. William R. "Sky" Brooks's observatory is still in use at William Smith College. Sky discovered 27 comets—more than any other American of his day.

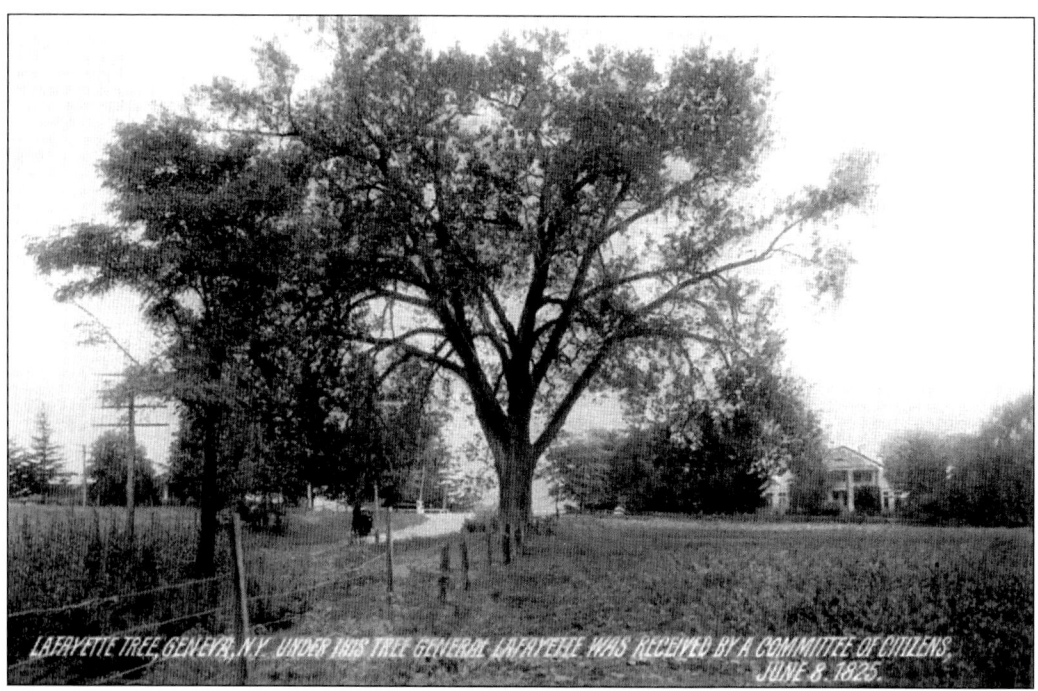

When Marquis de Lafayette made a wildly popular tour of America, he was the last major figure still active from a Revolution that was already passing into legend.

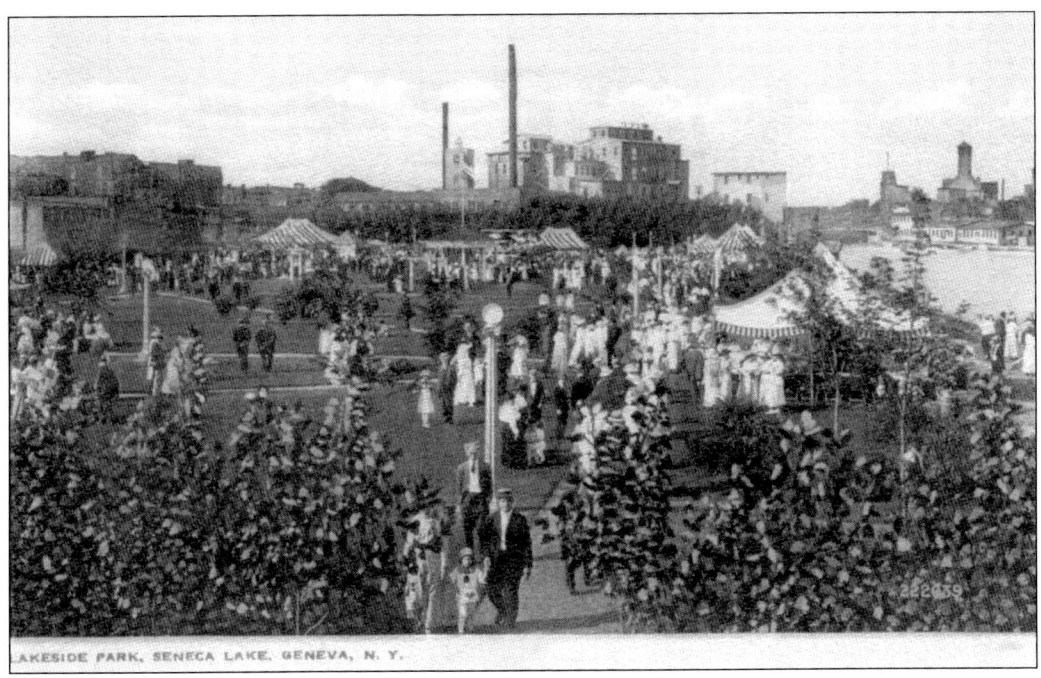

The waterfront park in Geneva is still home to such fun activities as the annual Seneca Lake Whale Watch. No luck yet, but that does not stop them from trying.

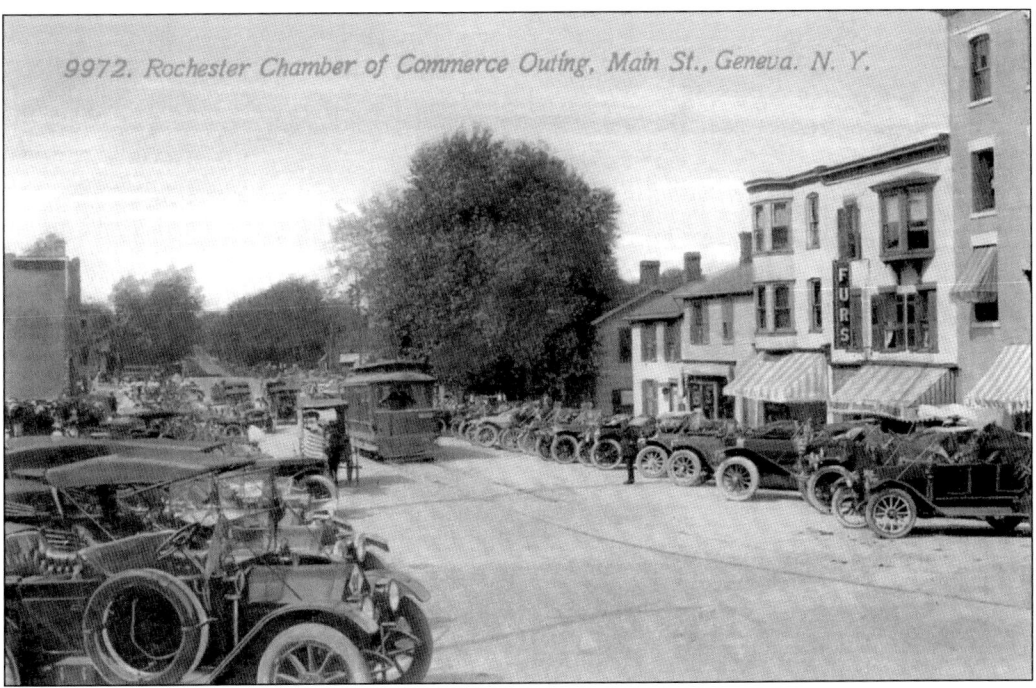

In the early days of traveling by motorcar, it was an adventure to drive from Rochester to Geneva. A gathering of automobiles would draw a crowd.

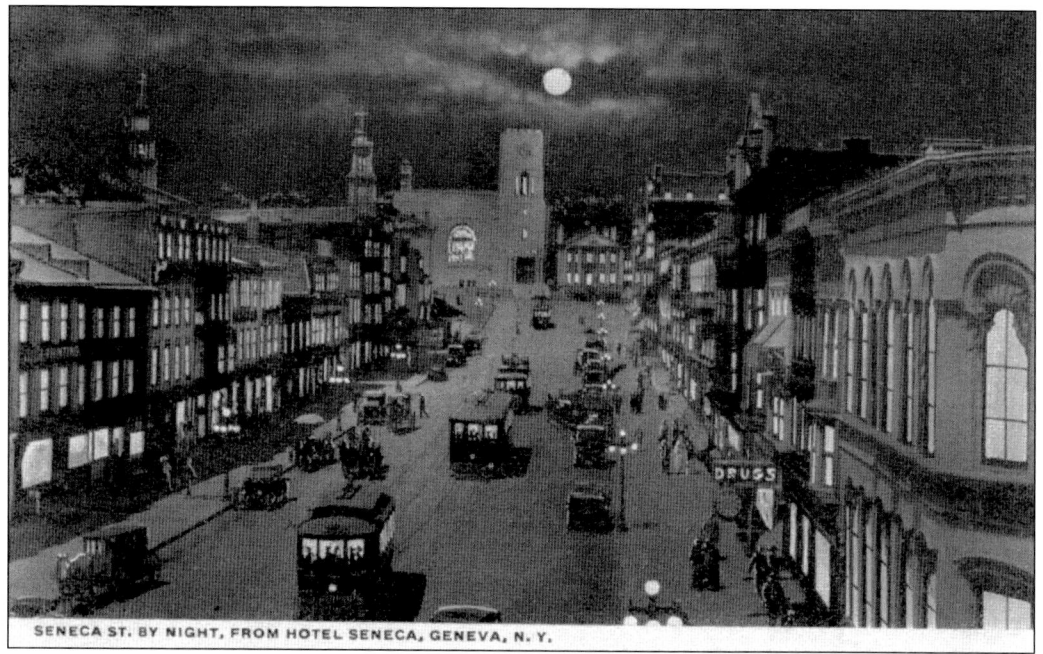

At 82 Seneca Street is the Smith Opera House (on the right), over 100 years old. The Smith is a lively cultural center, featuring concerts, plays, performers, and films.

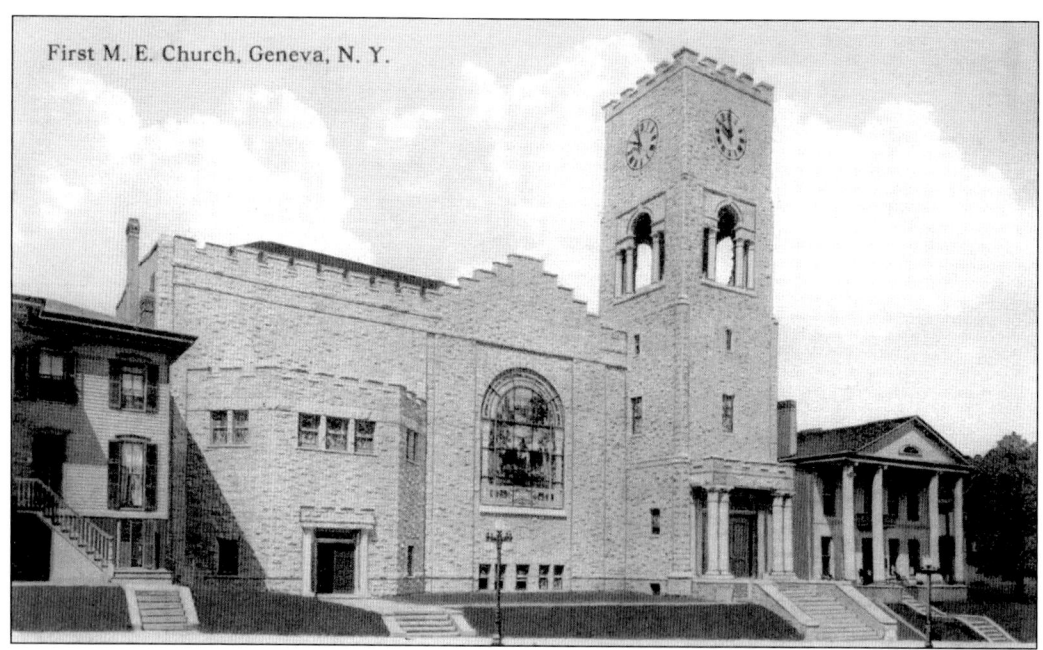

This church and the pillared building can be seen in the background of the previous image, just beneath the moon.

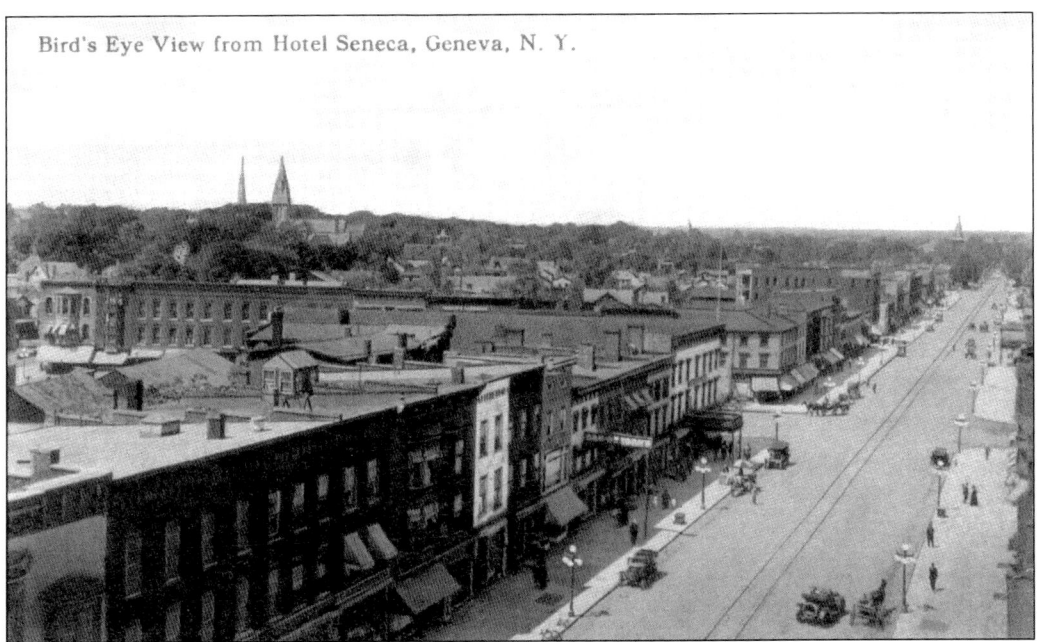

White settlers arrived in 1786, taking over the site that had been the Seneca town of Kanadesaga. Surveying errors that occurred soon after discouraged land speculators.

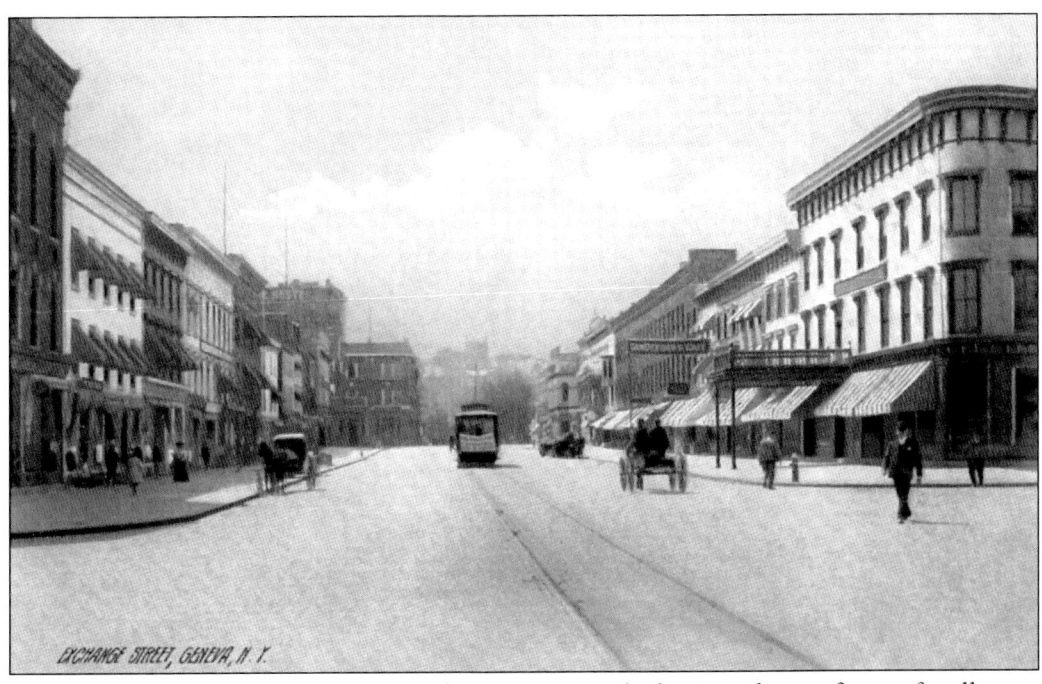

Someone had the foresight to make Exchange Street wide, leaving plenty of room for all types of traffic. The trolley once ran all the way to Rochester.

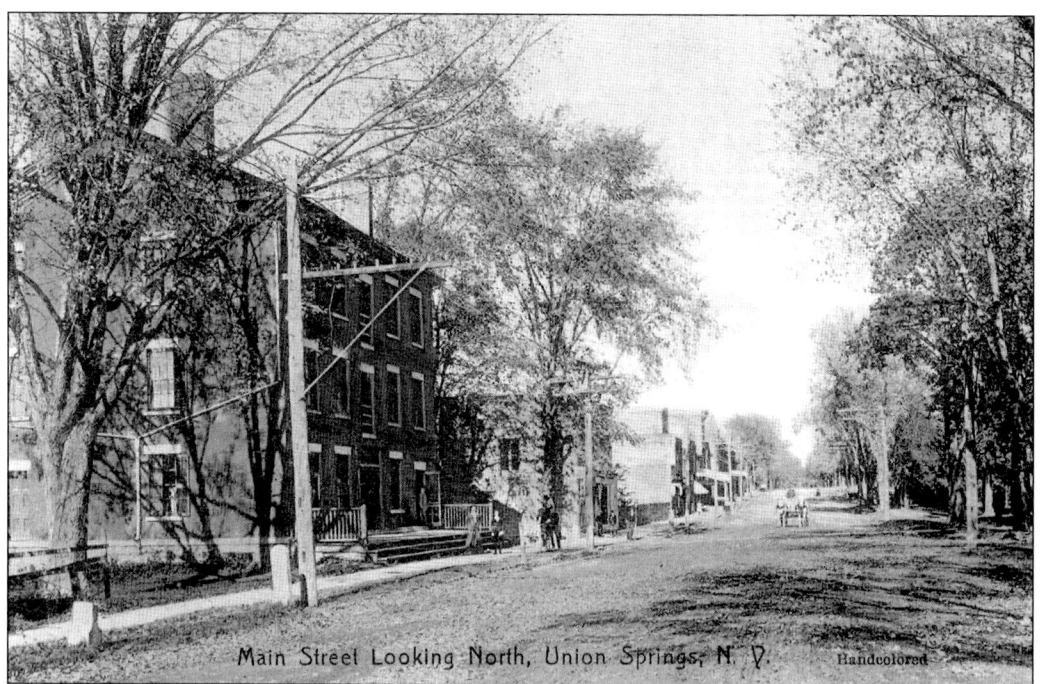

Notice the wagon pulled by a pair of matched horses in this view of Union Springs. Cayuga Castle, site of a major Cayuga Native American village, was nearby.

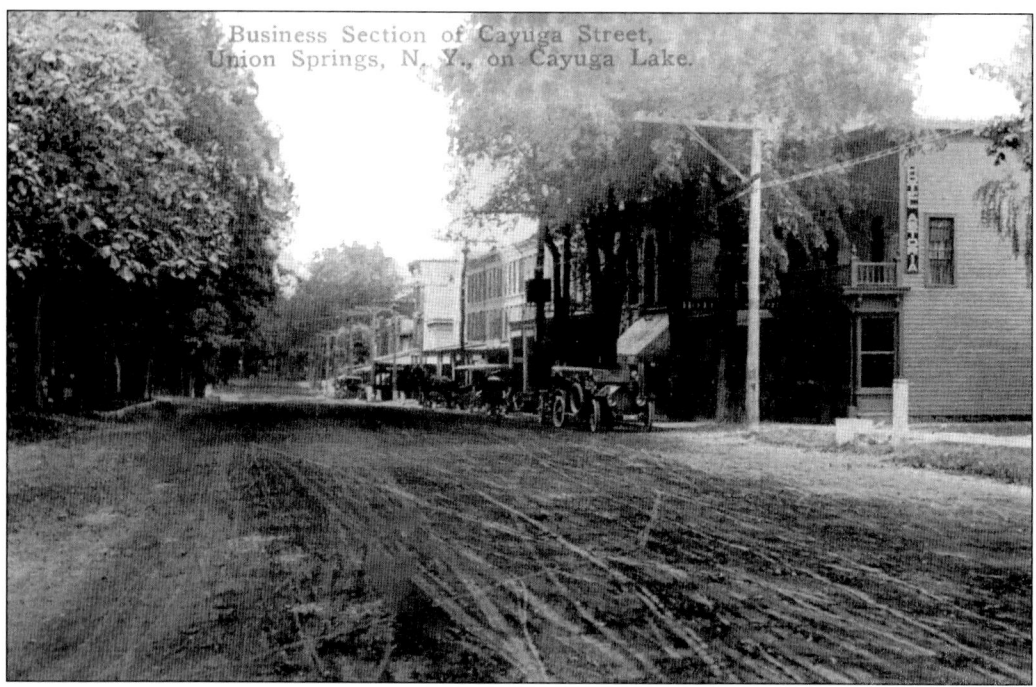

Cars, on the other hand, predominate around the Hotel Astoria. Cayuga Springs was named for the numerous salt and sulfur springs in the area.

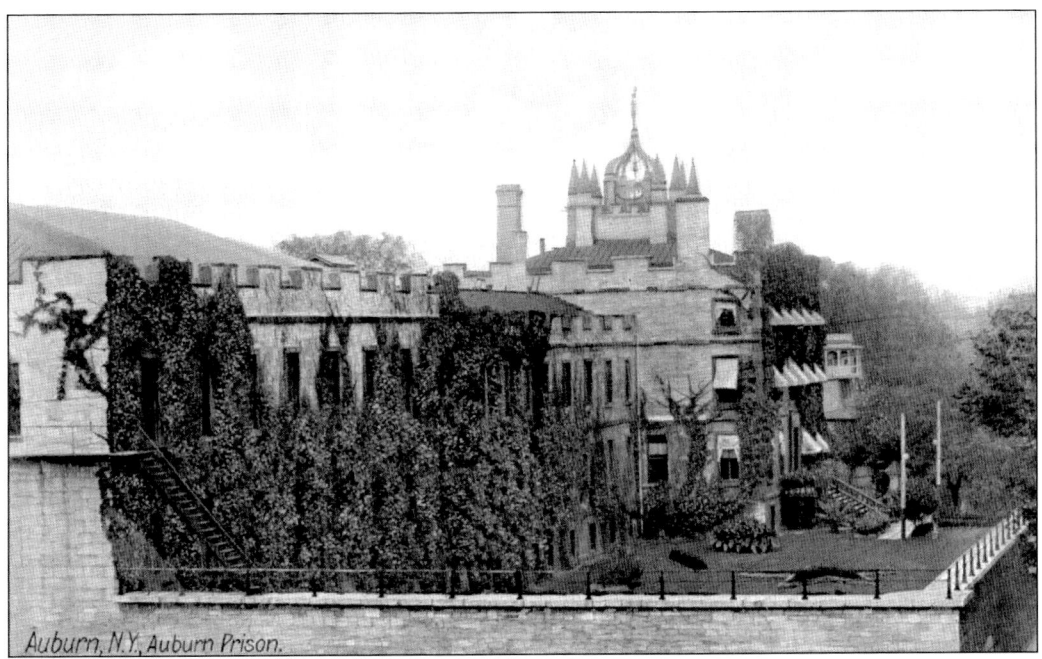

A state prison in Auburn started taking inmates in 1818; the reforming "Auburn System" attracted observers, including Charles Dickens and Alexis de Tocqueville. Auburn held the world's first execution by electric chair in 1890. Eleven years later, Leon Czolgosz met the same fate in "Old Sparkey," less than two months after shooting Pres. William McKinley.

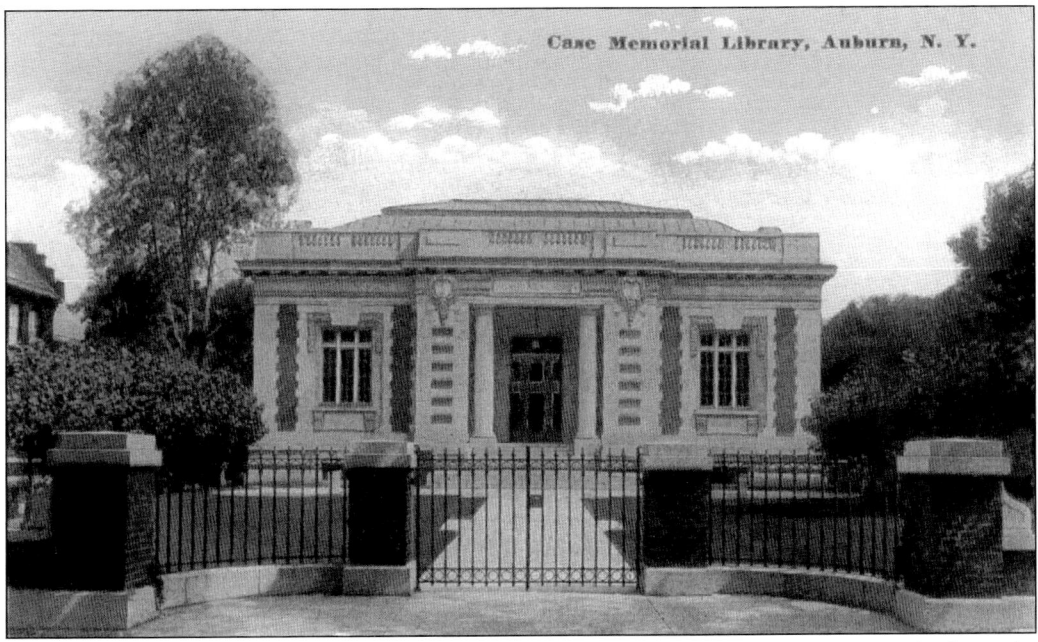

Willard E. Case, who made his fortune in electrochemistry, built the Case Memorial Library in 1896 in memory of his parents. It is now known as the Seymour Public Library after James S. Seymour, another public-spirited citizen.

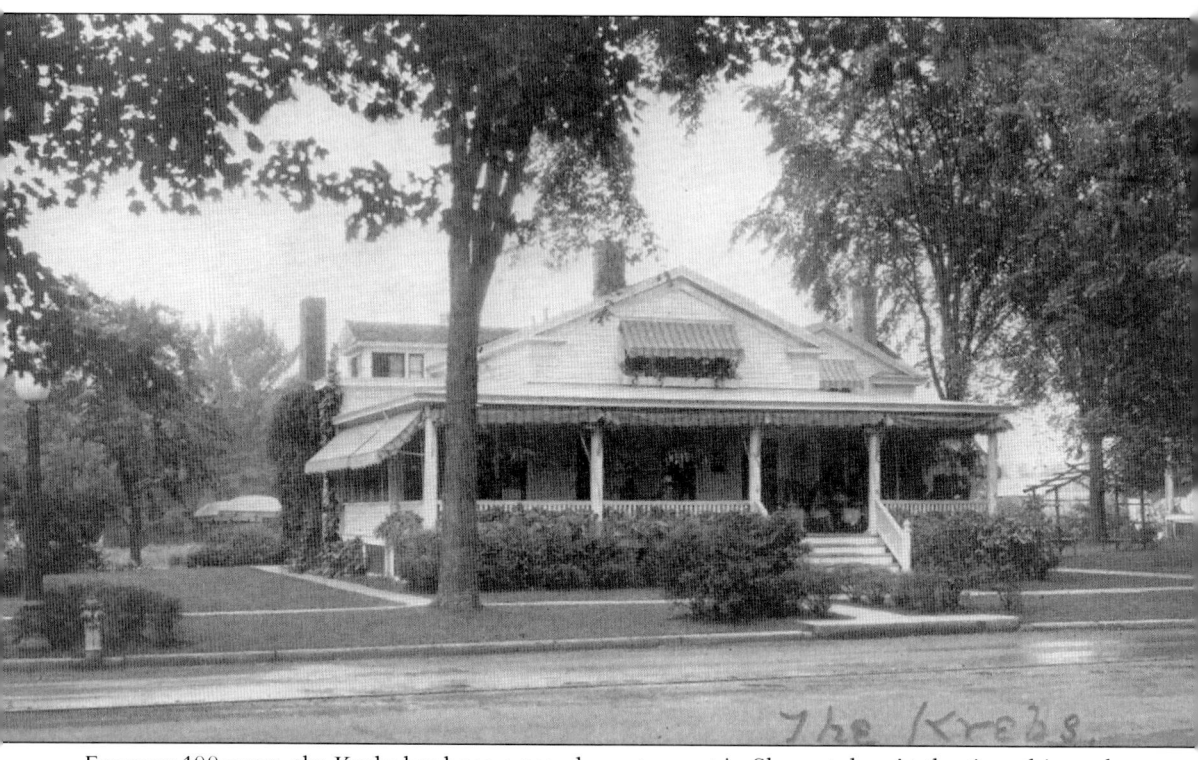

For over 100 years, the Krebs has been a popular restaurant in Skaneateles. At the time this card was made, the telephone number at the Krebs was 14.

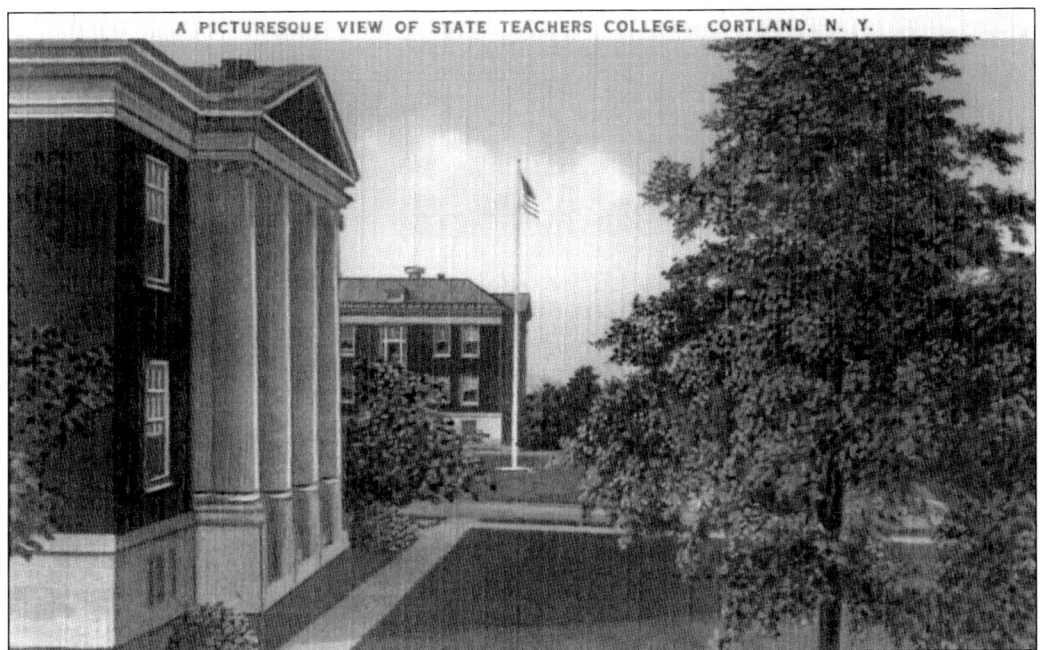

The Finger Lakes region is bracketed by State University of New York (SUNY) colleges at Geneseo on the west edge and Cortland on the east. Numerous community colleges and private colleges and universities make the region a magnet for college students.

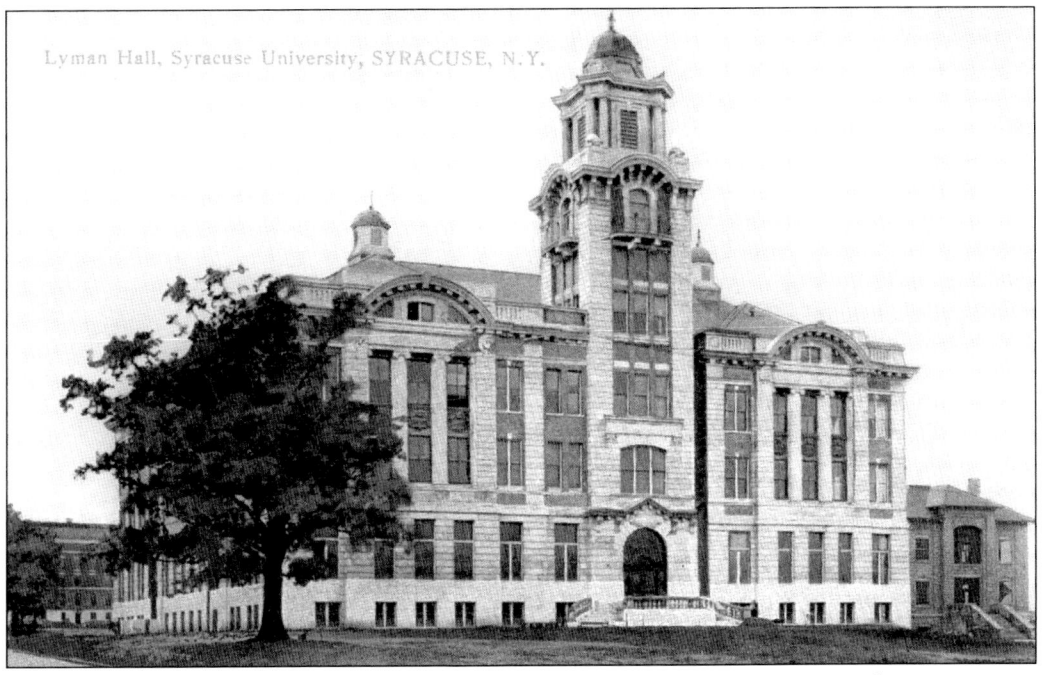

Syracuse University offered its first classes (in a rented building) in 1871. At that time it was a coeducational institution operated by the Methodist Episcopal Church. Nonsectarian since 1920, Syracuse is a world-renowned center of research and a nationally renowned powerhouse in football and basketball.

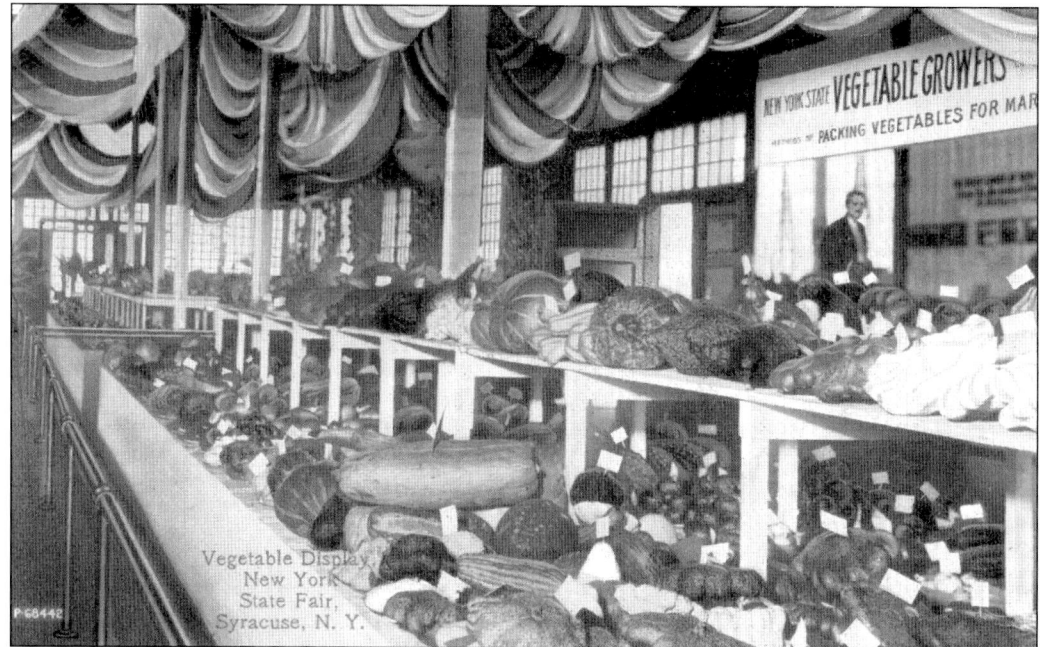

The great New York State Fair (America's first, which started in Syracuse in 1841) settled there permanently in 1890. While agriculture is still a strong feature, other offerings help bring in a million visitors a year, and two million use the facilities at other times. The fair itself lasts 12 days.

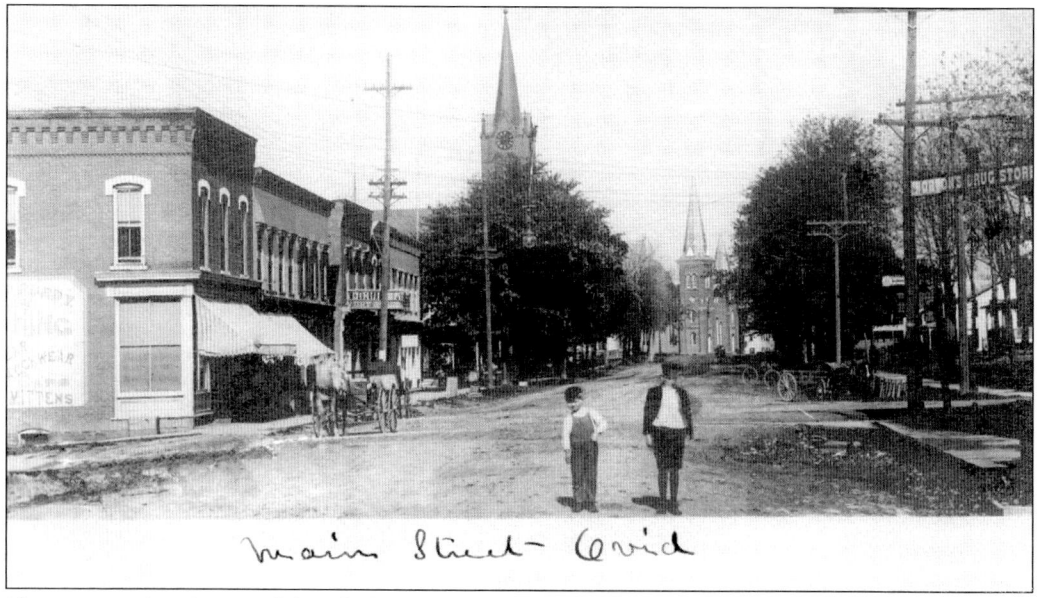

If one wanted a picture of their kids today, they probably would not pose in the street! But with the pace of traffic in those days, standing in the middle of Ovid's main thoroughfare was not particularly dangerous.

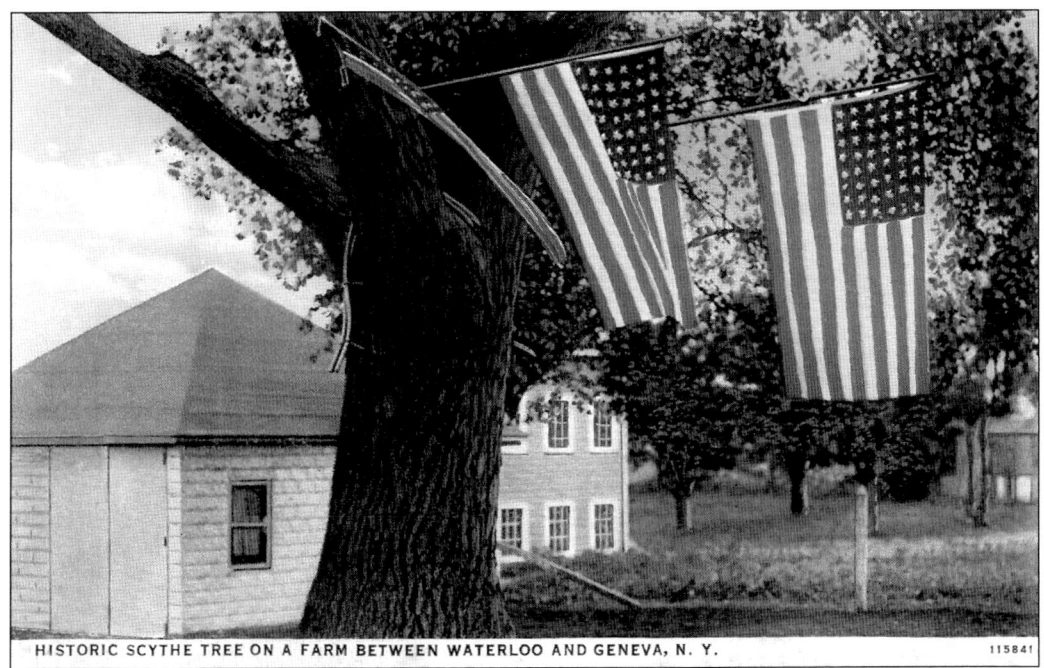

HISTORIC SCYTHE TREE ON A FARM BETWEEN WATERLOO AND GENEVA, N. Y.

Between Geneva and Waterloo, Wyman J. Johnson hung his scythe in a tree, telling his mother to leave it there until he returned from the Civil War; he never came home, and the scythe was never removed. The Schaffer brothers added their scythes in 1918, prompting the community to fly three flags. Two were removed to celebrate the Schaffers' safe return. With a little help from its friends, the historic tree—with its three scythes embedded—still stands.

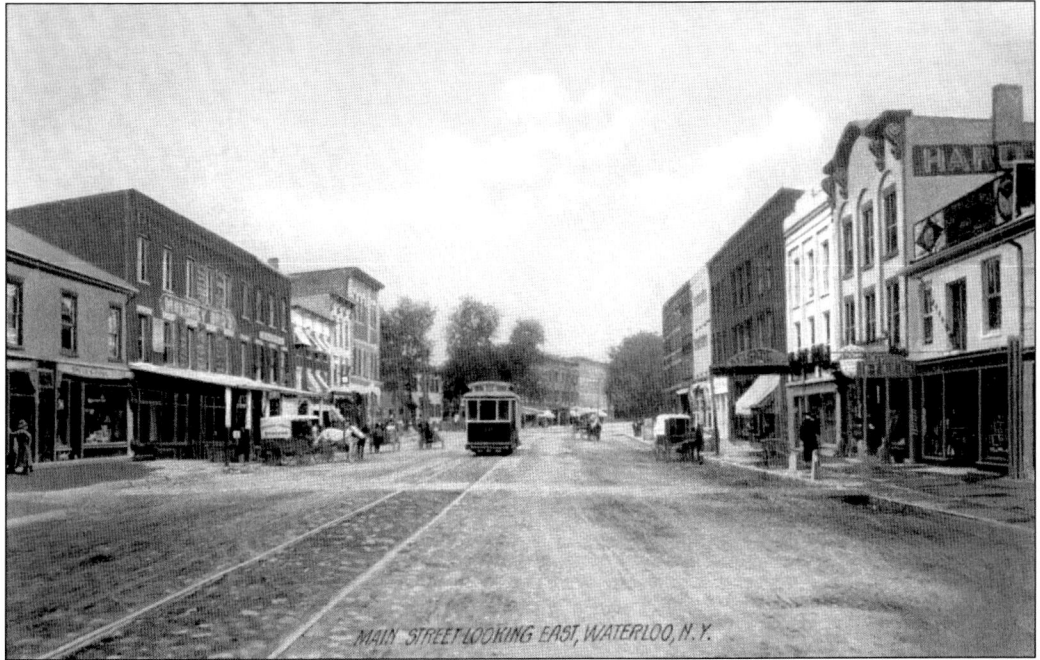

Waterloo is widely regarded as the birthplace of Memorial Day, which it always celebrates (as it did originally) on May 30.

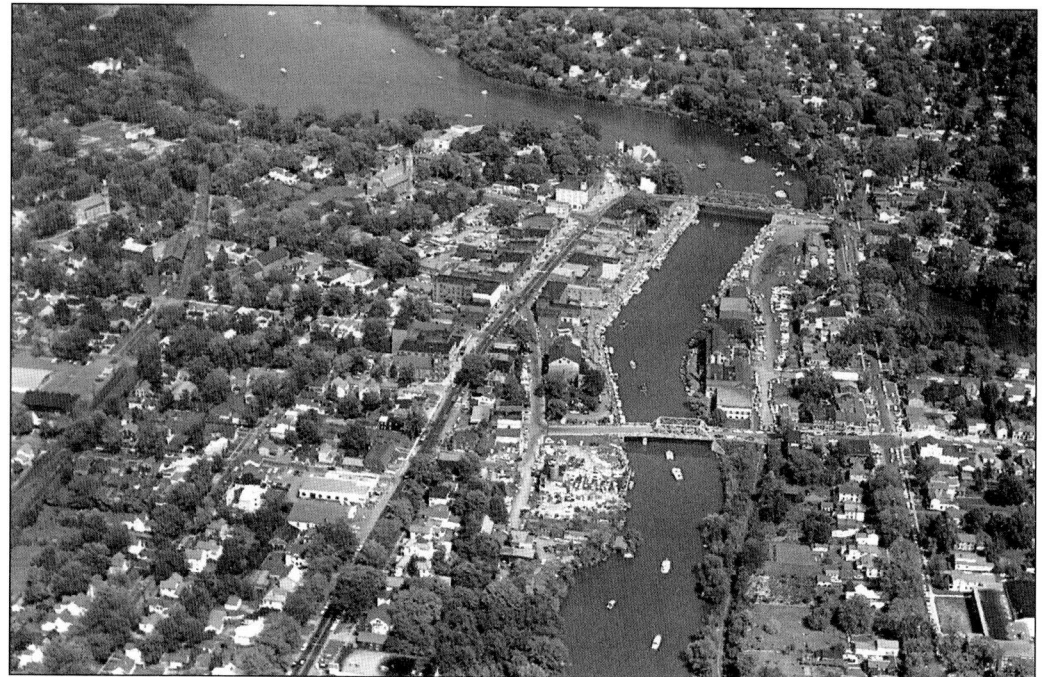

The original Seneca Falls disappeared when they were inundated by the canal (running top to bottom). On the street paralleling the canal to the left stands the ruined Wesleyan Chapel, site of the first women's rights convention in the revolutionary year of 1848.

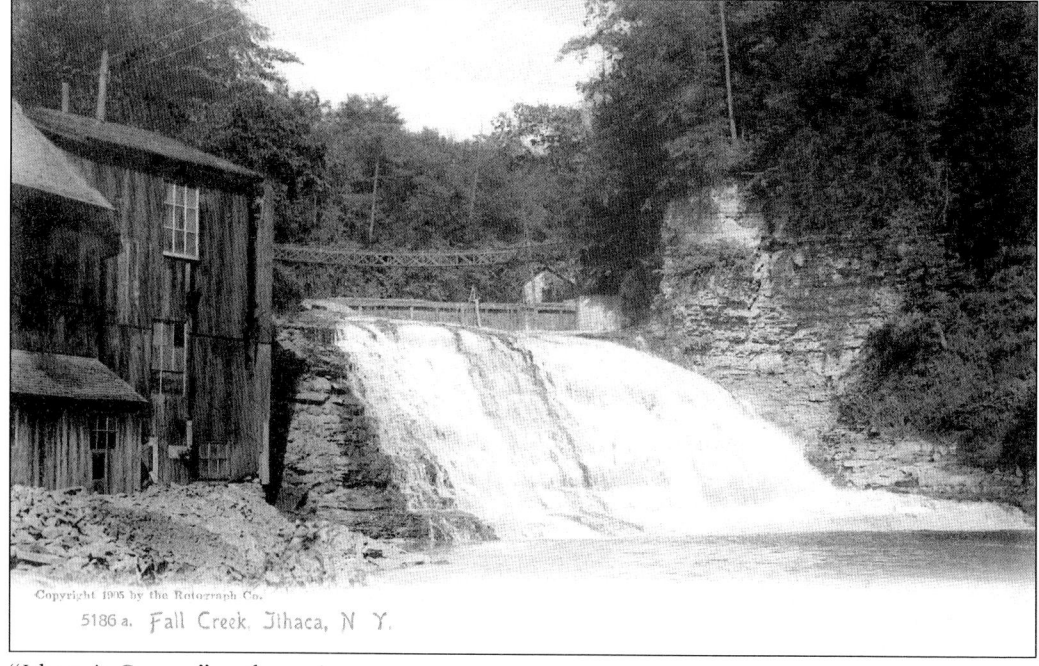

"Ithaca is Gorges," as the saying goes.

The falls and the gorges make it tricky to get from point to point, but most people seem to think they are worth it.

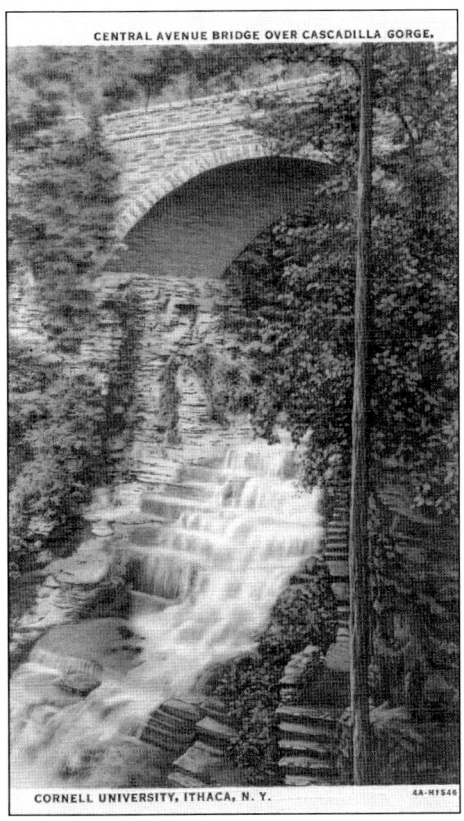

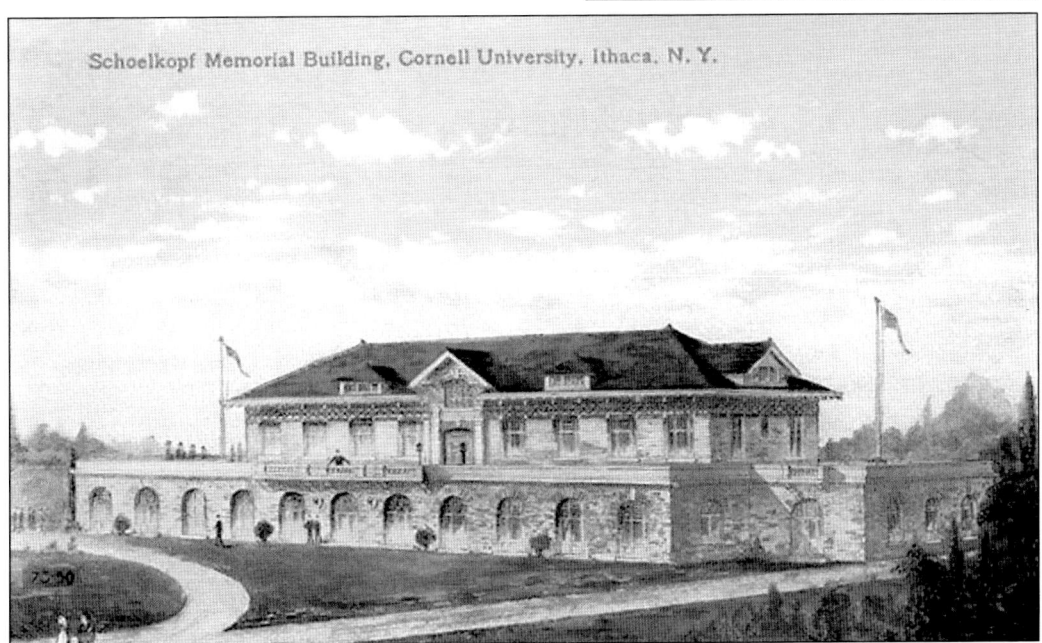

Cornell University opened its doors in 1868 as New York State's land-grant college. The Lehigh Valley Railroad carried so many Cornell students to campus that it adopted the Cornell colors for its own livery.

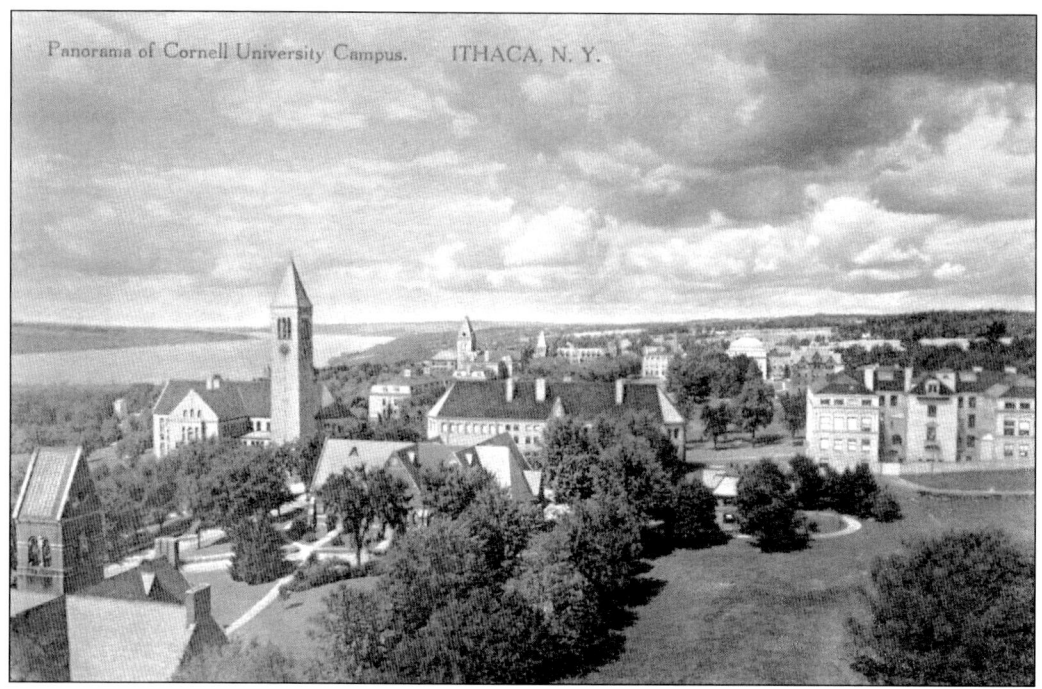

In 2002, the Cornell campus had 20,000 students and four Nobel laureates.

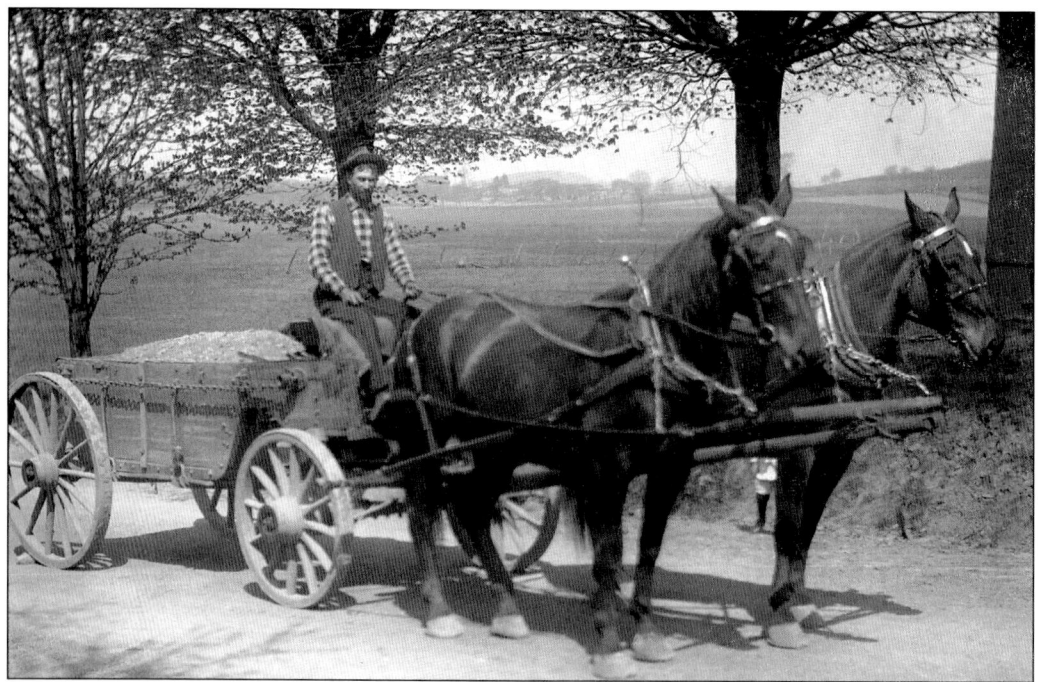

Over time, people have changed how they get around. This photograph was obviously posed—note the stone behind the wagon wheel and the boy's legs showing between the horses' front legs.

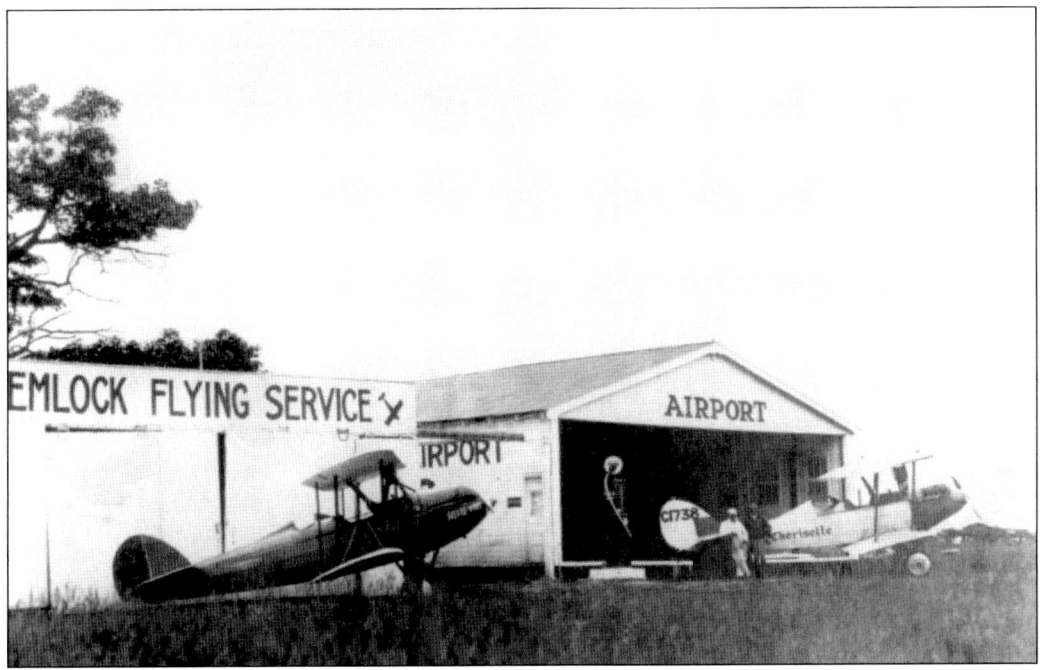

Between the wars small flying operations sprang up across the map. This one set up shop near Hemlock Lake.

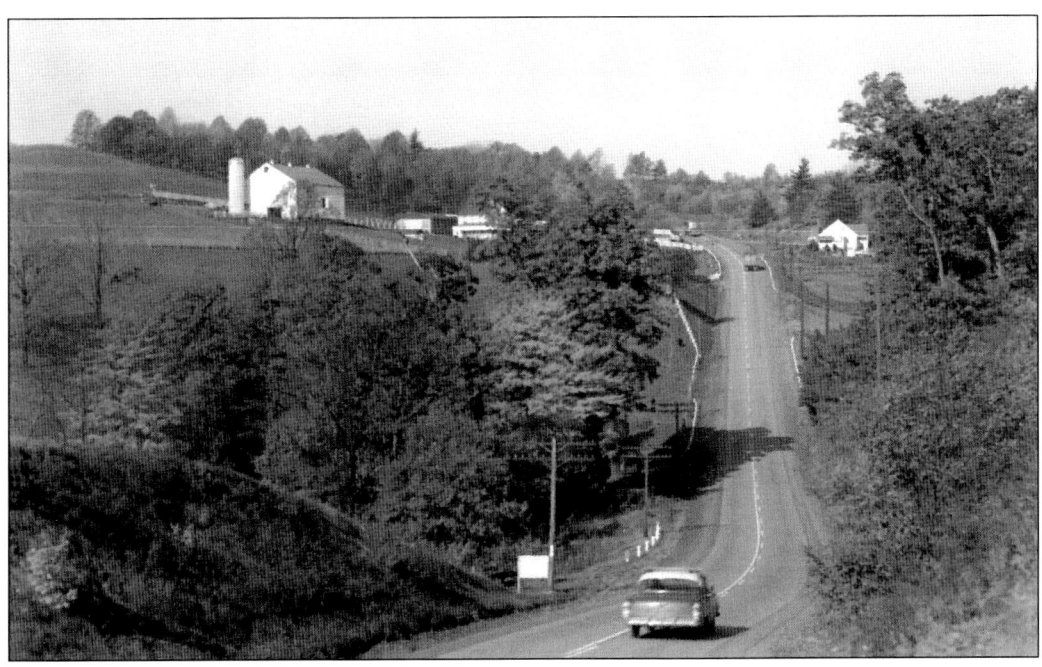

Either way, hop in—take a ride in the Finger Lakes.

# Discover Thousands of Local History Books Featuring Millions of Vintage Images

Arcadia Publishing, the leading local history publisher in the United States, is committed to making history accessible and meaningful through publishing books that celebrate and preserve the heritage of America's people and places.

Find more books like this at
**www.arcadiapublishing.com**

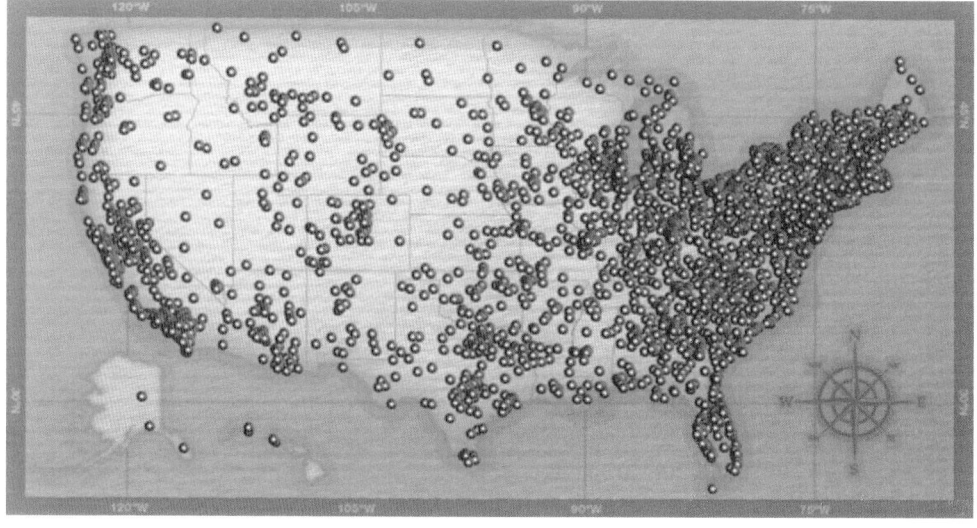

Search for your hometown history, your old stomping grounds, and even your favorite sports team.

Consistent with our mission to preserve history on a local level, this book was printed in South Carolina on American-made paper and manufactured entirely in the United States. Products carrying the accredited Forest Stewardship Council (FSC) label are printed on 100 percent FSC-certified paper.

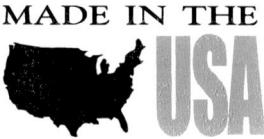